BEYOND ENTREPRENEURSHIP

Turning Your Business into an Enduring Great Company

James C. Collins
and
William C. Lazier

PRENTICE HALL
Englewood Cliffs, New Jersey 07632

Prentice-Hall International (UK) Limited, *London*
Prentice-Hall of Australia Pty. Limited, *Sydney*
Prentice-Hall Canada Inc., *Toronto*
Prentice-Hall Hispanoamericana, S.A., *Mexico*
Prentice-Hall of India Private Limited, *New Delhi*
Prentice-Hall of Japan, Inc., *Tokyo*
Simon & Schuster Asia Pte. Ltd., *Singapore*
Editora Prentice-Hall do Brasil, Ltda., *Rio de Janeiro*

© 1992 *by*
James C. Collins
and
William C. Lazier

10 9 8 7 6 5 4

Library of Congress Cataloging-in-Publication Data

Collins, James C. (James Charles)
    Beyond entrepreneurship : turning your business into an
enduring
great company / James C. Collins and William C. Lazier.
        p.   cm.
    Includes bibliographical references and index.
    ISBN 0-13-085366-6
    1. Small business–Management.   2. Organizational
effectiveness.
    I. Lazier, William C.   II. Title.
    HD62.7.C645   1992
    658.4–dc20   91-44606
                                                                  CIP

ISBN 0-13-085366-6

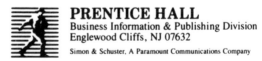

PRENTICE HALL
Business Information & Publishing Division
Englewood Cliffs, NJ 07632
Simon & Schuster, A Paramount Communications Company

Printed in the United States of America

Dedication

**For our best friends,
Joanne and Dorothy**

CONTENTS

PREFACE

When we first met Jim Gentes he was sleeping with his inventory.

Launching a new company out of his cramped, stuffy one bedroom apartment in San Jose, he had turned his bedroom into a warehouse for finished goods. His garage, packed tight with parts and equipment, was staffed with four youths working frantically in 100-degree heat to build bicycle helmets. When Gentes needed more space, he gave a helmet to a neighbor in exchange for use of his neighbor's garage, thus expanding from a single-garage to a double-garage start-up. Fortunately, his neighbors never complained about the daily visits of huge UPS semi-trucks pulling into the tiny driveway to deliver helmet shells and pick up new shipments.

"Headquarters" was the kitchen table, covered with papers, bicycle helmet prototypes, books, and computer printouts from a MacIntosh Computer that was tilted at a cockeyed angle in the corner. Sitting at that table, surrounded by cycling posters, Gentes, an intense man in his late twenties, told us that he expected to be out of this apartment and into his own building soon, and on his way to being a successful company.

Then he pointed to a stack of books on entrepreneurship and small business management. "They've been helpful for getting me off the ground," he said. "But they don't tell me what I really want to know."

"What's that?" we asked.

Gentes looked out the window and waited for 30 or 40 seconds. Then he turned and told us, "I want Giro to be a great company."

And the idea for this book was born.

This book is about how to turn an existing enterprise into an enduring great company. We've written it for people like Jim Gentes—people who want their company to be something special,

v

worthy of admiration and pride. Our focus is on helping them build an extraordinary organization, one that sustains high performance, plays a leadership role in shaping its industry, rises to the status of role model, and remains great for generations. If you're the leader of an enterprise that you want to turn into a great company, this book is for you.

This is *not* a book about how to start a business. We assume that you are (or plan to become) a key contributor to the further development of an existing, operating enterprise—one you started, bought, inherited, or joined.

Although many of the lessons in this book apply to any size company, we've written it primarily for leaders of small to mid-sized enterprises (which could include small enterprises within larger organizations). Why? The foundation of greatness is usually laid while the company is still small and malleable enough to be hand-crafted into an entity that fully embodies the values of its leaders.

IBM is great because of things Tom Watson did long before IBM became the monolith that it is today. NIKE is great because of things Phil Knight did when NIKE was a scrappy David taking on Goliaths. 3M is great because William McKnight bent the company to his values decades ago. L.L. Bean is great because of Leon Bean's actions when his tiny company operated out of a single building in Freeport, Maine. Patagonia is a candidate for greatness because of the indelible imprint left by Kristine McDivitt during the formative stages of the feisty, renegade company.

If you're the leader of a small to mid-sized enterprise, it's up to you to be the architect of greatness. This book is about being such an architect.

Although we have concentrated on for-profit companies, managers of non-profit organizations will also find much of the material in this book useful. The principles of building a great company generally apply to *any* organization that seeks enduring greatness.

What Is a Great Company?

We define a great company as one that meets the following four criteria:

1. Performance. A great company generates enough cash flow (through highly profitable operations) to be self-sustaining; it also has a solid track record of meeting other objectives set by its leaders and owners. Although it has ups and downs—and

perhaps even some dire times—a great company always recovers and eventually regains high performance.

2. Impact. A great company plays a significant leadership role in shaping its industry. It isn't necessarily the biggest company; it can influence by innovation as well as size.

3. Reputation. A great company is admired and respected by people outside its walls, often being used as a role model.

4. Longevity. A great company has staying power, remaining healthy for decades. The greatest companies are self-renewing institutions whose greatness endures for generations of management, transcending the presence of the individuals who originally shaped the company. When you think of enduring greatness, think of building a company that remains great for 100 years.

A company need not be perfect to be great. No company is perfect; all have their warts. A great company, like a great athlete, trips up now and then, briefly tarnishing its reputation. But a great company is also resilient, and bounces back from its difficult periods—just like a great athlete bounces back from a slump or an injury.

The Shape of This Book:
How to Make Your Company Great

Each chapter covers an essential element of attaining corporate greatness, presenting a framework of ideas and methods, supported by specific, vivid examples.

We begin Chapter 1 with *leadership style*. It's impossible to build a great company without an effective leadership style. It all starts with you.

In Chapter 2, we move to the function of effective corporate leadership: catalyzing a *vision*. Every great company has at its foundation a compelling vision. What *is* vision, *why* is it so important, and *how* do you set one? We answer these questions and present a useful framework for setting corporate vision.

In Chapter 3, we de-mystify the topic of *strategy*. Once the vision is clear, you need to make good decisions and have a road map for making the vision happen.

In Chapter 4, we move to an exciting and integral part of greatness: *innovation*. How do you stimulate creativity and keep your company innovative as it evolves? We present a framework and a plethora of specific suggestions and examples.

Finally, we finish in Chapter 5 with the importance of *tactical excellence:* how to translate vision and strategy into tactics and, most important, how to create an environment that produces consistent tactical excellence.

In writing this book, we drew heavily from our own practical business experience (we both worked in private industry before returning to Stanford Graduate School of Business to teach), academic research and theory, consulting work, and experience serving as directors for a number of companies. In addition, field research, case writing, and student projects have provided a continual source of examples and insights. The ideas in this book were shaped by our exposure to over 300 specific companies.

By the way, Jim Gentes no longer sleeps with his inventory. Giro has grown over a hundred fold since that meeting at his "headquarters" in 1986, and is well on its way to becoming an enduring, great company. To all of you who share Gentes' dream of corporate greatness, we wish you a similar fate.

James C. Collins
and
William C. Lazier

ACKNOWLEDGEMENTS

Writing a book is not a solo or even a two person effort. Although it's certainly true this book wouldn't exist without us, it's also true that it wouldn't exist in its present form without the help of many other people.

We are indebted to Paul Feyen and John Willig for seeing the potential in this book long before any of the chapters were written. John, our initial editor, gave us the confidence to write with bold conviction. He gave us helpful insight and guidance at crucial turning points during the writing of the manuscript.

Lee Anne Snedeker, our research assistant and casewriter, deserves the credit for coming up with the title "Beyond Entrepreneurship." Her creative assistance and thoughtful criticism on early drafts were immensely helpful.

Our always cheerful assistants, Karen Stock and Ellen Kitamura, were helpful during many phases of the project. Joan Patton—also known as "Quality Control Central"—did an excellent job of proofing, proofing, and proofing again various production versions of the text.

Janet Brockett applied her extraordinary creative and interpersonal talents to the development of our book cover and icons. Janet was a joy to work with.

We tip our hats to Sybil Grace and the rest of the team at Prentice-Hall who guided the manuscript with professionalism and care through production and out to the market.

We are intellectually indebted to the work of P. Ranganath Nayak and John M. Ketteringham and their book *Break-throughs* as a rich source of background material on the development of the 3M Post-It Notepads, the microwave oven, Tagamet, Federal Express, and the CT Scannner, which we use as examples in our chapter on innovation.

We are also indebted to Michael Ray and Rochelle Myers, first for being such outstanding teachers, and second, for allowing us to quote extensively from their book *Creativity in Business* and from transcripts of class visitors.

We are thankful for the permission to quote given to us by a wide range of individuals and companies: Bob Miller of MIPS Computer, Bill Hannemann and Jim Gentes of Giro Sport Design, Larry Ansin of Joan Fabrics, Kristine McDivitt of Patagonia, H. Irving Grousbeck of Continental Cablevision, Doug Stone formerly of Personal CAD Systems, Jim Swanson of Ramtek, Anne Bakar of Telecare, Bruce Pharriss of Celtrix Laboratories, David Kennedy of Kennedy-Jenks, Joe Bolin of Schlage Lock Company, Vinod Khosla co-founder of Sun Microsystems, Pete Schmidt of NIKE, Claude Rosenberg of Rosenberg Capital Management, Debi Coleman of Apple Computer, Mike Kaul of Advanced Decision Systems, Bob Bright formerly of America's Marathon, and Don Lyle of Tandem Computers.

We are particularly thankful to Bill Hewlett of Hewlett Packard Company, who graciously granted an interview about the early days of Hewlett Packard to Jim Collins and Jerry Porras, and to Steve Jobs of NeXT Computer for visiting our class and sharing his insights with us and our students. Both of these individuals significantly shaped our thinking, and earned our respect.

We were fortunate to have many thoughtful and dedicated readers of our drafts, who critically evaluated our work and provided helpful comments, encouragement, criticism, and suggestions. These include: Art Armstrong, Susan Bandura, Chris Buja, Roger Davisson, Shelly Floyd, Arthur Graham, Irv Grousbeck, Greg Hadley, Bill Hannemann, David Harman, Jim Hutchinson, Chris Jackson, Dirk Long, Bob Miller, Bruce Pharriss, Heidi Roizen, and Richard Wishner.

Finally, perhaps the greatest acknowledgement goes to the hundreds of bright, talented, inquisitive, and inspirational business executives and students who have taken our classes at Stanford's Graduate School of Business. They have shaped our thinking as much as—if not more than—we have shaped theirs. To all of these people who have held us to a high standard and who hold the dream of building an enduring great company, thank you.

J.C.
W.L.

Chapter 1

LEADERSHIP STYLE

The key to a leader's impact is sincerity. Before he can inspire with emotion he must be swayed by it himself. Before he can move their tears his own must flow. To convince them he must himself believe.

Winston Churchill

We call it the *M Syndrome*. M is the initial of a particularly ineffective CEO whom we observed. M is also the first letter of the word *malaise*.

M had an IQ of over 150. M had a Ph. D. and an MBA. M had 20 years of solid industry experience. M was on a first name basis with the top people in his industry. M worked 80 hours per week. M's market was growing at over 30% per year.

Yet M's company, after early success, floundered and was pulled into a dark downward spiral—into the gloom and malaise of mediocrity. Why? Because M's leadership style was so ineffective—so oppressive—that it hung over the organization like a cold, penetrating mist. It depressed people. It eroded their confidence. It gradually sucked the energy and inspiration out of them. It slowly killed the company, day by day, week by week.

What did M do wrong?

- M preached "respect for people" (because he had read about Hewlett-Packard's belief in respect), yet he never trusted people. M chanted teamwork, but defined team play as blind obedience.

- M was terribly indecisive. Confronted with an important decision, he would analyze it over and over, delaying action. Significant opportunities passed the company by and small problems developed into major crises.

- M had no clear priorities. He constantly hurled lists of 10 to 20 action items at people, telling them "*All* of them are top priority."

- M spent most of his time sealed safely away in his office, behind thick, closed doors. He seldom walked the halls or stopped by to see how people were doing.

- M constantly criticized people, yet never gave any positive reinforcement. A single mistake would haunt an employee forever—M would never give the person a chance to prove that he had learned from the mistake.

- M never effectively communicated the vision of the company. Hence, people felt that there was no vision, that the company was like a ship pounded by violent storms with no sense of direction.

- M spoke and wrote in turgid, technical language. Instead of inspiring people, he left them bored and confused.

- After the company reached a plateau of success (at about $15 million in revenues and 75 employees), M refused to move forward with anything new, bold, or risky. The company stagnated. Ambitious people left.

As in M's case, the primary barrier to greatness in many companies is ineffective leadership. The most advanced technology, the most thoughtful strategy, and the best tactical execution can be totally overshadowed by poor leadership style. This is true for all companies, but is particularly true of small to mid-sized companies where the top leaders have a dramatic daily impact, and must be the architects of corporate greatness.

Simply put, it's impossible to build a great company if you have a destructive leadership style.

The Multiplier Effect

If you are the top person, your style will set the tone for the entire organization. It is a multiplier effect—for better or worse—the tone you set at the top affects the behavior patterns of people throughout the company. If effective, your style will be a powerful factor in building a great company. If ineffective or negative, however, it will be like a heavy, wet blanket hanging over the company and weighing it down.

Different Styles

Should everyone have the same leadership style? No, of course not. Your leadership style will be a function of your own unique personality characteristics.

Indeed, there are many effective styles. Some effective leaders are quiet, shy, and reserved; whereas others are outgoing and gregarious. Some are hyperactive and impulsive; others are more methodical. Some are old, wise, and experienced; others are young, brash, and adventurous. Some love to give speeches; others are nervous in front of a crowd. Some are charismatic; others are not. (Do not confuse leadership with charisma. *Charisma does not equal leadership*, and some of the most effective leaders have very little charisma.)

Examine the spectrum of world leaders and notice how much their styles differ: Mahatma Gandhi (frail and soft-spoken), Abraham Lincoln (melancholy and thoughtful), Winston Churchill (the fierce and indomitable bulldog), Margaret Thatcher (stern and tenacious, the "Iron Lady"), Martin Luther King (impassioned, eloquent). Yet, in spite of the wide range of styles, each of these leaders was highly effective.

Cultivate your own style; don't try to be someone you're not or to take on a style that doesn't fit. Can you imagine Winston Churchill trying to imitate Gandhi's style, wearing a loincloth and speaking in a soft, almost inaudible voice? Conversely can you imagine Gandhi chewing on big fat cigars and growling, "Our policy is to wage war, by sea, land, and air, with all our might and all the strength God can give us ..."? These images are absurd. But they're no more absurd than if you try to ape someone else's style.

An effective style grows from within you. It should be entirely yours. No one except you should have a style exactly like yours.

Effective Leadership: Function Plus Style

Effective corporate leadership consists of two parts: leadership *function* and leadership *style*.

The function of leadership—the number-one responsibility of a leader—is to catalyze a clear and shared vision for the company and to secure commitment to and vigorous pursuit of that vision. This is a universal requirement of leadership, and no matter what your style, you must perform this function. (Chapter 2 explains the concept of vision and how to set one.)

In contrast, the style of leadership is unique to each individual. There are many styles that can be used to carry out the function of leadership. But herein lies a thorny paradox. On the one hand, we assert that your style should be peculiar to you, and that many styles can be effective. On the other hand, we have the dreaded M Syndrome, where M's style was the primary barrier to corporate greatness. How can we reconcile this paradox? Does this mean that, although each leader will have his or her own style, some styles are more effective than others?

To resolve the paradox, we have distilled the elements of style that we see in the most effective corporate leaders. Although each leader has a unique personal style, there are certain elements that tend to be common across a range of effective styles. See Figure 1.1 that follows.

EFFECTIVE CORPORATE LEADERSHIP

Leadership Function	Leadership Style	
Catalyze a clear and compelling vision that is shared by the group and is acted upon.	7 Elements of Effective Leadership Style** (Cut across all styles)	Individual Personality Characteristics (Unique to each individual)

** Authenticity, Decisiveness, Focus, Personal Touch, Hard/Soft People Skills, Communication, Ever Forward

Figure 1.1

An analogy will help clarify our solution to the paradox. Think for a moment about excellent writers. Each writer has his or her own style; William Faulkner's style is very different from Ernest Hemingway's, and Barbara Tuchman's style differs from that of William Manchester. Although style is personal to each individual writer, there are certain elements that tend to cut across the styles of all great writers: they engage the reader early in the work, capture the imagination with vivid detail, use language well, have good beginnings and endings, and so on.

Seven Elements of Leadership Style

In this chapter, we've identified the elements of style that are common among effective leaders. They are:

1. Authenticity

2. Decisiveness

3. Focus

4. Personal Touch

5. Hard/Soft People Skills

6. Communication

7. Ever Forward

Leadership Style Element 1: Authenticity

The most important element of leadership effectiveness is authentically living the vision of the company. The values and ambitions of a company are not instilled entirely by what leaders *say*; they're instilled primarily by what leaders *do*.

In a healthy company, there are no inconsistencies between what is said and what is believed deep down—the values come from *within* the leaders and imprint themselves on the organization through day-to-day activity. Think of it as kneading bread—constantly massaging the values into the very essence of the organization.

Granted, effective corporate leaders are aware of the practical benefits of their values. But they would behave consistently with those values in the *absence* of such benefits. And it is precisely this point that makes them so successful and effective.

When Bill Hewlett and Dave Packard started HP, they didn't sit down and ask, "What are the most pragmatic business values?" No. They deeply believed in having respect for people, and they simply acted out this belief in all that they did. It was as natural to them as breathing.

Show Your Conviction

We've observed that effective company leaders convey a ferocious intensity about their values, beliefs, and desires. They're unafraid to show the passion that is associated with these values, at times getting quite emotional.

Jim Gentes, founder of Giro Sport Design, is known to show quite touching emotion when speaking about how Giro's products saved a life or helped an athlete realize a dream.

Phil Knight, CEO of NIKE, is shy; he is *not* a jump-up-and-down cheerleader type. But when speaking to employees about his pride in them during a 1990 company meeting, his emotions were obvious. Knight, founder of one of the most successful companies of our era—a man driven by performance, competition, and winning—showed his tears and could barely finish his talk. It touched the NIKE people to the core because it was *real*.

Be the Best Role Model

Just speaking authentically isn't enough; you also have to *act* authentically. Each decision and action should dovetail with your philosophy, being in itself a statement of your core values.

People in your company are going to be extraordinarily influenced by what you do. As a corporate leader, you are like a parent or teacher, and, as such, people are likely to follow the example you set.

Don't underestimate the extent to which your actions influence those who work for you. Manners of speech, decision-making style, ways of behaving, and other attributes will rub off. For example, within a few weeks after John F. Kennedy came to office, White House staff members were speaking in Kennedy-like staccato sentences and jabbing the air with their fingers, the way he did.

Such is the nature of how people respond to authority figures. Inevitably, people will begin to emulate you. Even if you have a non-hierarchical environment, you'll still be perceived as an authority figure, and people will respond to you as such.

Therefore, *you've got to be a role model of the culture you want to create.*

Sam Walton, founder and primary leader of Wal-Mart during its rise from a single-store outlet to a successful chain of discount stores, understood the importance of being the consummate Wal-Mart role model. Walton, as portrayed .n Vance Trimble's book *Sam Walton,* believed that Wal-Mart's culture should be based largely on frugality—that extreme leanness and efficiency would create unbeatable strength.

Hence, as a role model of this philosophy, Walton wouldn't rent any car more expensive than a subcompact when travelling. When flying on commercial airlines, he flew coach. He ordered cold sandwiches and potato chips for Board of Directors meetings—board members had to bring along their own quarters for Coca-Cola. He obtained his coffee from the vending machine in the lobby, just like everyone else. He drove a beat up old pick-up truck, even when hosting English dignitaries (much to their chagrin).

Burton Stacy, of Walton's home town bank, said, "He [Walton] is not going to be seen in anything better than what his people are allowed ... Sam Walton is not going to stay in a better hotel ... nor eat in a better restaurant, nor drive a better car." Jack Stephens, an ex-board member at Wal-Mart, said, "Sam Walton—he lives and breathes efficiency."

Like all effective corporate leaders, Walton is a 100% pure genuine article—nothing artificial, nothing contrived.

In contrast, there is the example of Fortune Systems, a computer workstation business that failed miserably in the mid-1980s, squandering over $10 million in venture funding. A senior executive said, "We are all a team here, egalitarian in nature, working towards the same goals. We believe in concentrating on the task at hand, not on status symbols."

Yet, in flagrant violation of this sentiment, the senior managers had a separate "executive suite" and the CEO had a private parking space. When we saw this inconsistency, we knew the company was headed for mediocrity at best. It didn't even achieve that.

Like Walton, your stated corporate philosophy must ultimately be a genuine reflection of the values and beliefs you hold *in your own gut*. The values must be so much a part of you—of your core spirit—that you instinctively respond to situations in a way consistent with your stated philosophy. You shouldn't have to think about it. Likewise, when actions are taken by others that go against those values, it should eat at you on a gut level.

It's also important to carry this authenticity out to the major strategic decision made by the company. Just as you should be an exemplary role model of the values and beliefs through your day-to-day actions, the company itself should be a role model of its philosophy as exemplified by its major decisions.

Case Example:
Yvon Chouinard and Lost Arrow Corporation

At Lost Arrow Corporation (parent company of Patagonia), Yvon Chouinard held a deep conviction about the role his company should play in preserving the natural environment. He backed this up by donating 10% of pre-tax profits every year to environmental causes and sourcing fabrics from companies that used environmentally sound methods, even if those methods were more expensive.

Even more impressive is the long history of managing Lost Arrow in line with this belief. In the early 1970s (decades before being an environmentally-conscious company was fashionable), Chouinard set out to use his company to completely change the way rock climbers protect themselves on cliffs; he wanted them to use devices that leave the rock unscarred. He did this by introducing non-damaging protection devices called chocks or nuts.

At the time this was viewed by many as unwise. Few climbers wanted to switch from pitons (metal spikes pounded into the rock, thereby damaging it permanently) and most thought Chouinard was waging an uphill battle. Undaunted, Chouinard introduced the new gear and worked fanatically to get the climbing community to change.

And it worked. By 1975, virtually no one used pitons, and the cliffs were largely preserved for future generations. This action, led by Chouinard, attracted dedicated, loyal employees to the company. They knew that, unlike many companies that simply paid lip service to "concern for the environment," Chouinard *meant* it. And they were inspired by this.

Back Words with Action

We have no sympathy for managers who don't back their words with actions. Granted, no one is perfect, and we all fail to live 100% up to our ideals. But some company leaders don't even live up to 25% of their ideals. Their talk is rhetoric. Their insincerity is nauseating. They don't deserve to be leaders. And, indeed, they certainly will not build great companies.

Live what you say. Don't just talk about it, *do* it.

Leadership Style Element 2: Decisiveness

George C. Marshall pointed out that the greatest gift a leader can have is the ability to decide. Judging from how many executives suffer from chronic indecision, we think Marshall might be right.

Leaders who build great companies seldom suffer from indecision. The ability to decide—to somehow come to a decision, even in the absence of perfect information (and there will *never* be perfect information), is an essential attribute of well functioning teams and individual leaders.

Don't Let Analysis Prevent a Decision

Analysis allows us to say "maybe," but life (especially in a small to mid-sized company) does not.

Judicious use of analysis is good, as long as you don't fall prey to "analysis paralysis." There are seldom enough facts or data to eliminate all risk or to make a decision based solely on those facts. Furthermore, all business analysis is dramatically affected by your assumptions. Two people looking at the same set of facts will often come to entirely different conclusions about those facts. Why? Because they come at those facts with different assumptions.

For example, you can try this experiment. Ask a group of employees to assess the viability of a potential new product and make a go/no go decision. You provide them with a veritable forest full of facts. Now, they are all excellent employees with exactly the same business training. Yet, about half of them will say "go" and the other half say "no go." Why? To do their analysis, they have to make assumptions, and their assumptions drive their answers.

This is true in most business situations. You can do virtually an endless amount of analysis, but the analysis will seldom be conclusive. And you still have to make a decision.

We're not suggesting that you should be thoughtless about your actions and run off in a blind fury of impulsive activity. Facts, analyses, and probabilities all have their place in decision making. Just remember that the objective is to *make a decision,* not to pulverize it with analysis.

You have to sense when you've done enough analysis and gathered enough facts. Then get on with it. David Starr Jordan, founding president of Stanford University, captured this perfectly in his approach to decision making: "When all

the evidence seems to be in, I like to say yes or no at once
and take my chances."

Follow Your Gut

Jordan's "yes or no" approach still leaves an unanswered
question: precisely *how* do you make a final choice based on
imperfect information? Part of the answer lies in being willing
to follow your gut instinct—your intuition.

Admittedly, some people are uncomfortable with intuitive
decisions. Intuition seems unscientific and irrational, and its
use is awkward for those who are not well practiced. Yet the
most effective decision makers use a combination of hard-headed
analysis *and* intuition.

Paul Cook, founder and guiding force through the development of Raychem Corporation, is a good example. He told
an audience during a talk:

> Strangely enough, the company has made two or three
> big mistakes that it never would have made if I would
> have followed my intuition faithfully. I would not let
> that happen anymore. I've learned to trust my intuition
> faithfully. I really have. It's made a big difference.

Cook is not alone. Paul Galvin (founder of Motorola),
William McKnight (builder of 3M), Sam Walton (of Wal-Mart),
Kristine McDivitt (CEO for 17 years of Patagonia), and many
other corporate executives were comfortable and practiced with
their intuition.

There is no such thing as an unintuitive person; everyone
has intuition. The difficulty comes in recognizing and using
it. What does it take to effectively use your intuition? Here
are few suggestions.

- Go right to the heart of any problem or decision. Don't
  let a myriad of data, analysis, options, and probabilities
  overwhelm you and push you into catatonic indecision.

- Clear away the clutter—the long lists of pros and cons—and
  zero in on the central question. When confronted with
  a problem, say to yourself, "What's the essence of this?
  Never mind the details, what's the important thing?"
  Don't dwell incessantly on all the attributes and com-

plexities of a problem. Pare the situation down to its essential elements.

* A useful technique is to distill a decision down to its core and ask a simple question: Does your gut say "Yes" or "No"?

Over time you'll develop a finely tuned sense for what your intuition is saying. This "sense" has a special quality to it—you just *know* if something is right. One effective tool for developing this "sense" is to closely observe your internal reactions to the decisions you make.

For example, if you find yourself bogged down in elaborate columns of pros and cons, just randomly pick a decision and observe how you react. If you feel relief, then you probably made the right decision. If, on the other hand, you feel uneasy or tense—a "gnawing" in your stomach—then you probably made the wrong choice. You might try making a decision and living with it for 24 hours without telling anybody. This lets you observe how the decision feels before making it public.

Beware of the influence of fear on your gut instincts. Fear creates self-deception. What passes for an intuitive decision is sometimes a fear-driven decision in disguise. A fear-driven decision is one where, because of the risks involved, you are afraid to do what you know deep down is right. Fear-driven decisions can easily get confused with intuitive decisions because there is a false sense of relief that comes with pacifying the fear. (This false relief doesn't last, however, and the "gnawing" of your intuition eventually returns.)

If you find yourself saying, "I think this is the right thing to do, but I am afraid that ...," then you are in danger of making a decision that goes against your gut. To use your intuition effectively, you need the courage to do what you know is right, regardless of the risk.

A famous example of this comes from Harry Truman, one of the most decisive United States presidents, who went with his "gut feel" in making the unpopular decision to fire General MacArthur in 1951. The stakes were enormous, not only for Truman's political stature, but also for the rapidly escalating military conflict in Korea. But Truman fired Mac-Arthur anyway. Years later Truman reflected:

The only thing I learned from the whole MacArthur deal is that when there is something you know in your *gut* that you have to do, the sooner you get it over with, the better off everybody is.

A Bad Decision Is Often Better than No Decision

No matter how smart you are, it's impossible to have a 100% hit-rate with decisions. A good number of your decisions will be sub-optimal; that's just the nature of life. If you wait until you're absolutely sure before making a choice, you'll most certainly bog down in a quagmire of indecision.

Doing nothing can *feel* comfortable because it is without immediate risk. But, in the world of a small to mid-sized company that's got to keep moving, it is usually a recipe for disaster. If you've got a pressing problem, *make a decision and get on with it.*

Indecision is often worse than making a wrong decision. Get a jump on the problem; take the offensive rather than letting it back you into a corner where your hand will be forced. If you make a bad decision, so be it. It'll come back soon enough and smack you upside the head and then you can solve it right.

Unfortunately, most of us have a fear of being wrong, which makes it hard to follow this advice. Many of us carry around a strong fear of ridicule, blame, criticism, or being laughed at. In other words, the *psychological* consequences of making a mistake can seem worse than the actual consequences. We can be reluctant to make a decision for fear that we might—gasp—make a mistake.

You must learn to live with the fact that you will make mistakes—lots of mistakes—and that you will learn from them. Mistakes are in fact a great source of strength; making mistakes is analogous to building muscle in athletic training. Think about it for a minute: how does an athlete get stronger? By pushing to the point of failure. You do, say, three pull ups and fail on the fourth. The body adapts and gets stronger and the next time you can do four pull ups, and fail on the fifth. The next time out you can do five pull ups, and fail on the sixth, and so on.

The process of making decisions, some of which are "failures," and learning from them is "building muscle." If you don't ever make mistakes, you'll forever be stuck at three pull-ups.

Be proud of the fact that you periodically make mistakes. It shows that you're not one of the timid souls who are so terrified of making a mistake that they don't *do* anything worthwhile with their lives. As Paul Galvin, founder and architect of Motorola, said, "Do not fear mistakes. Wisdom is often born of such mistakes."

Be Decisive but not Bullheaded

Being decisive does *not* mean being inflexible or bullheaded. Yes, you've got to make decisions and commit to courses of action. But you've also got to be willing to make adjustments and adapt to new information or circumstances. If you need to change a decision, do it. It's far better to do that than to either stick doggedly to a bad decision or to never make a decision in the first place. Over the long run, it's far better to be right than consistent.

Group Decision Making

How much should you involve others in your decisions? In *Managing for Excellence,* David Bradford and Allan Cohen point out that there is a continuum of decision making styles. At one end of the continuum is *delegative decision making,* where the leader pushes the decision back to others, saying, "You make the decision."

Next is *pure consensus decision making,* with the decision coming from a group process that the leader facilitates. In a pure consensus style, the group makes the decision. The leader does not impose her solution, but rather seeks a choice that has "general agreement" among the entire group. The leader's skill is in asking questions, making observations, providing input, and catalyzing a decision. Effective consensus leaders guide the group to closure at just the right time—they don't cut off the process prematurely, nor do they let deliberations drag on unproductively.

Consensus does not equal unanimity! Too many managers have interpreted consensus to mean 100% unanimity. Not every person must agree with the decision for there to be consensus; there only needs to be general agreement. General agreement is significantly higher than a 51% majority, but usually falls short of 100% unanimity. It is something that is sensed, rather than quantified. Once a consensus is reached, those who disagreed during the process must agree or get off the ship.

Further along the continuum is *participative decision making,* with the leader asking for ideas, suggestions, evaluations of alternatives, and solutions. However, unlike the pure consensus style, the leader (not the group) ultimately makes the final choice. (An excellent case study of participative decision making is given in *Thirteen Days,* Robert F. Kennedy's book detailing the events of the Cuban Missile Crisis.)

The advantage of participative decision making is that it has the benefit of multiple points of view and vigorous discussion, yet allows an avenue for rapid decision. After an intense thrashing of the issues, the leader can state quickly and resolutely, "This is what we're going to do."

At the far end of the continuum is *autocratic decision making.* In this style, the leader gains only information from others (not suggestions or solutions). The leader does not involve others in the decision-making process or invite group debate of alternatives. The entire decision-making process remains in the leader's hands.

Which style is most effective for long term health and success? There is no single, clean answer, yet we can offer a few observations.

In general, the most effective leaders tend to make extensive use of participative decision making. The best decisions are made with some degree of participation—no one is brilliant or experienced enough to have all the answers. *No one.*

Bob Miller, CEO of MIPS Computer, a highly effective leader, explained:

> The best decisions come from facilitating ideas and suggestions from a group of great people. Get great people around you, involve them in the decisions, and you'll be right more often than not.

The degree of participation depends largely on the importance of the decision. If you seek wide participation on every single decision, even trivial decisions, people will spend all their time in meetings. However, as the importance of the decision increases, it's generally wise to invite the participation of a wider group.

People are more committed to decisions that they have a hand in shaping than to those that are decreed from above. True, it may take longer to go through a group process (either participative or consensus), but the decision will probably be more quickly and thoroughly acted upon. And it is the action that results from the decision that ultimately matters, not the decision itself. Keep in mind that it can take longer to sway people to accept a decision after it's been made than to involve them in the decision-making process in the first place.

Doesn't a group process invite disagreement among group members—disagreement that can be uncomfortable and difficult to resolve? Yes. And this is good.

To repeat: disagreement during the decision-making process is good. In making important decisions, it's wise to have constructive argument and differing points of view. Disagreement will clarify the issues and produce a more thought-out solution. Without disagreement, you probably don't fully understand the problem.

Referring to the example of the Cuban Missile Crisis, Robert Kennedy wrote about the importance of disagreement in reaching the best decisions:

> The fact that we were able to talk, debate, argue, disagree, and then debate some more was essential in choosing our ultimate course....Opinions, even fact itself, can best be judged by conflict, by debate. There is an important element missing when there is unanimity of viewpoint.

Leaders of great companies also tend to make extensive use of delegative decision making. To build a great company—a company that has effective leaders at all levels—you need to remove yourself from many of the decisions and force people to stand on their own feet. Granted, there are many decisions where you need to be involved, but there are many others where you're not essential. Furthermore, the most innovative companies tend to push decisions as far down in the organization as possible, giving people at all levels the opportunity to move fast, utilize their creativity, apply their intellect, and assume responsibility.

Delegating decisions doesn't mean being detached, nor does it mean standing idly by if the whole ship is going to crash into the rocks. It simply means giving people the power to make decisions that affect their area. It gives people a chance to test themselves and to build their own decision-making "muscle."

Keep in mind that no single style will work in all situations, and that it is helpful to be skilled across a range of methods. We offer the following rough guidelines for group decision making:

1. Whenever appropriate, delegate decisions downwards; give people a chance to build their decision-making "muscle." Be crystal clear about what decisions you have delegated, and hold people accountable for those decisions.

2. On important decisions that require widespread commitment for successful implementation, make the decision as a group, either participative or consensus. Enter the process with your own points of view, but be open to having your ideas influenced by others. Be clear whether the final decision is to be made by consensus or by you.

3. Encourage disagreement during the process.

4. Reserve autocratic decisions for situations where there's no time to invite participation (e.g. when the ship is crashing on the rocks), for trivial decisions, for decisions where you want to send a symbolic message to reinforce your values, and for the small set of decisions that you believe should always be made entirely by yourself.

5. Whatever style you use, be up front about it. Pretending to be participative or consensus-oriented in an effort to get "buy-in" to a decision that you've already made is terribly destructive. If you practice this type of deception, people will see it, be unimpressed and feel manipulated. Such deception creates cynicism and lack of genuine commitment. If you're going to be autocratic, then just be honest about it.

Accept Responsibility and Share Credit

Be prepared to shoulder full responsibility for poor decisions and, conversely, to share the credit for good decisions. If you do the opposite—if you take all the credit for good decisions but blame others for mistakes—you will quickly lose the respect of your people.

It takes courage when things go awry to say, "It's *my* responsibility." But that's exactly what you should say—at least if you want to garner people's lasting respect and commitment. Some executives try to explain away a bad decision by saying, "The idea was good, but its execution was botched by others." That may be true. But an effective leader will nonetheless shoulder the blame.

When things go well, give your team the glory and the credit. If you're a good leader, you'll have no need to take center stage and credit for your team's effort. Your contribution will be obvious. Just let it be. As the Chinese philosopher Lao-tzu pointed out 2,500 years ago, "True leaders inspire people to do great things and, when the work is done, their people proudly say, 'We did this ourselves.'"

Leadership Style Element 3: Focus

> **Do first things first—and second things not at all. The alternative is to get nothing done.**
>
> *Peter F. Drucker*

Effective leaders focus their efforts, keeping the number of priorities to a minimum and remaining resolutely fixed on them. You can't do everything; nor can a company on the path to greatness.

Take One Shot at a Time

Create a short list of key priorities and *keep the list short*. Some leaders have found it useful to have only one priority at any given time. They then concentrate on that single priority until they've dispensed with it.

If you must have more than one priority, then keep it to a maximum of three—any more than three priorities is an admission that you don't really have any priorities.

An illustration of this point was made by Bob Bright, executive director of a Chicago-based sporting events company that owned the Chicago Marathon. During Bright's tenure, the race grew from a regional, second-tier event to a first-class international event and the scene of world records. When asked what the key to his success was, Bright responded with the simple statement, "Never put your rifle on automatic."

We asked him to explain. He told us that he had been in the Marines in Vietnam for eight years. He was in the middle of many battles—he led "bait" teams directly into enemy camps. It was there that he learned one of the most important lessons of his life:

> Most people get killed when they put their weapon on automatic, and they just spray everyone around. When you have just a few people, and there is enemy all around you, the best thing is to say, "You take this section from here to here and you take this section from here to here, and *do not* fire on automatic. Take one shot at a time. Don't panic. Don't start spraying the whole area, because you are going to get nobody and they are going to be sitting on top of us."

> Well, the same thing applies to business—and it's really important. Keep yourself focused on one shot at a time. If you don't do that, you're going to end up in a lot of trouble.

Does this mean that you should only have one thing on your "to do" list? Yes and no. Clearly, it is virtually impossible to lead a company and have only one "to do" on your list. But you should be spending the bulk of your time on your number-one priority, concentrating your efforts on that priority until it is complete.

Manage Your Time, Not Your Work

The most constrained resource in your company is your time. Virtually every other resource can somehow be acquired or manufactured, but you cannot acquire or manufacture more time for yourself. There are only twenty-four hours in a day.

Kenneth Atchity, president of Atchity Entertainment International, observed that there is a vital difference between managing time and managing work: work is infinite; time is finite. Work expands to fill whatever time is allotted to it. To be productive, therefore, you must manage your time, *not* your work. The key question to ask yourself is not "What am I going to do?" but "How am I going to spend my time?"

It sounds topsy turvy, but it makes perfect sense if you think about it. The amount of work you have to do, especially if you are the leader of an organization, can expand indefinitely—it's simply not possible to do it all. Atchity hit the point perfectly in his book *A Writer's Time*:

> If your work is successful, it generates more work; as a result, the concept of "finishing your work" is a contradiction in terms so blatant and so dangerous that it can lead to nervous breakdowns—because it puts the pressure on the wrong places in your mind and habits.

How often have you felt that you just don't have enough time to get everything done? Probably a lot. We empathize. None of us have (or ever will have) enough time to get everything done. Every night we will go to sleep with work undone. If we lead productive lives, we will die with work undone.

Yet—and this is crucial—there is much more time available than we generally make good use of. If you manage your time wisely, you will probably "discover" many unused wells of productive time in your life.

The first step is to examine where your time actually goes. Periodically keep track of your time and analyze where it is being spent. Is it being spent on your top priorities? Or, is it being distracted and diverted into unimportant activities?

Is your time being spent primarily in activities that reinforce your vision or directly contribute to the pursuit of your strategy? If not, then you're not focused enough.

One sure way to force yourself to focus is to work *less*. J. Willard Marriott, founder of Marriott Corporation, had a useful philosophy that he applied to building his company from a single-unit restaurant to a major corporation: "Work hard. Make every minute on the job count. Work fewer hours—some of us waste half our time."

Winston Churchill, one of the most prolific individuals in history, took time to paint, lay bricks, feed the animals, and socialize. He then spent his work time (which often didn't begin until 11:00 P.M.) only on the most important items.

Hard Choices—Decisiveness Revisited

Setting priorities requires making tough choices as to what is really important. One reason so many people have such a difficult time getting focused is that they also have a difficult time making decisions: they balk at choosing which items will be left off their priority list. And you must be willing to take items off the list.

One CEO we worked with drove his management team insane because he was unable to choose priorities. He wanted *everything* done. But, alas, almost nothing got done. He would give people twenty "priorities," which, of course, was an impossible wish-list. One manager justifiably grumbled:

> We're supposed to "focus" on twenty items. That's just not possible. But when I go to our CEO and ask, "Which of these are the most important, because I can only do a sub-set of them?" he freezes. He just cannot make hard choices.

This CEO couldn't bring himself to *remove* things from the list, for that would have required a decision. But that is exactly what was needed. The company, not surprisingly, ran into serious difficulties shortly after the above interview.

Leadership Style Element 4: Personal Touch

Leaders who build great companies are "hands on"—always putting their personal touch on the business. There is simply no excuse for being detached, removed, distant, or uninvolved.

Build Relationships

Great companies have great relationships: relationships with customers, with suppliers, with investors, with employees, and with the general community. The emphasis in all dealings is on developing and nurturing long-term, constructive relationships.

(Note: This is very different from the half-hearted disingenuous attention given to "employee relations" or "customer relations." In most companies, "employee relations" has the aim of pacifying people, rather than building a relationship with them. We are writing about something quite different here.)

In a great company, employees have a relationship with the firm that goes far beyond the traditional, "I get paid in exchange for work" mentality. Even former employees feel that they still have a relationship with the company well after their employment has ended. Have you ever noticed that employees who have left certain companies still say "we" when talking about that company?

Customers of great companies have a closer tie than the traditional, "I pay you for product" exchange. They believe that they have a personal relationship with the company. Keep in mind what Leon Bean did with L.L. Bean Corporation, as described in a *Saturday Evening Post* article: "...each of his customers seems to share the illusion that L. L. Bean is a personal discovery, and very probably a personal friend."

These close relationships develop because the company's leaders invest their personal time in helping to shape the relationships.

Joanne Ernst is an athlete who had a contractual arrangement with NIKE for seven years. During this time, NIKE leadership invested in building a long-term relationship with Ernst. She even received personal, handwritten notes and Christmas greetings from Chairman Phil Knight.

This personal investment in the relationship created an intense loyalty and commitment to NIKE. And, as a result, Ernst went to great lengths to be a good spokesperson for the company, often going out of her way—far beyond her contractual obligation—to do something "just right." She explained:

> It was never just a pure business transaction. I've always identified with NIKE's spirit—the spirit of competition and the magic of sports. But it's more than that. If I were to do a bad job, I felt that I would be letting down personal friends. That's really the way I felt about it. Even after retiring from sports and ending my formal connection with the company, I still feel part of the NIKE family. I'll always feel that.

Think of every interaction as an opportunity to establish or further develop a long-term, positive relationship. You can only do this with a personal touch. You don't build relationships with employees by writing stale, formal memos; you do it by interacting in a more personal way.

Get out and talk to people. Walk around. Sit in the lunchroom and eat with all levels of people. Get to know the names of as many people as you can. (Some people, like Kristine McDivitt at Patagonia, learn the names of every employee.) Say hello to people by their first names.

Here is an example of what *not* to do. The general manager of a computer company became convinced that he should "do a little of this personal touch stuff." He had read about MBWA (management by walking around) and told his secretary to arrange for meetings with employees in his office. He wanted to schedule some management by walking around so that he didn't really have to go out and walk around!

You may be wondering if that really happened. It did. And, although it's an extreme case, it's by no means isolated. It is also inexcusable. There is simply no justification for not getting out of the office and interacting personally with people on an informal basis.

Larry Ansin, who completely revitalized Joan Fabrics Corporation after taking it over from his father, told us:

> You've got to get out from behind your desk and see for yourself what's going on. Go out and talk to people. Listen to them. Be visible. Don't wall yourself off with a blizzard of corporate memos.

Ansin was much more successful at building a great company than the general manager who "scheduled" management by walking around in his private office.

Use Informal Communication

A powerful way to add your personal touch is to use quick, informal communication. One particularly effective method is to keep a stack of personal note paper with you at all times. Use it to jot brief, handwritten notes to people. You'd be amazed what a difference this can make. And it hardly takes any time; sometimes it only takes a minute to jot a personal note and sixty seconds is a small amount of time compared to the impact. It lets people know that you're aware of them and what they're doing, and that you care.

Bill tells of how this particular method made a huge difference to him personally in his relationship with Stanford:

> I was in the middle of a particularly grueling quarter of teaching, and was completely exhausted. I also felt a bit depressed because a number of projects I was working on weren't going all that well. Dejected, I stumbled into my office and shuffled through the stack of mail on my desk. I opened an interoffice mail envelope and, to my surprise and delight, found a short handwritten note from the dean thanking me for my efforts on one of my courses. That one note, which probably took him no more than thirty seconds to write, did a lot to solidify my feelings about Stanford and to boost my morale.

Obviously, face-to-face comments or phone calls are also effective methods of providing informal feedback. Whatever method you use, it should be informal, timely, thoughtful, and honest.

Be Accessible and Approachable

There is no benefit to stiff formality. Set a tone of being approachable. Go on a first name basis. Keep the "status barriers" to a minimum. Private parking spaces, ostentatious offices, and flagrant "executives only" privileges should be avoided or downplayed. Executive status symbols put distance between you and the rest of the company.

Figure out how to make yourself accessible. If people feel that there is a moat (complete with alligators in the form of surly secretaries) surrounding your office, you'll certainly begin to lose the personal touch. People at all levels should feel that they can have direct contact with the top executives of the firm.

Does this hold true even as the company grows larger? Does accessibility, direct contact, and personal touch make sense once the firm grows past a certain size?

The answer is yes, and we only have to look at IBM as an example. Even after Thomas J. Watson, Jr. took over from his father (when IBM was already well over a billion dollars), he held fast to the renowned "open door policy." Watson, Jr. wrote in *Father, Son & Company:*

> The open door policy was a practice of Dad's that traced back to the early 1920s. Disgruntled IBM employees were first expected to take up their gripes with their managers. But if they got no satisfaction they had the right to come directly to me. ... On at least one occasion a single protest led to a substantial change in the way we did business.

As the company grew, Watson's office handled 200–300 cases each year. To keep it manageable, he used personal assistants, who were chosen among IBM's most promising young managers. Even after IBM had grown to over 100,000 employees, Watson would still handle some employee complaints himself " ... so that word would get around that the head man was still available."

If the Watsons could be accessible and keep a personal touch on the business as IBM grew, then saying "we are too big for that stuff" is a lame excuse indeed.

Know What's Going On

Reject the common wisdom that as your company grows you should become detached and removed from what's happening on the firing line. Yes, you need to delegate authority. Yes, you should overcome the compulsive impulse to direct every single decision. True, your time will be stretched and increasingly dominated by "high level" meetings.

However, you should still find time for firsthand exposure to the rhythms and activities of the company. The only way to do this is to see with your own eyes and listen with your own ears. See for yourself what the problems are, what is going well, and how people feel.

For example, Sam Walton constantly sought ways to keep his own fingers on the pulse of the enterprise. Walton would drop in on Wal-Mart sites, unannounced, sometimes as many as ten in a single day. In one instance, Walton awoke at 2:30 A.M., bought a box of doughnuts, took them to a warehouse loading dock, and shared them with dock workers while asking them how things could be done better. In another instance, he unexpectedly jumped in the cab of a Wal-Mart semi-truck and rode 100 miles to obtain direct personal insight into Wal-Mart's transportation system.

Walton's behavior is not unusual among the most effective corporate leaders. Granted it is time consuming to go out and see for yourself, especially as the company grows. But it is not impossible. The best corporate leaders *make* time for it. They know that people on the shop floor, in the field, or in the lab are just as important to listen to as other executives.

Reinforce Values with Symbolic Details

There is a paradox evident in those who build the great companies. On one hand, they concentrate on high level vision and strategy while, on the other hand, they involve themselves with seemingly trivial details. The acceptance of the paradox lies in understanding that details are not trivial. Details matter. The most effective leaders are obsessed with both vision *and* details. They are fanatical about getting the details right.

How you deal with certain details is actually a very high level statement—a statement about the core values of the company. Involving yourself with certain details can send a very powerful symbolic message.

Case Example: Debbie Fields

Debbie Fields, founder of Mrs. Fields Cookies, wrote in her book *One Smart Cookie* that she walked into one of her stores unannounced (a common practice of hers) and noticed " ... a very unhappy-looking batch of cookies laid out for the customers."

> They were flat and overbaked. A perfect Mrs. Fields Cookie is half an inch in thickness, and these were a quarter of an inch. A perfect Mrs. Fields cookie is three inches in diameter, and these appeared to measure three and one quarter inches. They were also a little more golden brown than they should have been.

The cookies were only off by a quarter of an inch in each direction—a quarter of an inch! But what really hammered home the importance of detail, and reinforced the underlying Mrs. Fields philosophy, was the way she handled the situation.

She could have fired the store manager on the spot, which she didn't do. She could have sent out a corporate memo reemphasizing proper cookie size and color, but she didn't do that either. She did something much more powerful and symbolic:

> I turned to the young man standing next to me and said, "Tell me, what do you think of these cookies?"
>
> "Aw," he said, "they're good enough."
>
> I nodded. I had my answer. One tray at a time, I took the cookies—five or six hundred dollars' worth— and slid them gently into the garbage can. "You know," I said to him, "good enough never is."

Think of reinforcing values as analogous to kneading bread. Your personal involvement with specific details is part of the kneading process. Like Debbie Fields' trashing of six hundred dollars worth of cookies, your personal touch on a seemingly mundane detail can take on mythic proportions and ingrain itself in people's minds as a vivid symbol of the company's philosophy.

We have a close relationship with Hewlett-Packard Company. Through this relationship we've heard a vast number of stories called "Bill and Dave stories." Each story vividly portrays how Hewlett or Packard dealt with a specific incident in the formative stages of the company.

In one story, according to HP legend, Bill Hewlett, while wandering through a division, noticed a little detail: the stockroom was locked with a chain and padlock. Furious, Hewlett obtained a pair of bolt cutters, destroyed the chain, and left the remnants on the division manager's desk, along with a note: "This isn't how we do things around here. We trust our people. Bill Hewlett."

When asked if this story was true, Hewlett responded simply, "It could be." He then explained that he did a lot of things like the bolt cutter incident in the early days of the company—so many in fact that he couldn't remember them all.

Personal Touch versus Micro-management

Don't confuse personal touch with micro-management; they are not the same. Micro-management—a horribly destructive behavior—is illustrated in the following description of a certain CEO's management style:

> Our CEO tries to control and direct every single little detail. Instead of feeling like you're competent and trusted, you feel that you are being "watched over." He nit-picks everything and it drives us all crazy. Some of our best people have left for other companies because he's so demoralizing. You know the old saying about seeing the forest for the trees? Well, this guy is so far down in the trees that he's trying to control the direction and size of *each pine needle.*

This CEO's style is clearly oppressive, but how is it different from personal touch? Are we being consistent? At first we admonish you to "know what's going on" and to "reinforce values with specific details"; then we admonish you to not "micro-manage." How do these fit together?

The difference is simply this: A micro-manager doesn't trust his people, and seeks to *control* every single detail and decision; he believes that ultimately only he will make the right choices. A personal-touch leader, on the other hand, trusts his people to make basically good choices; he respects their abilities.

A micro-manager doesn't respect his people's abilities. A micro-manager makes people feel like they are being suffocated—the way a twenty-year-old would feel if his parents still dictated bedtime. Anyone who has been micro-managed can attest that it has a terribly demoralizing effect.

Micro-managing also limits people's development. Instead of being a guide or role model, a dominant micro-manager seeks to control people and eventually finds himself surrounded by stunted dwarfs who ask, "Why should I learn to think for myself, when he wants to do all the thinking for me?"

Yes, you should be fanatical about getting the details right. Yes, you should shape the group's values with symbolic acts on certain specific details, but not on *every* detail. The symbolic acts are meant to lead the way—to guide, to show, to set an example. They are meant to leave a lasting impression so that you don't need to tightly control people—so that people will behave *of their own accord* consistent with the core philosophy.

You can be hands-on without stifling people; you can have your fingers on the pulse of the organization, yet not suffocate folks. Indeed, a non-controlling personal touch has just the opposite effect of micro-management. Instead of demoralizing people, it elevates and inspires them to perhaps do more than they would otherwise think possible, which leads us right into our next leadership style element.

Leadership Style Element 5: Hard/Soft People Skills

Leaders who build great companies master the paradox of hard and soft. They hold people to incredibly high standards of performance (hard) yet they go to great lengths to build people up—to make them feel good about themselves and about what they are capable of achieving (soft).

The Importance of Feedback

If we had to pick the single most underused element of effective corporate leadership, it would be feedback—especially *positive* feedback.

It's a fact of human nature that people perform better when they have a positive self-image. Psychologists in a variety of experiments have found that people's performance—*objectively measured*—improves or declines depending on the type of feedback they get. Positive feedback tends to improve performance, whereas negative feedback tends to decrease performance.

Yet, all too often, people get precious little feedback from company leaders—positive *or* negative. This absence of feedback sends a message: We don't care about you. And when people feel you don't care about them they're not going to give their best effort. Why should they?

Great sports coaches—those who have mastered the craft of catalyzing people to perform to their highest possible level—have always known the importance of giving feedback to their athletes and showing that they care.

Tommy Lasorda, Manager of the Los Angeles Dodgers for four National League pennants and two World Series championships, said in an interview with *Fortune Magazine:*

> Happy people give better performances. I want my players to know that I appreciate what they do for me. See, I believe in hugging my players. I believe in patting them on the back. People say, "God you mean to tell me you've got a guy making a million and half dollars a year and got to motivate him?" I say, absolutely. Everybody needs to be motivated, from the President of the United States on down to the guy who works in the clubhouse.

John Wooden, the most accomplished college basketball coach in history (ten NCAA Championships at UCLA in twelve years), believed in always looking for a way to build his players up and, at the same time, continually challenge them to be better. He held a simple philosophy: "People," he said, "need models, not critics." One of his personal admonitions was, " ... to end practice on a happy note. I always tried to counterbalance any criticism in practice with a bit of praise."

Another great coach, Bill Walsh (who oversaw three Super Bowl Championship teams at the San Francisco 49ers), emphasized the importance of personal and positive encouragement. Walsh would shake hands and say a positive personal word of encouragement to every player just before each game. He also asked his assistant coaches to acknowledge each player, shake his hand, and offer supportive thoughts.

These coaches are good role models for business executives. They clearly live up to incredibly high standards, and they make dispassionate, objective assessments of people. Yet, they still use positive reinforcement.

Implicit in this, of course, is the assumption that you genuinely care about the people in your organization—that you have compassion, empathy, and respect for them. And, indeed, this is a requirement for effective corporate leadership. An organization run by individuals who don't care about or respect the people working for them is unlikely to attain enduring greatness.

We attribute much of John Wooden's incredible success to his sincere concern for each player. "My love for young people," he wrote, "is the main reason I have stayed in coaching and have refused positions that would have been far more lucrative."

What about negative or critical feedback? You can't run a company and give only positive feedback. Obviously, there are times when critical feedback is necessary. And, certainly, it's essential to give only *honest* feedback. If you fabricate positive feedback just to make someone feel good, it will lose credibility. In addition, there are times when someone's output needs to be critically evaluated, as that person's performance might be falling far short of expectations.

In his book *Building a Champion,* Bill Walsh wrote:

> The stylish, graceful, easy-going, affable, "players' coach" will get you up to 80 percent of the job done. The final 20 percent is attributable to making tough decisions, demanding a high standard of performance, meeting expectations, paying attention to details, and "grabbing and shaking" when necessary.

All that being said, however, we've observed that *poor* leaders err on the side of too much critical feedback and too little positive feedback. In all too many companies, people only get feedback when they do something wrong, rather than all the times that they do something right.

Furthermore, the best leaders are always looking for ways to put people in positions where they'll do well—where they'll perform at levels that merit positive reinforcement. They're always looking for ways to build people up, rather than tearing them down.

Indeed, if you find that you have someone who is not performing well, you might first ask the question, "Do we have this person in the right job?" It's common to find that an employee who languishes in one job, flourishes in a different role. For example, excellent engineers and sales people often flounder in management roles.

Finally, be aware that when things are going poorly is not necessarily the time to be the most critical. Indeed, harshly berating people who probably already know that things are not going well can be counter-productive. In grim circumstances people often need a little encouragement and support.

Case Example: Russell S. Reynolds

An interesting example is how Russ Reynolds, founder of Russell Reynolds Associates, handled a visit to a poorly performing office. The entire office was absolutely terrified of Reynolds's pending visit, fearing that he would criticize and perhaps fire people. Everyone was on edge, partly because of the office director's statement that "If you can't deliver, then I'm sure Russ will get rid of you and find someone who can."

At the appointed hour, employees assembled in the main conference room, expecting the worst. Reynolds started off the meeting by just chatting with people. After about 30 minutes, the office director tried to plunge into a more serious discussion of the problems at hand. Reynolds pulled the discussion back to a lighter, more positive tone. Finally, in exasperation, the office director asked, "Don't you want to get down to business and deal with our problems here?"

"No," responded Reynolds, "I can see that you're doing everything you can. I'm sure that if you just keep working at it, something will break and the office will turn around. You're good people here, and I have every confidence in you. Just keep at it."

It was absolutely brilliant. Reynolds knew that people needed to be built up at this point, not torn down. People in the office responded by saying, "Hey, this guy *believes* in us. We *can't* let him down." His belief in them was well-founded; the office rebounded and became a very successful unit.

Leader as Teacher

The most constructive approach to critical feedback follows from the concept of leader as teacher. When you need to provide corrective or negative guidance, think not of yourself as a critic—or even a boss—but as a guide, mentor, and teacher.

The process of critique should be an educational experience that contributes to the further development of the individual.

Case Example: H. Irving Grousbeck

Irv Grousbeck, co-founder and President of Continental Cablevision, has developed a very effective approach to Hard/Soft people skills. During a conversation with us, he explained his philosophy and style:

> I've always operated from the model of manager as teacher. I'm interested in how mistakes can be used to improve people's capabilities.
>
> First—and this is important—you don't criticize the person. Instead, you *examine the event*. It's analogous to doing a good job of raising children; you address the issue of a messy closet, rather than criticizing your child for being a messy person.
>
> The same is true in managing. I always ask for the individual's side of the story. I ask him to give me an idea of what happened to make the event turn out the way it did. Then, I'll ask him what options he considered, and I'll present some other options and ask if he considered those. I toss out suggestions in the form of questions.
>
> The whole process is one of education and development. I make it clear that we are sitting on the same side of the table, that there is no problem with him as a person and that there is no problem between him and me. I emphasize that everyone makes mistakes, sometimes illustrating the point by referring to mistakes that I have made.
>
> But I also make it clear that I want the person to learn how the event could have been better handled, so that it can be done better in the future. That way, he is continually developing his capabilities, and the entire company benefits.

Grousbeck has a soft style in providing corrective feedback. Yet, he is resolutely dedicated to a high standard of excellence—both in himself and others. And, more often than not, this standard is attained.

The Role of High Standards

Do not interpret the importance of building people up and helping them learn from mistakes as meaning that you should permit incompetent, poor, or irresponsible performance. Hand in hand with the need for positive reinforcement is the need for high standards.

Just as giving people positive reinforcement tends to increase their performance, so does the presence of challenge and high expectations. Good teachers have always known that students generally *want* to be challenged, and that they generally respond favorably to high expectations. Think back for a moment about the best teachers you ever had. They are probably the ones that held very stringent standards for the class. The same principle applies to effective corporate leadership.

Like a good teacher, a good leader assumes that people from all walks of life and backgrounds *can* perform at high levels and that, deep down, they want to. A good leader doesn't *demand* high performance (demanding implies that people are basically lazy and are inclined to withhold their best effort—that it must be extracted out of them, like pulling teeth).

No, a good leader offers people the opportunity to test themselves, to grow, and to do their best work.

There is no shortage of people interested in doing something in which they can take pride. But there is a vast shortage of leaders who provide the stimulation of stiff challenge and high standards, combined with the uncompromising belief that seemingly ordinary people can do extraordinary things.

Put people in positions where they're required to rise to a high standard, and let them know that you believe they will do so. Keep in mind the approach Trammell Crow took in building his company: betting on people and having faith in them. in *Trammell Crow* by Robert Sobel, a young developer told of his experience with Crow:

> I remember when he took me into a meeting with the contractors and all the lenders and introduced me to them. He built me up as though I was something that I really wasn't, which I think demonstrated confidence in my abilities. I couldn't believe that he would give someone as young and as inexperienced [as I was] that level of responsibility.

This combination of push/pull, yin/yang, hard/soft, high standards/positive reinforcement is the essence of stimulating people to exercise their full capacity. By helping each person to reach his maximum capability, whatever level that might be (and there is a spectrum of abilities across any group of people), you can stimulate the entire company to jump over a very high bar.

Leadership Style Element 6: Communication

We know it sounds trite to underscore the need for communication—and indeed we wish it were trite. The unfortunate fact is that many company leaders are poor communicators. It's not that they can't communicate; it's that they don't.

A great company thrives on communication. Effective leaders stimulate constant communication: up, down, sideways, group, individual, company-wide, written, oral, formal, informal. They work towards having a continual hum of communication throughout the organization.

Communicate Vision and Strategy

In the next chapter, we hammer home the importance of developing a clear vision and strategy for the company. But just developing it is not enough; you also have to communicate the vision and strategy.

You don't have to be a spectacular orator or eloquent writer to communicate effectively. Don't worry about how to communicate where the company is headed, just say it. And say it a lot. Speak it. Write it. Draw it. Say it again. Never let the vision fall from sight; keep it in front of people at all times. Refer to it constantly.

For example, when Jim Burke was CEO at Johnson & Johnson, he estimated that he spent 40% (yes, that is *forty* percent) of his time communicating the J&J Credo (the company's core values and beliefs).

In watching Doug Stone, former CEO of Personal CAD Systems, move about the company, we noticed that he drew pictures of the company's strategy on flip charts in offices and conference rooms throughout the building. During nearly

every meeting he somehow got around to drawing these di-
agrams, and he left these little drawings all over: on scraps
of paper, on people's note pads, on flip charts, on white boards,
on bulletin boards, on lunchroom napkins. When asked about
this, he said:

> I leave those drawings around on purpose. It's really
> hard to get an entire organization to understand where
> it's going, so you've got to keep hammering at the
> message. I leave those drawings around so that people
> will continually bump into them and perhaps refer to
> them during meetings. I guess it's kind of like subliminal
> suggestion.

Use Analogies and Images

Use vivid images to convey what the company is trying
to do. Use concrete examples to illustrate how the company
is actually succeeding in moving towards its vision. Tell stories
that illustrate the values and spirit of the organization.

Analogies, parables, and metaphors, graphically described,
are a powerful form of communication. Use them.

In 1940, Franklin Roosevelt somehow needed to effectively
communicate the concept and necessity of "Lend-Lease" (a program whereby the United States would provide supplies to
a beleaguered Britain during the early phases of World War
II). He could have gone into all the financial complexities of
Lend-Lease, but that would have failed to capture the imagination of the American public. Instead, he resorted to a parable:

> Suppose my neighbor's house catches on fire, and I
> have a length of garden hose. If he can take my garden
> hose and connect it up with his hydrant, I may help
> him put out the fire. Now what do I do? I don't say
> to him before the operation, "Neighbor, my garden hose
> cost me fifteen dollars; you have to pay me fifteen
> dollars for it." ... I don't want fifteen dollars—I want
> my garden hose back after the fire is over.

One of our favorite business examples is that of Steve
Jobs conveying the essence of Apple's vision. In 1980 (before
the Macintosh had been created), he said during a talk at
Stanford:

[Apple] is based on the principle that one person and one computer is fundamentally different from 10 people and one computer. It's like the capital equipment cost of a passenger train: you can buy 1,000 Volkswagens, and, yeah, they're not as comfortable, and they're not quite as fast, but those 1,000 people can go wherever they want, when they want. That's what our industry is all about.

The best analogy ... is that man on a bicycle is twice as efficient as a condor [the most efficient animal]. Man can make tools that will amplify the inherent ability he has. That's what these computers are all about; they're bicycles.

Get out of the literal. Draw pictures. Tell stories. Use inexact analogies. Be vivid. Don't worry about whether the analogy is logically correct—the point is to communicate effectively, not to be logically correct.

Add Personal Touch to Formal Communication

Most business writing and speaking is dull, turgid, and sterile. It has no life, no spark. There's no personality in it. In an effort to be businesslike or presidential, certain managers eliminate any hope they have of communicating effectively.

Have you ever noticed that a good writer makes you feel that she is having a personal conversation with you? Or that a good speaker draws you in, creating an intimacy between you and him, even though there may be many (perhaps thousands) in the audience? This is the effect you should strive to create.

There are two basic ways to achieving this effect.

- First, reveal yourself. Don't be afraid to share stories from your own experience and observations. Telling something about yourself, your own experience, or your unique view of the world creates intimacy, even though there may not be personal contact between you and the writer or speaker.

- Second, use a direct, personal, and unpretentious style. Use words like we, you, and I rather than depersonalized words like one. Use warm words like friends and comrades.

Speak or write directly to the listener as if he's sitting right in front of you. Shorten your sentences. Be vigorous. Use clear language. Use crisp words.

Don't say: "One can see that there are some dissatisfactions with the methods applied to the labor relations situation." Say: "I can see that you folks are angry about the way you've been treated."

Don't say: "It's our policy to maximize the value chain and quality vector for our malt beverage products." Say: "We make a great beer."

Don't say: "The matter at hand is the reduction of financial resources due to litigation-specific economic predation." Say: "Lawsuits are costing us a lot of money."

Call a Duck a Duck—And Don't Hide

It's a big mistake to present unpleasant news in a sugar coated package and a worse mistake to hide from the responsibility of communicating disagreeable facts. It's far better to be honest and direct.

For example, consider the following memo:

To: Director of Personnel

Fr: CEO

Re: Staff Readjustment

With the decline in our business, it's time to cut expenses. Therefore, we must perform a staff readjustment. Attached is a list of individuals that need to be terminated in the next 60 days. Please discuss the situation with their managers.

Emphasize that this is not a layoff. Rather, tell people that it's simply time to eliminate lower performers.

Since this is the first time in our history that we have had a staff readjustment, please handle the situation with care. I expect you to minimize the disruption.

Think for a minute: what's wrong with this? There are at least four problems with the memo:

1. If something looks like a duck, quacks like a duck, and waddles like a duck, then it's probably a duck. No matter how you phrase it, this staff readjustment is a layoff, and only dullards won't recognize it for what it is.

2. The CEO is hiding. Instead of taking responsibility for announcing an unpleasant decision, he is shunting it off onto the director of personnel.

3. Since the layoff isn't being dealt with in a direct and open way, most people will get their information through rumors. This will magnify their fears and cause them to feel very insecure: "How many will there be? Am I one of them? How long will this go on? Should I start to look for a new job?" In addition, they will be resentful: "Do they think I'm an idiot? Why doesn't our CEO tell us about this? Doesn't he have any respect for us?"

4. The outcome is predictable: some of the very best people—the ones that the company most wants to keep—will choose to leave. Those who remain will expend countless hours of nervous energy worrying about their situation, rather than doing productive work.

People hate being misled. They hate being taken for dullards. They quickly lose respect for leaders who don't deal with them honestly and directly.

What should the CEO have done differently? He should have communicated such a painful decision himself. Here is an example of what a more effective leader might do.

My business friends and partners,

I've always believed in communicating with one another for better or for worse, and being up-front and open with most everything that affects our company. In line with that philosophy, I must address one of the most difficult decisions I've had to make in our entire history.

As you know, we've experienced a dramatic decline in our business. This decline has put us in a situation where we must cut expenses in all areas, including staff. We have therefore decided to have a ten percent layoff.

I know that this must come as a shock; we've never had to do this before. And, God knows, I hope we never have to do it again. But in order to ensure survival of the company, which is at stake, we've concluded that this painful step is necessary.

I want you to know that we've decided to implement the layoff in one wave. You have my word that we fully expect this to be the only layoff; we do not have any other layoffs planned. We'd rather take the bitter medicine in one large dose than drag out the agony and uncertainty over an extended period of time.

No matter how it's presented, the news of a layoff is going to be painful, especially for the unfortunate employees who lose their jobs. However, the more direct approach is likely to produce less disruption and garner greater respect than the first approach.

Calling a duck a duck is not only good communication, it also conveys respect for your people. Always assume that people at all levels have nearly infallible duck detectors, and that they prefer leaders who step forward and shoulder the burden of direct, honest communication.

Stimulate Communication in Others

Communication shouldn't flow only from top to bottom. It should be taking place at all levels and in all directions. Be aware that your style can inhibit communication in others. Conversely, it can also induce excellent communication. Remember, you set the tone.

Here are a few things you might consider for stimulating communication throughout the organization:

- Ask a lot of questions and leave people time to answer the questions.

- Ask people to come to staff meetings (which should be scheduled at regular intervals) with at least one major point that they think everyone should know.

- Ask people to come to staff meetings with at least one question they would like to ask. Encourage them to ask any questions that are on their minds. Respond to questions by saying, "Good question. I'm glad you asked that." There's nothing that will shut down communication quicker than if you make people feel stupid for asking questions.

- Ask people in both informal and formal meetings to "speak what is really on your mind."

- When someone disagrees with the group, ensure that the person gets a fair hearing for his disagreement.

- Be spontaneous. Encourage people to get together on the spur of the moment to work on problems. Impromptu informal meetings are some of the best communication vehicles.

- Reduce oppressive, stiff formality. Make people feel comfortable. Loosen your top button and tie. Roll up your sleeves. Kick off your shoes.

- When there are factions or tensions, don't play "go-between." Tell the factions to get together in the same room and discuss the problem themselves, rather than using you as a conduit. People in companies are often like kids in a family—they come running to mom or dad to complain, rather than dealing with a problem directly. Don't encourage this.

- Encourage people to express their feelings as well as their thoughts. We all have strong feelings about things. When feelings are suppressed, real communication cannot take place. Feelings in business? Yes, absolutely. Business, after all, is done by people and people have feelings.

- Don't let one or two personalities dominate all discussion. Draw out the more reticent members of your team by asking them what their views are.

- Thank people for raising key issues, even if those issues are uncomfortable.

Again, it may seem trite to harp on communication. But it's incredibly important, and so many executives are terrible at it. If you're going to err, err on the side of too much communication. You can't overinvest in it.

Leadership Style Element 7: Ever Forward

We would like to emphasize one final element of effective leadership style: an "ever forward" mentality. Leaders of great companies are always moving forward—progressing—as individuals (personal growth) and they pass this ever forward psychology along to the company. They have a high energy level and never become complacent.

Hard Work

There's no getting around the need for hard work. It's a given. It comes with the territory.

However, there is a big difference between hard work and workaholism. You work hard to get something done. A workaholic, on the other hand, works out of compulsion—fear of some sort. Workaholism is unhealthy and destructive. Hard work is healthy, invigorating, and can be practiced up until the day you die, whereas workaholism leads to burn-out.

We know some effective leaders who work only 40–50 hours per week, but who we nonetheless classify as very hard workers—their level of intensity and concentration when at work is incredibly high. Conversely, we know some workaholics who work 90 hours per week and are basically ineffective. More is not necessarily better.

Improve with Each Day

Never stop trying to become a more effective leader. You can always be better. There is always a higher standard. Never stop learning or developing your skills. Remain resolutely committed to the constant pursuit of a higher standard. Try, with each day, to be better than the day before.

Pay attention to your weaknesses and shortcomings. Ask for brutal feedback on where you are weak and what you should work on. Ask for candid criticism of your leadership style from those who work with you and for you. Also ask brutally objective outsiders to observe your leadership style and make comment. (This is something we have done for a number of CEOs, and they have found it to be immensely helpful; but it is also painful.) Put objective, honest outsiders on your board of directors.

None of us find it pleasant to have our shortcomings pointed out. It hurts. We therefore tend to avoid getting feedback that we know will expose our shortcomings. But, like distasteful medicine, it's necessary. To be a really exceptional leader, you've got to be committed to continual self-improvement.

Keep the Energy Up

If you become stale, so will your organization. The moment you cease to be excited and energetic about your work you will simultaneously cease to be effective as a leader. People who build great companies remain energetic their whole tenure. They never "retire on the job." Indeed, some of them never retire at all. They cannot imagine spending their years of wisdom as flaccid, unproductive retirees.

Take care of yourself physically, emotionally, and spiritually. Get enough sleep. Stay healthy. Get some exercise. Have diversions. Read. Converse with interesting people. Expose yourself to new ideas. Spend time in solitary, renewing activities. Set new challenges for yourself. Do whatever is necessary to keep yourself vibrant, stimulated, growing, and alive as a human being.

You've also got to like what you're doing. We've never met an effective small company leader who doesn't basically enjoy his or her work. Doing things you don't enjoy ultimately leads to low energy levels and burn-out.

Finally, one of the best ways to maintain a high energy level is to constantly *change*. Try new things, get involved with new projects, change the way you do things, experiment; do whatever it takes to keep things fresh. Some people think that making changes costs energy. After all, isn't it easier just to keep things the way they are? Ah, but here is the secret: yes, change costs energy but it adds more energy than it uses up.

Have you ever noticed that when you move to a new office or a new house there is an increased level of excitement and energy? You might even complain about the inconvenience

of moving, yet the newness of the situation is nonetheless
stimulating and invigorating. The same principle applies to
work.

Optimism and Tenacity

Psychological research has shown that the most productive
and happy people have a basically optimistic view of the future.
We believe the same is true of companies.

Certainly, you should in no way discount the difficulties
that must be faced, the setbacks that might be encountered,
the pain to be endured, and the possibility of failure. Rose-
colored glasses are dangerous indeed. However, you cannot
afford to doubt that the company has the ability to make
itself and its own future better than it is today. You've got
to believe in your company and its future. If you don't, who
will?

Optimism, however, is not enough; it must go hand in
hand with tenacity and persistence.

When we first met Bob Miller, who took over as CEO
of MIPS Computer in 1987 (when the company was heading
toward insolvency), and successfully led it out of the "dark
days," we were amazed to discover his quiet style. At first,
you might even describe him as low key or soft spoken. How,
we wondered, did he succeed in galvanizing MIPS forward?

After a few minutes, we began to understand. As he
talked, we could sense his resolute, firm conviction that MIPS
had the potential to shape its industry. Combined with this
was a clear and resolute determination that, as long as he
was there, he would never give up. Miller described his view
of business as like being on a mission, and that he never
let obstacles deter him from persistently pressing onward.

Keep the Company Moving "Ever Forward"

Paul Galvin, founder of Motorola, continually pointed out
that, "Everything will turn out all right if we just keep in
motion, moving forward." William McKnight, primary architect
of 3M in its early days, emphasized that many of the company's
product successes came from stumbling onto something, but
that "you can only stumble if you are moving."

Like Galvin and McKnight, corporate leaders who have shaped great companies—people like the Watsons, Leon Gorman and his grandfather Leon Bean, Sam Walton, Bill Hewlett, Akio Morita, William Procter, Walt Disney, and Henry Ford— believed in "ever forward" motion for their companies.

One of the distinguishing characteristics of a great company is that it doesn't stop trying to change, improve, and do new things. A great company never arrives, never believes that it is good enough.

Greatness is not an endpoint, it's a path—a long arduous, tortuous trail of continual development and improvement. A great company reaches one plateau and then seeks new challenges, new risks, new adventures, new standards. A great company celebrates its successes, savors them, enjoys them—but only as brief stopping points along a never completed journey.

Ever forward. If one thing fails, try another. Fix. Try. Do. Adjust. Move. Act. As Henry Ford said, "You've got to keep doing and going."

Touch the Spirit

The essence of leadership, as we have mentioned before, is to catalyze a clear vision that is shared and acted on by the group. But there is one additional element: touching people's spirit.

There is a spiritual side to all of us. For some, it's hidden below case-hardened cynicism, whereas for others it's near the surface. But in all cases it's there to be tapped.

By spiritual we do not necessarily mean religious. We are speaking of the higher side of people; the side that brings a lump to our throats when the underdog prevails; the side that wants to see the good guys win; the side that wants the world to be a better place for our children; the side that compels us to return the extra change when a clerk has given us too much; the side that hopes we would not let our comrades down in battle; the side that causes us to feel outrage at cheating and unfairness; the side that pushes us late into the night to complete an arduous task simply because we gave our word; the side that jumps instinctively into an icy river to save a drowning victim; the side that makes us heroes.

Granted, this is only one side of us. There is another side—the side that Joseph Conrad wrote about in *The Heart of Darkness*. It's the side that breaks commitments, lets our comrades down, keeps the extra change, seeks to crush those less fortunate, pursues expediency over excellence, turns a blind eye to our own inconsistencies and weaknesses. All of us have both sides. A leader, however, appeals to the higher side, stimulating people to take the high road. A leader speaks to the finer qualities we all possess and challenges people to express these qualities. Ultimately, a leader changes people.

Again, we return to our analogy of leader-as-teacher, and we ask you to think about the teachers who have changed your life. Chances are they helped you to see more in yourself than you had seen before. They tapped something inside you that sparked new perceptions of yourself, new expectations of yourself; your ideals for yourself rose to a new level.

Like such a teacher, a leader idealizes people and has resolute conviction that people can rise to this ideal. A leader grabs the spirit in people, pulling it forward and waking it up. A leader changes people's perceptions of themselves, getting them to see *themselves* in the idealized way that *he* sees them.

The leader conveys the message: "We can accomplish our big, hairy goals. I know we can do it, because *I believe in you*."

Chapter 2

VISION

The basic question is, what vision do you aspire to?

Abraham Maslow

$\mathbf{T}$he function of leadership—the number-one responsibility of a leader—is to catalyze a clear and shared vision for the company and to secure commitment to and vigorous pursuit of that vision. As we discussed earlier, this is a universal requirement of leadership, and no matter what your style, you must perform this function.

Why is vision so important? What exactly is vision? And how do you go about setting one?

Answering these questions is the topic of this chapter. We hope to inspire you to put "catalyze a shared vision" as your number one priority. We will then present the "Collins-Porras Vision Framework"—a useful, concrete framework that removes the fuzziness that surrounds the topic yet, at the same time, preserves the magic or spark that's an essential quality of vision. Throughout this chapter, we will provide specific pointers on the process of catalyzing a shared vision.

Before launching into the benefits of vision, we'd like to provide you a quick snapshot of the overall structure that we will be using throughout this chapter and the rest of the book.

Figure 2-1 shows the basic flow: you begin with vision, move to strategy, and then to tactics. It also shows that vision is composed of three basic parts: core values and beliefs, purpose, and mission.

Diagram of Vision, Strategy, Tactics

Figure 2-1

We will explain each of these parts later in the chapter, and give many examples. But first we will explain why you should take on the challenging task of setting a vision.

Vision Is Essential to Greatness

> Consider any great organization—one that has
> lasted over the years—and I think you will
> find that it owes its resiliency to the power
> of what we call beliefs, and the appeal these
> beliefs have for its people ... The basic phi-
> losophy, spirit, and drive of an organization
> have far more to do with its achievements
> than resources, structure, innovation, and
> timing.
>
> *Thomas J. Watson, Jr.*
> *Former CEO, IBM Corporation*

Instilling your company with a lasting corporate vision is a challenging task. As one manager told us, "By asking me to do this you're setting the bar at a very high level." And indeed we are. It is *difficult,* we do not deny.

But vision is essential to attaining corporate greatness. Notice that in the above quote Tom Watson didn't say, "Consider any organization ... "; he said, "Consider any *great* organization ... "

Vision isn't necessary to make money; you can certainly create a profitable business without it. There are plenty of people who have made a lot of money, yet had no compelling vision. But if you want to do *more* than just make a lot of money—if you want to build an enduring, great company—then you need a vision.

If you examine closely the historical evolution of great companies—companies like IBM, L. L. Bean, Hewlett-Packard, Merck, Herman Miller, 3M, McKinsey & Company, Sony, McDonald's, NIKE, Wal-Mart, Disney, Marriott, Procter & Gamble, Boeing, Johnson & Johnson, Motorola, Federal Express, Russell Reynolds Associates, General Electric, PepsiCo, Pioneer Hi-Bred, among others—you will find that, at some point, *while the company was still relatively small,* key leaders instilled a compelling vision into the organization.

In some cases, like Federal Express, the vision was put in at the founding of the company. In other cases, the company was founded by entrepreneurs to fill a specific need (such as to work for themselves or to bring a specific product to market) and they didn't articulate a broader vision until a few years down the road. Minnesota, Mining, and Manufacturing Company, for example, was founded simply to mine corundum (a hard substance similar to emeralds) from a small lake in Minnesota. It was only after that initial venture failed and the company groped around for a few years, that CEO William McKnight developed a broad, clear vision of 3M Company, and its potential impact on the world.

But, in every case, whether at the founding or a few years down the road, key leaders in great companies catalyze and articulate a shared vision for the entire organization.

Four Great Examples

IBM

Thomas J. Watson, Jr., CEO at IBM from 1956 to 1971, felt that the vision of IBM was the single most important ingredient in IBM's rise from a small company on the brink of bankruptcy in 1914 through the perilous phases of growth to its position as one of the most widely admired and consistently successful corporations in history.

Watson felt this so strongly that he published an entire book on the subject: *A Business and its Beliefs—The Ideas That Helped Build IBM,* wherein he writes:

> Any organization, in order to survive and achieve success, must have a sound set of beliefs on which it premises all its policies and actions. I believe the most important single factor in corporate success is faithful adherence to those beliefs. Finally, the organization must be prepared to change everything about itself *except* those beliefs.

Watson's father, Tom Watson, Sr., primary architect of IBM, emphasized the importance of vision to IBM. In 1936, he wrote in a letter to his son that the number one asset a leader should develop is "vision."

(You'll notice that terms mission, vision, purpose, values, objectives, beliefs, culture, and philosophy seem to be used interchangeably and somewhat loosely by different authors and managers. Some make extensive use of the word mission. Others use the term vision and still others use purpose, goals, overall aim, objectives, or culture. For the moment, don't get distracted by terminology and spend a lot of time trying to figure out if vision is different from mission is different from values, etc. We will unravel and clarify these with the Collins-Porras Vision Framework presented later in the chapter.)

Johnson & Johnson

After Robert W. Johnson, Jr. took over from his father as CEO of Johnson & Johnson, he put a great deal of thought into drafting a clear statement of company beliefs. Known thereafter as the "Johnson & Johnson Credo," it became the backdrop for all future planning and decision making in the company.

McKinsey & Company

Marvin Bower, chief architect of McKinsey & Company, the world's most successful management consulting firm, placed a great deal of emphasis on the development and communication of a shared vision from the early days of the firm.

In 1937, when McKinsey was a small firm with only two offices (by 1990 it had 48 offices worldwide), Bower dedicated tremendous amounts of time to codify and articulate the McKinsey vision. At the 1953 Annual Firm Conference, Bower unveiled a "Diagram of the Firm's Principal Personality Characteristics," which was used for years as a blueprint for the "McKinsey Approach." Bower later wrote a book on McKinsey, which emphasized McKinsey's vision. The words "our philosophy," "our approach," "we had to think in visionary terms," "we believe," and "our principles" appear extensively throughout the book, and in the chapter titles.

Hewlett-Packard

During the mid-1950s, when the Hewlett-Packard company was only 15 years old and still relatively small, Bill Hewlett and Dave Packard took their management team off-site to the wine country in Sonoma, California, to codify HP's principles and permanent objectives. Referred to thereafter as the "Sonoma Conferences," these meetings solidified the underlying precepts of HP.

You might be thinking, "But my company is small; I'm not sure all this vision talk applies to us. We're not HP, IBM, J&J, or McKinsey. We're just trying to make a go of it."

Good point. But remember, each of the above companies once was a small, struggling enterprise and, *in every case,* the vision was laid in place *when the company was still small.* It's not that these companies are big and therefore have the luxury of vision; it's that vision helped them become great in the first place. Vision precedes greatness, not vice versa.

A caveat: we don't mean to imply that vision is necessary only if you want to become big. We understand that you might want to remain a small company. If that's what you want, then you still need a vision. Why? Because if you're good, there will be opportunities to grow. The only way to remain small (if that's what you want), is to have a clear vision about what you want the company to be in the first place.

For example, we worked with the owner of a small company that had a serious crisis due to the lack of a clear vision. She tells the story:

> We were nearing the completion of the exhausting development phase of a new product with tremendous market potential. We were then a ten-person company, and this new product would catapult us to at least three or four times that size. Sounds great, huh?
>
> It was the worst experience of my life! As the product neared completion, we began to run around like chickens with our heads cut off getting ready for the influx of orders. I kept having this feeling in my stomach that something wasn't right; that I didn't really want this.
>
> But we just kept pushing ahead, moving inexorably towards a product launch that would forever change the character of the company. No sane person would turn away such a great opportunity—growth, profits, wild success, admiration of others, right? Nonetheless, I kept feeling worse and worse, until I reached the end of my rope, completely burned out.

Then it occurred to me: what we were doing was absolutely contrary to what I wanted for myself, my family, and the company. The problem was that I had never articulated what I wanted our company to be, and we had never talked about it among ourselves. We just kept moving down the day-to-day path of one opportunity after another. Social norms dictated that to grow and become a big overnight success is what we should do. And that's what was driving us. But it wasn't *our* vision for the company, and it wasn't what we wanted out of life. When the stress level finally reached an unbearable peak, we cut the product, and were much happier.

Had we been clear in our minds that our vision was to remain small—a profitable and happy *little* company with a nice lifestyle—we wouldn't have made the decision to do the product, and we never would have gotten ourselves into that horrible mess in the first place.

The Benefits of Vision

Let's now turn our attention to the four primary benefits of corporate vision:

1. Vision forms the basis of extraordinary human effort.
2. Vision provides a context for strategic and tactical decisions.
3. Shared vision creates cohesion, teamwork, and community.
4. Vision lays the groundwork for the company to evolve past dependence on a few key individuals.

A Basis for Extraordinary Human Effort

Human beings respond to values, ideals, dreams, and exhilarating challenges. It's our nature. We will go to phenomenal lengths in an effort to live up to the ideals of our organization, peer group, or society if we share those ideals and consider them worthy. Managers who build their organizations based on a set of worthy values, sound beliefs, and a compelling mission are laying the groundwork for extraordinary human effort.

Most people want to do more than bring home a paycheck. They want work they can believe in and that has meaning.

This may not be true of all people, but it's certainly true of the people most likely to be solid contributors to a great company. Tap into the basic human desire for meaningful work and the traditional management problem of "how to motivate employees" largely evaporates. People will be self-motivated when doing work they believe in.

Motivation depends greatly on the extent to which a person can frame her work within a broader overall purpose. This even applies to routine jobs. During a visit to Giro Sport Design, an assembly worker proudly pointed to a bulletin board. Posted there were letters describing serious bicycle crashes, and how Giro helmets saved people from serious brain injury. "Fortunately," wrote one person, "the helmet shattered, instead of my head. Thank you for being in business."

"That's what we do," said the assembly worker. "We're not just making helmets. We're making people's lives better."

A guiding overall aim, when clear and shared, is so powerful that it can even form the backbone of motivation for an entire country. Writing about Israel in 1967, Barbara Tuchman remarked:

> With all its problems, Israel has one commanding advantage: a sense of purpose. Israelis may not have affluence, or television, or enough water, or the quiet life. But they have what affluence tends to smother: a motive.

Creating this motive is your task as a leader. You do this by creating the vision—by creating what Tuchman calls the "exhilarating task" that bonds a group together.

Think of how the British people rallied in a supreme effort to defeat Hitler in the World War II. Think of how NASA overcame the odds against putting a man on the moon by the end of the 1960s. Think of how Boeing employees dedicated themselves to the "impossible" task of making the revolutionary 747 Jumbo Jet a commercial reality. Think of how engineers at Apple worked 80 hour weeks to bring out a computer that would change the world.

A Context for Strategic and Tactical Decisions

Corporate vision provides a context within which people at all levels can make decisions. *The importance of this cannot be overemphasized.*

A shared vision is like having a compass and distant destination in the mountains. If you give a group of people a compass and destination point and then turn them loose in the mountains to reach that destination, they will probably figure out a way to get there.

They may encounter obstacles, detours, bad turns, and side canyons along the way. However, with the general directions of the compass, a clear end-goal, and the belief that they are working towards a worthy destination, they will probably reach the target.

In contrast, companies without a shared overall aim have no context, and their people wander aimlessly in the side canyons and take detours to nowhere. Such companies resemble overworked fire departments, with people responding to crises and revenue opportunities as they emerge, rather than proactively making decisions within a coherent conception of what the organization is ultimately trying to do.

Case Example:
How Bob Miller Saved MIPS Computer

MIPS Computer was founded in the mid-1980s to capitalize on significant advances in computer technology. It had over $10 million of venture capital financing, state-of-the-art technology, and the promise of growing market demand for powerful computers. Yet, four years after its founding, it was in turmoil and on the brink of bankruptcy. Why?

MIPS had no clear idea of what precisely it was trying to do. It had no clear idea of what it wanted to become. Instead, the sales department blindly pursued every revenue opportunity, without asking the question: what revenue opportunities make the most sense within the context of what we are trying to achieve?

This, in turn, drove R&D to develop (at great cost) a plethora of unrelated products, without asking the question: how do these products help us attain our vision? MIPS leaders pursued joint ventures that severely limited the opportunity to distribute overseas, without ever asking the question: how does the overseas market fit with our vision?

Of course, they *couldn't* ask that question, as there was no clear vision. There was no focal point of united effort, and the organization gradually disintegrated into factions. Each faction blamed others for the perilous position of the organization. Morale declined. Good people left for better opportunities. Investors and customers lost confidence and, hence, cash flow went negative.

It took the leadership of a new CEO, Bob Miller, to save the company. Commenting on how he successfully pulled the company out of its malaise to a prominent position in the RISC Technology industry, Miller commented:

> The most important question is: what do you want to be five to ten years from now? The company had never asked or clearly answered that question. That may seem simplistic, but posing that question was the basic solution. Only then could we make good strategic decisions.

Miller's comment leads to a very important point: Strategy is impossible without first setting a vision.

There are thousands of pages in management literature written about strategy. Strategic Management is a required course at most business schools. Large consulting firms build client lists by selling "strategy solutions." There is good reason for this: sound strategy is essential to attaining greatness.

But think for a minute about the word strategy. What does it really mean? Strategy is *how* one intends to go about attaining a desired end. It is the *means* to an end. Thus, it is wholly impossible to have an effective strategy unless you are clear—absolutely crystal clear—about what the end point is. Strategy is a *path* to attaining your vision. Knowing how to get "there" is impossible if you can't articulate what "there" is.

Most companies (we believe that most organizations do indeed lack clarity of vision) let crises, firefights, and tactical decisions drive the company. We refer to this as "tactics-driving strategy." Vision should drive strategy and strategy, in turn, should drive tactics, not the other way around.

This may seem obvious, and you may be wondering why we're harping on it. We agree. It *is* obvious. However, its practice is also extraordinarily rare. We've noticed that in almost every company with significant organizational problems, one of the root difficulties is the lack of a clear vision. Indeed, it always strikes us as incredible how seriously some organizations suffer from this root problem.

Even in situations of national importance, the phenomenon of tactical success but overall failure due to the lack of a clear overall aim can be played out.

Case Example:
The United States War in Vietnam.

You know, you never defeated us on the battlefield.

An American Colonel, Hanoi, 1975

That may be so. But it is also irrelevant.

North Vietnamese Colonel in response

In terms of tactics and logistics, according to Harry G. Summers in the book *On Strategy*, the United States Army was successful in Vietnam. Over a million soldiers a year were transported to and from Vietnam, and they were sustained in the field better than any army in history. In tactical engagements, the army had an extraordinary success rate, with enemy forces thrown back with terrible losses in engagement after engagement. Even so, it was North Vietnam that emerged victorious. How could the United States have succeeded so well, yet failed so miserably?

A wide range of authors on the subject all came to a startlingly simple conclusion: the United States didn't know precisely what it was trying to achieve, and it was therefore impossible to have an effective strategy. A 1974 survey of Army generals who had commanded in Vietnam found that almost 70% of them were uncertain of United States objectives.

"This confusion over objectives," Summers concluded, "had a devastating effect on [United States] ability to conduct the war."

"The principals never defined either the mission or the number of troops," wrote David Halbertsam, author of *The Best and the Brightest.* "It seems incredible in retrospect, but it is true. Hence, there was never a clear demonstration of what the strategy would be."

Halberstam might have pointed out that without this clarity of aim, it would have been absolutely impossible to even have a strategy in the first place.

Don't get us wrong. We don't mean to imply that tactical excellence (as the United States had in Vietnam) is unimportant. It's essential, but it should be within the context of a clear overall vision. Vision, then strategy, then tactics.

Cohesion, Teamwork, and Community

As coach John Wooden of the UCLA Bruins pointed out, you have to build up each player to be his best as a guard, center, or forward, but it is even more important to develop the individual player's pride and belief in the whole team and its goals. Coaches like Wooden successfully reconcile the two by having very clear shared goals and an underlying set of principles and values that hold the team together.

Without a shared vision, any organization can easily degenerate into factions. Disparate agendas, turf wars, empire building, and petty politics become prevalent; destructive infighting saps people's energies, rather than working for a common aim and towards the strengthening of the entire organization. It becomes impossible to maintain a strong and positive sense of community.

Companies are usually founded with a clear, vibrant sense of purpose. Yet as companies mature, they often disintegrate into squabbling factions. Institutional self-enhancement and turf wars smother the spark and spirit of the early sense of purpose.

In one company, we interviewed the top ten managers separately and asked: "What's this company all about? What are you trying to become? What are you trying to achieve?" No two people gave the same answer. As one explained: "We are a collection of ten individuals with personal agendas, ready to charge in the opposite direction from everyone else. No wonder we have problems."

The company erupted into a devastating series of internal battles, complete with secret pacts among key players to gang up on other players. The company was eventually acquired (for a low price) by a large corporation, leaving one of the VPs to comment:

> We had such potential, and we just squandered it. Once we lost a sense of unified purpose, we put all our creative energies into fighting among ourselves, rather than winning in the market place. It's sad.

Conversely, we've seen companies on the brink of destruction, pull together with common purpose and overcome incredible odds. Ramtek Corporation, for example, had filed for Chapter 11 bankruptcy protection. A new CEO, Jim Swanson, took over the company and resurrected it to new life and steered it out of bankruptcy. (Most companies that file Chapter 11 die on the operating table.)

"Our mission," said Swanson, "was to get out of bankruptcy. It was such a challenging task that it unified the team to put forth supreme efforts and beat the odds."

Soon after emerging from bankruptcy, Swanson took his team off-site to set a new mission. "We had a big challenge," he said. "We met it. Now we need a new one or else we'll lose that sense of team spirit."

In Chapter 4, Innovation, we stress the importance of decentralization and autonomy. The problem, of course, is how to unleash individual creativity and, at the same time, move in a unified direction. Vision is the link. If all people in the company have a guiding star on which to sight (a common vision), they can be dispersed in hundreds of independent little boats, rowing in the same direction.

Evolving Past Dependence
on a Few Key Individuals

In the early phases of an organization, a company's vision comes directly from its early leaders; it is very much their personal vision. To become great, however, a company must progress past excessive dependence on one or a few key individuals. The vision must become *shared as a community,* and become *identified primarily with the organization* rather than with certain individuals running the organization. The vision must actually transcend the founders.

To illustrate this point, we like to use the powerful historical example of the founding and subsequent development of the United States. Instead of creating a country that depended on the continued presence of the then living leaders (Washington, Jefferson, Adams, et al.), the founders put in place a set of basic principles that would guide the country for centuries after their death.

In essence, they codified the vision of the country in the Declaration of Independence and the United States Constitution. They thereby ensured that the future of the United States would come close to living up to their beliefs about how the country should run and, just as important, would not require the continued presence of these individuals.

Those fellows in Philadelphia in 1787 were very smart: by instituting the enduring principles of the Constitution, they created the "glue" that would hold the country together even in the absence of a common enemy or the single "great dictator." Students of history will agree that this is very rare indeed.

[Note: We realize that the United States Constitution is not a perfect document. Our purpose here is not to deify the Constitution per se but rather to illustrate the idea of creating a self-renewing society that derives its strength more from an enduring set of principles than from the presence of specific leaders.]

It's interesting to note that when Tom Watson, Jr. took over IBM from his father in 1956, he had the Constitution in mind when he took the top executives off-site to create the "Williamsburg Plan," as he wrote in *Father, Son & Company:*

> I picked Williamsburg [Virginia] because it is a historical place and this meeting was meant to be a kind of constitutional convention for IBM.

In contrast, there is the example of Duncan Syme and Vermont Castings. Syme had a vision: to make the best wood stoves in the world. He believed in this so much that he would personally stand on the production line to ensure that each stove met his exacting standards. During the 1970s, Vermont Castings became the fastest growing company in the wood stove industry, reaching sales of $29 million and margins as high as 60%.

Then, in the early 1980s, Syme stepped away from daily operations and turned the company over to professional managers (day-to-day management, Syme admitted, was not his strength).

But there was a critical problem: Syme's vision went into retirement with Syme. In his absence, the company lowered quality standards, diluted its traditional focus on wood stoves, reduced customer service, and pulled the company away from its original vision. Sales and profit growth flattened, the company lost its ability to bring out innovative new products, and many felt the company had lost its greatness.

Syme returned to Vermont Castings in 1986 and got it back on track, reinstalling his vision and regaining the company's position as the premier wood stovemaker.

This time, however, he took an entirely different approach, as he explained in *Inc.* magazine. Instead of relying solely on himself to be the guardian of the "Vermont Castings Way," he began a process of institutionalizing his vision. He wrote a "Statement of Vermont Castings Vision and Creed" and began the long process of ensuring that it was expressed in all operational decisions.

Creating a company with a vision (rather than a company with a single visionary leader on whom everything depends) is difficult for some leaders. They like being the "visionary"—the hero or great leader—on whom everything depends. The truly visionary managers are those who make the vision *property of the entire enterprise* and instill it in such a way that its remains strong and intact well after the leader departs from daily operations.

A Vision Framework

The word vision conjures up all kinds of images. We think of outstanding achievement. We think of deeply held values and beliefs that bond the people in a society together. We think of audacious, exhilarating goals that galvanize people. We think of something eternal—the underlying reasons for an organization's existence. We think of something that reaches inside us and pulls out our best efforts.

And therein lies a problem. Vision has a nice feel. We can agree that it's essential to greatness. But what exactly *is* it?

The Collins-Porras Vision Framework

A number of CEOs have told us that they can't seem to get their hands on what vision is. They've heard lots of terms like mission, purpose, values, strategic intent, but no one has given them a satisfactory way of looking at it that will transcend the morass of words and set a coherent vision for the company.

Out of this frustration, the Collins-Porras Vision Framework was developed. Much of the material in this chapter is based on extensive research at Stanford and the article, "Organizational Vision and Visionary Organizations" *(California Management Review,* Fall 1991). We need not go into all of the theoretical underpinnings and background research of the framework here. The essence of it is that a good vision consists of:

1. CORE VALUES AND BELIEFS
2. PURPOSE
3. MISSION

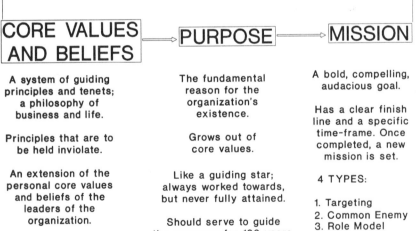

Collins-Porras Vision Framework

VISION

CORE VALUES AND BELIEFS	PURPOSE	MISSION
A system of guiding principles and tenets; a philosophy of business and life.	The fundamental reason for the organization's existence.	A bold, compelling, audacious goal.
Principles that are to be held inviolate.	Grows out of core values.	Has a clear finish line and a specific time-frame. Once completed, a new mission is set.
An extension of the personal core values and beliefs of the leaders of the organization.	Like a guiding star; always worked towards, but never fully attained. Should serve to guide the company for 100 years.	4 TYPES: 1. Targeting 2. Common Enemy 3. Role Model 4. Internal Transformation

Figure 2-2

We've found that people quickly grasp the concept of core values and beliefs. However, the difference between purpose and mission often causes confusion.

To quickly grasp the difference between purpose and mission, think of pursuing a guiding star across a mountain range. Your *purpose* is the guiding star, always out there on the horizon, never attainable, but always pulling you forward. Your *mission*, on the other hand, is the specific mountain you are climbing at any moment. While assaulting that mountain, all your focus and energy goes into that specific ascent. But once you reach the top, you sight again on the guiding star (your purpose) and pick yet another mountain to climb (another mission). And, of course, throughout the entire adventure, you remain true to your core values and beliefs.

With these as models, you can set and codify your own corporate vision from the following examples.

Vision Component 1: Core Values and Beliefs

Core values and beliefs are where vision begins. Core values and beliefs are like an ether that permeates an organization—its decisions, its policies, its actions—throughout all phases of its evolution. Some companies refer to this as their "guiding philosophy."

Core values and beliefs form a system of fundamental motivating principles and tenets—precepts about what is important in both business and life, how business should be conducted, its view of humanity, its role in society, the way the world works, what is to be held inviolate, and so on. You can think of it as analogous to the "philosophy of life" that an individual might have. Core values and beliefs are analogous to a biological organism's "genetic code"—they are in the background, but always present as a shaping force.

The core values and beliefs come from *inside* you. You, as a leader of the company, imprint your personal values and beliefs about life and business through your daily actions.

And therein lies the crucial aspect of core values and beliefs: they must be an *absolutely authentic* extension of the values and beliefs you hold in your own gut. You don't "set" values. The proper question isn't, "What values and beliefs *should* we have?" but rather "What values and beliefs *do we actually hold in our gut?*"

Ultimately, core values and beliefs get instilled by what you *do*, by specific, concrete actions, not by what you say.

For example, L. L. Bean was built on the core values and beliefs espoused by Leon Leonwood Bean. Bean, who founded the company in 1911, had a deeply held personal philosophy, summed up simply as, "Sell good merchandise at a reasonable price, treat your customers like you would your friends, and the business will take care of itself."

Nice sentiment. But the foundation of Bean's strength isn't sentiment; it's the actions that reflect the sincerity of the sentiment. He implemented a 100% guarantee of absolute satisfaction via a no-questions-asked refund policy. (In one instance, the company refunded the full purchase price of a never-worn shirt purchased 32 years earlier.) He decided Bean would never close, keeping the phone-order lines open 24 hours a day, 365 days per year. He demanded that all products be manufactured to exacting standards, and that customers be charged a fair price.

"But that's not values," you might be thinking. "That's just good business." We agree. It is good business.

But the power of Bean's mystique—the reason for its dedicated employees and its fanatically loyal customer base —is the fact that behind its actions are a set of genuine values. Ol' L. L. sincerely believed in treating customers like friends. He wouldn't have done it any other way!

Some Examples

Examples of core values and beliefs from Herman Miller, Telecare Corporation, Merck, Hewlett-Packard, and Johnson & Johnson follow. We believe we can best illustrate core values and beliefs with specific, detailed examples. Some of these examples come from discussions with managers of those companies, documents, or observations of their actions. We're not suggesting that the specific values and beliefs in our examples should be yours. They are illustrations.

Herman Miller, Inc.
Core Values and Beliefs*

We are a research-driven product company; we are not a market-driven company.

We intend to make a contribution to society, through our products, services, and the way we deliver them.

We are dedicated to quality; quality of product, quality of service, quality of relationships, quality of our communications, quality of our promises.

We believe that we should be, for all who are involved, a place of realized potential.

We cannot live our lives isolated from the needs of society.

We are deeply committed to the Scanlon idea, a plan for practicing participative management, including productivity and profit sharing.

Profit, like breathing, is indispensable. While it is not the sole goal of our lives, in the context of our opportunities, profit must be a result of our contribution.

* Abstracted from *Leadership Is an Art*, by Herman Miller CEO Max DePree. Published by Doubleday, 1989.

Telecare Corporation
Core Values and Beliefs

We believe in doing a really outstanding job—we simply don't want to do anything without high quality.

We believe in having a long term commitment to employee development.

We believe that we have a responsibility to society and that our service is vitally needed by individuals, families, and the community. We believe that Telecare, in particular, is needed because no one can provide this service as well as we can.

We believe that we should help patients rehabilitate to their highest level, regardless of their level of impairment.

We believe in hard work and the enjoyment of it.

We believe in growth both for ourselves as individuals and, over the long term, of the organization.

We do not exist to maximize profit, yet we must nonetheless be an efficient, productive, and profitable business, or else we limit our ability to be of service.

The Johnson & Johnson Credo*

We believe that our first responsibility is to our customers.

Our second responsibility is to our employees.

Our third responsibility is to our management.

Our fourth responsibility is to the communities in which we live. We must be a good citizen.

Our fifth and last responsibility is to our stockholders. Business must make a sound profit. When we operate according to our principles, stockholders should realize a fair return.

We are determined with the help of God's grace to fulfill these obligations to the best of our ability.

* Paraphrased from the Johnson & Johnson Credo, by R.W. Johnson, 1943.

Hewlett-Packard Core Values and Beliefs*

In the words of Dave Packard: "The HP Way says, 'Do unto others as you would have them do unto you.' That's really what it's all about."

In the words of Bill Hewlett: "Fundamentally, the HP way is respect for the individual. If you give him a chance, the individual will do a lot more than you think he can. So you give him the freedom. Respect for the individual—not just employees, but customers and the works."

* From interviews with Bill Hewlett and Dave Packard.

Merck & Company
*Core Values and Beliefs**

We value above all our ability to serve the patient.

We are committed to the highest standards of ethics and integrity.

We are responsible to our customers, to our employees, and to the societies we serve ... Our interactions with all segments of society—customers, suppliers, governments, and the general public—must reflect the high standards we profess.

We are committed to research that matches science to the needs of humanity.

Since our future as a company rests squarely on the knowledge, imagination, skills, teamwork, and integrity of our employees, we value these qualities most highly.

We expect profit, but profit from work that benefits humanity.

* Abstracted from Merck & Company "Statement of Corporate Purpose," 1989.

The Role of Profit

Notice that the companies in our examples tend to view profit as a necessity, rather than as the ultimate goal of the business. What do you make of that? How does this fit with the classic business school doctrine that the purpose of a business—the primary responsibility of its managers—is to maximize shareholder wealth?

To become a great company, we ask you to reject the classic business school doctrine. "Maximize shareholder wealth" is a simple theoretical way of looking at business, but it's not supported by the reality of many great companies. Most great companies are formed to meet the goals and express the values of their founders, which is not always the same as maximizing shareholder wealth. For them, profit is simply a strategic necessity rather than the supreme end point.

This may be a jolting concept, we realize. But we're certainly not the only management writers who have come to the same conclusion. Peter F. Drucker, in his classic text, *Management:*

Task, Responsibilities, Practices, reached the same conclusion years ago:

> Business cannot be defined or explained in terms of profit... The concept of profit maximization is, in fact, meaningless... The first test of any business is *not* the maximization of profit, but the achievement of sufficient profit to cover the risks of economic activity...

We don't deny—and neither do the companies we've worked with and studied—that profit is essential. Actually, it's not profit per se that's essential, but the cash flow that it generates. A business cannot exist without adequate cash flow, and to have an eternal, self-generating source of cash, the company must be profitable.

But profitability and cash flow are not what work is ultimately all about. Profit maximization doesn't provide the type of inspirational aim that people throughout the company are willing to put their full energies towards, to commit a part of their spirit to. We are not saying that profit is bad. Yes, absolutely profit is needed, but profit in and of itself does not provide meaning.

Tom Chappell, founder of Tom's of Maine, a highly profitable company, explained in *Inc.* magazine how the pursuit of numbers alone is an endless treadmill:

> Quantitative goals can't invest purpose in a process that has none. The quest simply for *more* of anything is inherently unsatisfying. If there is no point or joy in what your are doing, or if you lose sight of the point, then just measuring your progress can't make it worthwhile or fun. If I can organize people around purpose, that is the most powerful form of leadership.

Returning to our example of L. L. Bean, we see that Leon Leonwood Bean was motivated primarily by his love of the outdoors, his passion for his products, and a desire to do business in a way that reflected his values. He grew the business slowly, taking 55 years to reach the size of 160 employees. Profit as a percentage of sales in 1966 was only 2.2%, with significant room for improvement (as demonstrated by the fact that profitability improved dramatically after his grandson took over).

Yes, Bean could have had a bigger company, and a more profitable company. But this was not his purpose. As ol' L.L.

used to say in expressing satisfaction with his life, "I'm already eating three meals a day, and couldn't eat a fourth."

But if profit maximization is not necessarily the purpose of the business, then what is? This brings us to the next component of a good vision: purpose.

Vision Component 2: Purpose

Purpose, the second primary part of a good vision, is an outgrowth of your core values and beliefs. Purpose is the fundamental reason for your company's existence—its ultimate reason for being. Your company's purpose dovetails with the sense of personal purpose that you and other members of the company hold deep within you, and thereby provides meaning to work.

A crucial aspect of purpose is that it's always worked towards, but never fully achieved, like chasing the earth's horizon or pursuing a guiding star. The enduring aspect of purpose is well illustrated by Steve Jobs, co-founder of Apple and founder of NeXT:

I don't feel that I'll ever be done. There are lots of hurdles out there, and there's always a hurdle that I'll never reach in my lifetime. The point is to keep working toward it.

To make a personal analogy, purpose plays the role that a sense of life purpose can provide an individual. A person with a purpose will never be at a loss for meaningful work.

Have you ever noticed that extraordinary people—people like Michelangelo, Churchill, Roosevelt, and Maslow—led productive, fulfilled lives right up to their deaths? They had a sense of personal purpose that could never be completed; they would never be done; they could never submit themselves to the oblivion of unproductive retirement. Purpose in a company plays a similar motivating role.

The Statement of Purpose

You should be able to articulate your company's purpose succinctly, in one or two sentences. This is called a "Statement of Purpose." A statement of purpose should quickly and clearly convey why your company exists, how it fills basic human needs and impacts the world.

A good purpose statement is broad, fundamental, inspirational, and enduring. It should serve to guide your organization for at least 100 years.

Again, we turn to examples from actual organizations. Refer to the following representative list of purpose statements.

Statements of Purpose

Merck

We are in the business of preserving and improving human life. All of our actions must be measured by our success in achieving this.

Schlage Lock Company

To make the world more secure.

Giro Sport Design

Giro exists to make people's lives better through innovative, high quality products.

Celtrix Laboratories

To improve the quality of life through innovative human therapeutics.

Lost Arrow/Patagonia

To be a role model and tool for social change.

Pioneer Hi-Bred International

To create agricultural science products that may very well be critical to sustaining mankind in the future.

Telecare Corporation

To help people with mental impairments realize their full potential.

McKinsey & Company

To help leading corporations and governments be more successful.

Mary Kay Cosmetics

To be a company that gives unlimited opportunity to women.

Kennedy-Jenks

Our purpose is to provide solutions that protect the environment and improve the quality of life.

Advanced Decision Systems

To enhance decision making power.

Stanford University

To enhance and disseminate knowledge that improves human kind.

Discovering Purpose: The "Five Whys"

When articulating purpose, don't make the error of simply writing a specific description of your current product lines or customer segments. "We exist to make computers for knowledge workers" is not a good purpose statement. It's neither compelling nor flexible enough to last for 100 years. It's merely descriptive of what a certain company currently does.

A far better purpose would be:

Our purpose is to make a contribution by creating great tools for the mind that advance humankind.

Does this mean you should avoid mentioning your products or customers in your purpose statement? Yes and no. Yes, you should avoid sterile, descriptive, bland, dull statements like, "We exist to make X products for Y customers."

On the other hand, if you can tie your products to a more fundamental need, and if you are clear that you are only going to do that type of product for the next 100 years, then you might produce a purpose statement like Celtrix Laboratories. Celtrix was tempted to state its purpose as, "To develop, manufacture, and sell human therapeutics products." Wisely, however, CEO Bruce Pharriss took it a step further and asked, "*Why* do we want to do this? *Why* is this important? *Why* do we want to dedicate a portion of our lives to this?" In response, Celtrix created the following purpose statement:

To improve the quality of human life through innovative human therapeutics.

This process of asking multiple layers of "why" is powerful for getting at purpose. One very powerful "why" question is:

"Why should we continue to exist? What would the world lose if we ceased to exist?" [Note: this may seem like an odd question, but it's very effective for quickly getting to the core of purpose: why the company exists.]

Another powerful approach is to start with the statement, "We make X products" and then ask "why" five times. We call this the "five whys" approach. After five whys, you'll find that you're getting down to the fundamental purpose of the business.

Here's an example of how the five whys lead from products to Patagonia's purpose.

"We make outdoor clothing."

"Why?"

"Because it's what we know best and what we like to do."

"Why is that important?"

"Because it's the best way to make innovative, high quality products that people will pay well for."

"Why is that important?"

"Because that is how we can continue to be financially successful."

"Why is that important?"

"Because we need the credibility of being a successful business, and the resources to do business in the way we think it ought to be done."

"Why is that important?"

"Because we ultimately exist to be a role model and tool for social change, and the only way we can do that is to be financially viable and successful enough to have the rest of the business community looking to us as a role model."

You Already Have A Purpose

Does every company need a statement of purpose?

In answering this question, let us be clear about one thing: every company *has* a purpose—a reason for being. It's just that most companies have never formally articulated it. Nevertheless, a purpose exists, whether written down or not. Often it's unstated and implicit, but always there, in the woodwork.

For instance, NIKE has existed for years without a formally articulated statement of purpose. Yet, NIKE is driven by a powerful purpose that permeates the entire company: to be a vehicle for competition and victory, both in corporate life and in athletic combat. Although it's not specified in a single-sentence statement, this underlying purpose, which comes from the competitive spirit of founder Phil Knight, is the core driving force of NIKE. (In fact, NIKE's name is that of the Goddess of Victory in Greek mythology.)

Even though you already have a purpose, it's nonetheless a valuable exercise to think through the question: what exactly *is* our purpose? Keeping your answer to a *short and direct* sentence helps to clarify what the business is ultimately all about. And, once clarified, it acts as a test for all decisions: is this action consistent with our purpose?

Purpose Need Not Be Unique

You've undoubtedly noticed that some of the purpose examples we've given could apply to numerous organizations—they don't necessarily differentiate one company from another. That's ok. Purpose is a motivating factor, not a differentiating factor. It's entirely possible for two companies to have the same purpose.

Your mission, on the other hand, will certainly differentiate you from everyone else.

Vision Component 3: Mission

Mission, the third key part of an effective vision, is a clear and compelling overall goal that serves as a focal point of effort.

To quickly grasp the concept of mission, think of the NASA moon mission as articulated by President Kennedy in 1961:

This nation should dedicate itself to achieving the goal, before this decade is out, of landing a man on the moon and returning him safely to earth.

Unlike purpose, which is never achieved, a mission should be achievable. It translates values and purpose into an energizing, highly focused goal—like the moon mission. It is crisp, clear, bold, exhilarating. It reaches out and grabs people in the gut. It requires little or no explanation; people "get it" right away. Once a mission is fulfilled, you return to purpose to set a new mission.

Remember the analogy of pursuing a guiding star across a mountain range. Your purpose is the guiding star, always out there on the horizon, never attainable, but always pulling you forward. Your mission is the specific mountain you are climbing at any moment. Once you reach the top, you sight again on the guiding star and pick yet another mountain to climb.

A good mission has a finish line—you must be able to know when you've done it, like the moon mission or a mountain top. A good mission is risky, falling in the grey area where reason says, "This is unreasonable," and intuition says, "But we believe we can do it nonetheless."

We like to use the following phrase to convey the idea of mission:

big, hairy, audacious goal.

Finally—and this is important—a good mission has a *specific time frame* for its achievement.

The moon project was a beautiful example of just such a mission. It was exciting. It was big, hairy, and audacious, yet achievable. It had a clear finish line and it had a time frame.

Reject the Standard Mission Statement

We realize that our definition of mission is different from that used at most companies. Please, reject the standard approach! Most corporate mission statements are terrible. They're all too often nothing more than a description, and a bland one at that, of the operations of the company—a boring stream of words that evokes the response, "True, but who cares?" Managers draft a bunch of words that make sense, but that have all the appeal of snuggling up to a cold, dead fish. They smack of corporate double-speak and are incapable of tapping people's spirit.

Here are some examples of typically ineffective mission statements (from actual companies):

> The Corporation is committed to providing innovative engineering solutions to specialized problems where technology and close attention to customer service can differentiate it from commodity of production or job shop operations.

Just makes you want to go out and conquer the world, doesn't it?

> We provide our customers with retail banking, real estate, finance, and corporate banking products which will meet their credit, investment, security and liquidity needs.

Now, *that* is really exciting!

> [The company] is in the business of applying microelectronics and computer technology in two general areas: computer-related hardware; and computer enhancing services, which include computation, information, education, and finance.

This sends a tingle down the spine; we can hardly sit still.

We know we're being a bit sarcastic and harsh. Nevertheless, we've got to get across the point that mission statements like these just don't work. They will not inspire or galvanize your company. As an employee of one of the above companies told us in response to his company's mission statement:

> This is ridiculous. The statement is very long and very boring. By the time I finished reading it, I was totally uninspired and had lost confidence in the people at the top of this organization. I mean, blah—who wants to read this stuff? It's dreary. If they don't show any excitement for what the organization is trying to do, then how can they expect any one else to get inspired?

Be Compelling and Passionate in Your Mission

Your mission must meet one overriding criterion: it must be *compelling*. The best missions have an element of genuine passion in them.
Don't set a mission like this:

To make and sell athletic shoes on a worldwide basis.

Set a mission like this:

Crush Reebok

Don't set a mission like this:

To make high end reduced instruction set micro-processors for a wide range of applications.

Set a mission like this:

Make the MIPS architecture pervasive worldwide by the mid-1990s

Don't set a mission like this:

To be a producer of automotive products that meet consumer needs and provide an adequate return to shareholders.

Set a mission like Henry Ford's in 1909:

We're going to democratize the automobile

One of our favorite examples of a good mission statement is Britain's mission in 1940, as articulated by Winston Churchill:

Our whole people and empire have vowed themselves to the single task of cleansing Europe of the Nazi pestilence and saving the world from the new dark ages. We seek to beat the life and soul out of Hitler and Hitlerism. That alone. That all the time. That to the end.

Now *that* is a mission. Granted, Britain's mission in 1940 is hardly the type of goal that could be taken on by a small company. Nevertheless it conveys the idea that a mission should have an element of passion.

Risk, Commitment, and the Zone of Discomfort

But isn't setting such an audacious mission risky? Yes. A good mission should be difficult to achieve. There should be a chance you'll fail, combined with an off-setting belief that you'll make it anyway. That's part of what makes it a real mission.

What about highly conservative companies that have attained greatness? They don't run themselves like "bet the farm" entrepreneurial ventures, do they? Actually, some of the most conservative companies have set highly risky missions. Let's look briefly at three examples: IBM, Boeing, and Procter & Gamble.

- In the early 1960s, IBM bet the company on a big mission: to remake the computer industry with the IBM 360. It was the largest privately financed commercial project ever undertaken, and required more resources than it took to build the first Atomic Bomb. *Fortune* magazine called it " ... perhaps the riskiest business judgement of recent times." During the 360 introduction, IBM built up nearly 600 million dollars of work in process inventory and almost needed emergency loans to meet payroll.

- Boeing has pushed itself to the limit with risky missions, such as one set in the 1950s: to create a successful commercial jet aircraft. Boeing invested a substantial portion of its net worth in the project which, had it failed, would have jeopardized the company's solvency. The Boeing 707 was the result. A decade later, Boeing made a similar gamble with the 747.

- Procter & Gamble, known as one of the most conservative of all companies, has a history of committing to risky goals. For example, in the early 1900s, P&G established an internal mission: to reach a point where it could provide steady employment for its workers, rather than the hire and fire swings forced by seasonal demands.

These swings were caused by the demands of wholesalers, who ordered in large quantities and then, like a snake digesting a large meal, would lie dormant. To achieve the mission, P&G took the audacious step of setting up a sales force to sell directly to retailers—a move that at the time was thought by industry observers to be insane. But CEO Richard Deupree had a simple philosophy about bold, audacious moves:

> We like to try the impractical and impossible and prove it to be both practical and possible. You do something you think is right. If it clicks, you give it a ride. If you hit, mortgage the farm and go for broke.

Common to each of these companies was 1) a belief that they could fulfill the mission, and 2) a willingness to go for it. This willingness to put it on the line is part of the vision-setting process. Your task is to pick a mission that falls in a zone of discomfort—where it's not a sure bet, yet you believe deep down the company can do it.

You set a mission not by pure analysis, but by analysis plus intuition. You'll never be able to prove ahead of time that an audacious mission is going to be 100% achievable. You have to know in your gut that it can be done, recognizing this simple truth: once committed to a bold challenge, the probabilities of success change.

When Kennedy first proposed the moon mission, he was advised that there was only a 50/50 chance of success. He believed in America's ability to achieve the mission, to somehow turn the odds. He knew that if the country committed to the mission, it would somehow find a way.

Think of it this way. If someone puts you on a difficult mountain climb and leaves you an easy avenue of retreat, the probabilities of success would be at a certain level, say, for the sake of argument, 50%. Now suppose you are on the same mountain and the avenue of escape is removed; if you don't succeed, you die. The probabilities of success change to closer to 100%. Why? Because you are committed. You'll fight, scratch, invent, or somehow figure out a way to the top because you have no other choice.

Be Sincere

Like your values and purpose, your mission has to be sincere and authentic—something that you want to obtain badly enough that you're willing to make personal sacrifices for its attainment. We've seen cases where the leaders of a company outline a great-sounding mission that's not an honest reflection of their real aims for the business. This never works and, in fact, is counter-productive.

In one situation, the CEO kept talking about "Our mission ..." when all he was really working towards was to sell the company and cash out his stock options. Not only did he lose the dedication of most employees, he lost their respect. As one individual put it: "There was no way we could get excited when he wasn't honest with us. I mean, we're not that stupid."

Four Types of Mission

There are four basic types of mission to choose from:

1. Targeting
2. Common Enemy
3. Role Model
4. Internal Transformation.

Mission Type 1: Targeting

Targeting is just as the name implies: setting a clear, well- defined target and aiming for it. The NASA moon project is a target mission. Ford's aim "To democratize the automobile" and MIPS's aim to make its architecture "pervasive worldwide by the mid-1990s" are also target missions.

Another approach to targeting is to set the goal of taking the company to an entirely new level of overall prestige, success, dominance, or industry position. Here are some examples:

> *Merck:* "To establish Merck as the preeminent drug-maker worldwide in the 1980s." (Set in 1979.)

> *Coors:* "To be number three in the beer industry by the end of the 1980s." (Set in 1980.) "To be number two in the beer industry by the end of the 1990s." (Set in 1990.)

> *Schlage Lock:* "To become the dominant lock supplier in the United States by the year 2000." (Set in 1990.)

Have you ever heard of Tokyo Tsushin Kogyo? Probably not. In 1952, it was a tiny, struggling seven-year-old company, and its founders were wrestling with the question of how to propel itself along the path to greatness. They decided to set a bold, audacious mission:

To create a product that becomes pervasive worldwide.

The company then implemented the mission by creating and marketing the first radio small enough to fit in a shirt pocket. Today, the company is known as SONY Corporation.

You've probably noticed that none of our target examples are defined with numbers. Can a quantitative target be an effective mission? Yes, *but with caution.*

For example, Home Depot's mission set in the late 1980s was:

To go national with $10 billion in sales and 350 locations by 1995.

In 1977, Wal-Mart's founder Sam Walton set the mission:

To become a $1 billion company by 1980.

This was a mission to more than double the company's size, yet Wal-Mart achieved the mission on schedule with sales of $1.2 billion in 1980.

So why did we say, "Yes, but with caution"?

Because we've found that quantitative missions are often less exciting to people throughout the company than, say, democratizing the automobile or becoming the preeminent company in your industry. Just stating, "Our mission is $50 million in revenues in 1995" won't necessarily excite people. If you use a quantitative mission, be sure to tie it to something meaningful to everyone.

Jack Stack makes extensive use of quantitative target missions at his company, Springfield Remanufacturing Company. He also makes sure to put the numbers in a larger context, as he explained in an *Inc.* magazine interview:

Our goals are always based on the security of the company, so the larger meaning is to create jobs and keep people working. Each goal is a must, not a want. We're trying to create a company that will last 30, 40, or 50 years.

Remember, the aim here is not just to create a precise target, but to create one that will galvanize people.

Mission Type 2: Common Enemy

Setting out to defeat a common enemy is a particularly powerful, albeit uncreative, form of mission. It appeals to people's competitive instincts. Picking a common enemy to seek out and destroy—especially if you are the underdog—can create extraordinary unity of purpose. Britain's mission in 1940 (to beat the life and soul out of Hitler) is an excellent historical example. The same type of mission can be set in business.

Pepsi's mission at one point was to "Beat Coke!" A senior executive at Pepsi described the impact of having this mission:

> We always believed, since the early seventies, when Pepsi was widely viewed as the perennial also-ran, that we could do it. All of us started out with that objective, and we never took our eyes off it. ... It put us on a search-and-destroy mission against a Goliath.

In one of our all-time favorite examples, Honda, when faced with Yamaha's having overtaken them as the number one motorcycle manufacturer in the world, responded with:

Yamaha wo tsubusu!

(We will crush, squash, slaughter Yamaha!)

Soon after Honda established this mission, it so demolished Yamaha that later Yamaha publicly apologized to Honda for having claimed that it would dominate Honda.

NIKE has thrived for years on common enemy missions. First, it set out to beat Adidas in the United States. It did. Then, after the unexpected rise of Reebok, they established the mission of crushing Reebok in the competitive "sneaker wars." (During an interview about the "Sneaker Wars," on ABC's 20/20 aired August 19, 1988, NIKE CEO Phil Knight was asked if he knew the president of Reebok. Knight said yes. The interviewer then asked if he liked the President of Reebok. Knight replied, "No. And I don't want to like him." A board member of NIKE once remarked, "Our idea of a perfect day is to get up in the morning and throw rocks at our competitors.")

Common enemy missions are typically set by companies that are striving to become number one, but have not yet achieved it; they play nicely into a David versus Goliath motivation.

An extremely powerful effect of common enemy missions is that they can convert an organization whose back is against the wall—that is concerned about its very survival—to a "we shall prevail" mode. People don't like to "just survive," they like to win. And a common enemy mission taps into this basic human motivation.

Micron Technology provides an excellent illustration. In 1985, Japanese companies' illegal dumping of their product below cost nearly put the little semi-conductor company out of business. CEO Joseph Parkinson used the existence of an outside foe as a unifying force to pull the company through what he calls "the dark days." Parkinson told us in an interview:

> When things were going bad, I was trying to keep everyone motivated to keep us alive. At first, I wasn't scoring a lot of points, but then it occurred to me to key off the fact that people like to win. I mean, who likes to just survive? So with our backs to the wall, we went on the offensive. Yes, it was a tremendous advantage to have a bitter enemy. But it was more than that. We were sworn to *prevail* over that enemy. And this shift from a survival mode to a "we shall prevail" mode—beating the odds as the underdog—is something everyone can get behind, from assembly-line workers to VPs.

A word of caution: in spite of its obvious advantages, there are negative aspects of common enemy missions. It's difficult to spend your entire life at war. What do you do when you've defeated the enemy and become number one? What happens when you are no longer David, and have become Goliath? NIKE, for example, went into a slump after it defeated Adidas. It didn't rebound from that slump until Reebok had slipped by them and became a worthy target of NIKE's competitive wrath.

Mission Type 3: Role Model

Another useful type of mission is corporate role models. Use organizations that you admire as images of what you want your company to become. Role-model missions are excellent for small to mid-sized companies with bright prospects.

For example, in its early years, Trammell Crow had the mission "To be the IBM of the real estate industry." Jim Gentes at Giro Sport talks about becoming to the cycling industry what NIKE is to athletic shoes and Apple is to computers. Norwest Corporation of Minneapolis, aims to be "The Wal-Mart of banking."

And speaking of Wal-Mart, it's interesting to note that Sam Walton used J.C. Penney as his role model, including directly copying Penney's seven principles of business management into the early days of Wal-Mart.

Mission Type 4: Internal Transformation

Internal transformation missions are rare. They're usually best in organizations that need a dramatic restructuring.

For example, the United States had an internal transformation mission in the late 1800s: to reconstruct the Union after the civil war. The Soviet Union's attempt in the late 20th century to become a more free-market economy is another societal example of an internal transformation mission. An excellent corporate example comes from Jack Welch at General Electric:

> We are committed to developing the sensitivity, the leanness, the simplicity and the agility of a small company.

For a company the size of GE, this is indeed big, hairy, and audacious.

Since internal transformation missions tend to be most appropriate for large, stagnant organizations, we've encountered very few good examples in small to mid-sized companies.

How Far in the Future?

We've emphasized the importance of having a specific time frame affixed to your mission. How far into the future should a mission stretch? Should it be something that can be fulfilled in six months? A year? Three years? A Decade? Fifty years?

There's no definitive answer. Some missions take 30 years or more to fulfill. Others might be fulfilled in a year or less. A good rule of thumb is a 5- to 15-year horizon, perhaps longer if the mission is particularly challenging. Of course, some missions can be fulfilled faster than five years, and it may be appropriate and effective to have a short time frame.

Whatever time-length mission you set, be sure to recognize when you've fulfilled it and, most important, set a new one. Otherwise, you may fall into one of the most dangerous of traps: the "We've Arrived Syndrome."

Beware the "We've Arrived" Syndrome

It's absolutely essential to recognize when you've fulfilled a mission and therefore need to set a new one.

When a mission has been fulfilled, people will tend to set their own directions and fragment the whole. A classic historical example is that of the World War II allied effort between Russia, England, and the United States. The allies were able to work together remarkably well while they had in common the mission to defeat Hitler. But, alas, once Hitler's fate was assured, the alliance broke apart, plunging the world into the cold war.

Furthermore, you need new missions to keep the company galvanized towards new challenges. Just as individual people can become lost, adrift, and aimless once they've reached a goal, the same is true of companies. This is what we mean by the "We've Arrived Syndrome."

Jan Carlzon learned this lesson the hard way as CEO of Scandinavian Airlines, after the company reached its first mission. In an interview with *Inc.* magazine, he said:

> We had a dream, and we reached it, and we reached it very quickly. But we didn't have another long term objective. So people started to produce their own new objectives. You see, it had all been a little too easy. And we created frustration, because this is a psychological game. Do you know the song Peggy Lee sings, 'Is That All There Is?'

> I learned that before you reach an objective you must be ready with a new one, and you must start to communicate it to the organization.

> It's not the goal itself that's important. It's the fight to get there.

THE "WE'VE ARRIVED" SYNDROME

THE COMPANY HAS A COMPELLING MISSION
(SOMETIMES IT IS SO COMPELLING
AND SO OBVIOUS THAT IT ISN'T EVEN
EXPLICITLY ARTICULATED)

COHESION, TEAMWORK,
PERFORMANCE, ENTHUSIASM

FULFILL MISSION, BUT
A NEW ONE IS NOT SET
("WE'VE ARRIVED")

NO BOLD NEW CHALLENGE

MALAISE, COMPLACENCY, FACTIONS
FEELING THAT "SOMETHING IS MISSING"

Figure 2-3

The We've Arrived Syndrome is particularly common in early stage or turnaround companies that are galvanized by the challenge of reaching a point where survival is no longer in question. Because survival in such situations is itself such an overriding goal, the mission to survive often isn't even made explicit—everyone *knows* this is the mission without anyone saying it.

Therein lies the problem. Because it isn't explicit, there isn't the explicit recognition of its fulfillment. No new mission is created to replace the old one. Complacency sets in and factions become prevalent.

Case Example:
Strategic Software, Inc.

Founded in 1976 with no outside venture financing, Strategic Software's founders were dedicated to building a company that would provide excellent software products, financial stability for employees and owners, and a stimulating work environment. For the first seven years, employees and managers worked twelve-hour days in tiny cubicles. "It was us against the world," explained one of the founders. "We were a great team then."

Gradually, year by year, the company attained financial success (reaching $25 million in annual revenue with healthy profit margins) and a stable customer base. In 1983, it moved into a prestigious office complex with modern sculptures, perfectly manicured green lawns, water ponds, thick carpets, handcrafted cherry-wood furniture, and its own parking lot.

Then the whole place fell apart. One founder described:

> What was once a great esprit de corps degenerated into intense factions and we lost all sense of team spirit. People began working 9 to 5 and, worse, they acquired a 9 to 5 attitude! We looked around and found that success had brought malaise. We just didn't have that same fighting spirit. From there it was all downhill.

What happened, of course, is that the organization had fulfilled its first big mission (to reach a point where survival was no longer in question). It seemed like there was nothing more to work for. It had arrived. Its leaders should have created a new mission, but they didn't. And the organization stagnated, eventually putting itself up for sale.

The Potential Impact of New Facilities

In the above case example, we made a specific point about the new building. Facilities may not seem like a very important topic; but they are.

We've seen a number of companies, such as the one above, encounter difficulty soon after moving into beautiful new buildings and offices. It's not that new offices are in themselves bad. But they send a signal: "We've arrived. We're successful. We've made it."

Greg Hadley, an experienced turnaround artist, described the impact of a new building on the psychology of a company that he took over:

> It was like the Taj Mahal. People looked around, and said, "Hey, look at this. We *must* be good. We must already be successful." And then they started paying more attention to their golf game than the business.

Gavilan Computer Company, which squandered over $40 million in venture capital without ever getting a product out the door, had exquisite corporate offices. As one employee told us, "I felt like I was already working in the FORTUNE 500. It diluted any real sense of urgency. And, you know, it wasn't anywhere near as much fun as some other start-ups I've been with."

Do we mean to imply that you shouldn't have nice places to work? No, of course not; but you should be aware that a beautiful new edifice *symbolizes* having crossed a threshold, having "made it," having completed a mission.

The point of all this is that your company will cross many finish lines in its life, and there will be symbols of these finish lines (a public offering, new buildings, industry awards, or whatever). Your job is to make sure that these symbols lead to continual work towards a compelling mission.

When you reach the top of a mountain peak, begin looking for the next one. Set a new mission. If you just sit there, you'll get cold and die.

Putting It All Together

We've now covered the three basic elements of a good vision: core values and beliefs, purpose, and mission. To further illustrate vision, we've included two examples of how these components of vision fit together: Giro Sport Design (a small company) and Merck (a large company).

EXAMPLE OF VISION: GIRO SPORT DESIGN

CORE VALUES AND BELIEFS

Giro's fundamental, inviolable Values and Beliefs are these:

GREAT PRODUCTS. Every product we introduce must be a unique contribution to the market, not one that is introduced just for the purpose of making money. It must therefore be *innovative, high quality,* and the *unquestioned best* in its category.

GREAT CUSTOMER SERVICE. Our service standards are as stiff as our product standards. We should treat our customers as we would our best friends.

GOLDEN RULE. We should treat those with whom we have dealings as we ourselves would like to be treated.

TEAMWORK. No individual should be indispensable. Think we; not I.

BEST EFFORT. Each person should do her very best in each task undertaken. Strive for an A, not a B+.

DETAILS. The little things matter; God is in the details.

INTEGRITY. We are honest. We honor our commitments. We are consistent and fair.

PURPOSE

Giro exists to make people's lives better through innovative, high quality products.

MISSION (Set in 1990)

Giro's mission is to be a great company. We aim to be the most respected and admired company in the worldwide bicycling industry by the year 2000.

EXAMPLE OF VISION: MERCK

CORE VALUES AND BELIEFS

We value above all our ability to serve the patient.

We are committed to the highest standards
of ethics and integrity.

We are responsible to our customers, to our employees,
and to the societies we serve.

Our interactions with all segments of society—
customers, suppliers, governments, the general public—
must reflect the high standards we profess.

We are committed to research that matches science
to the needs of humanity.

Since our future as a company rests squarely
on the knowledge, imagination, skills, teamwork
and integrity of our employees, we value these qualities
most highly.

We expect profit, but profit
from work that benefits humanity.

PURPOSE

We are in the business of preserving and improving
human life. All of our actions must be measured
by our success in achieving this.

MISSION (Set in 1979)

To establish Merck as the preeminent drug-maker
worldwide in the 1980s.

Write It Down

It's good practice to codify your vision on paper. Writing it down forces you to think rigorously about what exactly you are trying to do. Even more important, it's a critical step in making it the *organization's* vision, rather than the vision of a single leader.

As Steve Bostic of American Photo Group put it in an interview with *Inc.* magazine:

> You have to get [your vision] on paper. That's key. If people never see the vision—or if it's here today, gone tomorrow—there's no way they can get into it. There are severe limits to what companies that are one man shows can achieve.

Bostic is not alone in this view. R.W. Johnson codified the J&J credo for future generations of J&J leaders. Tom Watson wrote *A Business and Its Beliefs* to codify the basic principles of IBM. Marvin Bower wrote about the McKinsey Vision in a book, *Perspective on McKinsey*. Bill Hannemann at Giro keeps a written version of Giro's vision near him at all times. We even know of one company (Stew Leonard's Dairy) that literally chiseled its enduring principles into stone.

What about flexibility? Don't you want to maintain flexibility to change with times? Does all this "enduring principles" and "100 year purpose" philosophy really make sense? Isn't chiseling your principles in stone a bit limiting?

Change is good, we agree. The question is: what should change, and what should be held tight? The answer lies partially in the hierarchy from values to tactics:

Core Values and Beliefs:	Change seldom, if ever.
Purpose:	Should last for 100 years.
Mission:	Changes whenever one mission is completed and a new one needs to be set (usually every five to fifteen years).
Strategy:	Revised annually, then totally recast with each new mission.
Tactics:	In constant flux, to adjust to changing conditions.

A Vivid, Compelling Description:
Paint a Picture with Your Words

It's essential to be able to communicate the vision in vibrant, engaging, and specific words—in words that provoke emotion and generate excitement. Think of it as translating the vision from words into pictures, of creating an image that people can carry around in their heads. We call this "painting a picture with your words."

When you have a mission like, "To be a great company by the year 2000" you need to vividly describe what that means, and then say, "Our mission is to make that picture happen."

Use specific, vivid images. Observe how Jim Gentes describes Giro's aim to become a great company:

> The best riders in the world will be using our products in world-class competition. Winners of the Tour de France, the World Championships, and the Olympic Gold Medal will win while wearing Giro helmets. We will receive unsolicited phone calls and letters from customers who say, "Thank you for being in business; one of your helmets saved my life." Our employees will feel that this is the best place they've ever worked. When you ask people to name the top company in the cycling business, the vast majority will say Giro.

Here's how Henry Ford painted a picture with his words to communicate the mission, "To democratize the automobile":

> I will build a motor car for the great multitude. It will be so low in price that no man making a good salary will be unable to own one—and enjoy with his family the blessing of hours of pleasure in God's great open spaces. The horse will have disappeared from our highways, the automobile will be taken for granted.

Note the specifics: "enjoy with his family the blessing of hours of pleasure in God's great open spaces" and "the horse will have disappeared from our highways." This is what we mean by "painting a picture with your words."

One of our favorite examples of the power of painting pictures with words comes from Churchill, one of the best vision communicators the world has ever known:

Hitler knows that he will have to break us on this
island or lose the war.

If we can stand up to him all Europe may be free
and the life of the world may move forward
into broad, sunlit uplands.

But if we fail, then the whole world,
including the United States,
including all we have known and cared for,

Will sink into the abyss of a new Dark Age
made more sinister, and perhaps more protracted,
by the lights of perverted science.

Let us therefore brace ourselves to our duties,
and so bear ourselves
that if the British Empire and its Commonwealth
last for a thousand years

Men will still say:
"This was their finest hour."

"But that's Churchill," you say. "I'm not Churchill. I could
never communicate like Churchill. And besides, it would be
easy to communicate like Churchill if we had a foe like Hitler.
But we don't, and never will."

True. Few of us can communicate like Churchill. But we
can *learn* from Churchill, and Ford, and others. Churchill
wasn't born eloquent. The words did not flow; he worked at
it. He labored for hours over his speeches and writings, shaping
each phrase with the care Michelangelo might have lavished
on the David or Pieta. He paid attention to the details, the
specific, vivid images that would stick in people's minds, like
"broad sunlit uplands" and "abyss of a new Dark Age."

Although few of us can hope to be as eloquent as Churchiil,
we can nonetheless use him as a role model for communicating
our visions.

Clear and Shared

To be effective, a vision must fulfill two key criteria: it
must be *clear* (well understood) and *shared* by all the key
people in the organization.

This raises a vexing question: should the vision be dictated from the top (from, say, the founder or CEO) or should it be derived from a group process?

The disadvantage of a vision that is dictated from above is that, although usually clear, it may not be widely shared. On the other hand, a vision developed by group process can easily turn out to be an uninspirational "camel"—a "vision by committee" that lacks clarity and spark.

Each company, within the context of its own norms and style, must come to its own conclusion. There is no universally right answer to this dilemma.

We've seen situations where a clear and shared vision is set entirely by group process. To those who are skeptical as to whether a group process can work, we point you again to the founding of the United States of America. Although there certainly were strong leaders present (Washington, Jefferson, Madison, and Adams), the vision of the country was set entirely by a *group* process. In fact, George Washington hardly said a word during the entire Constitutional Convention.

On the other hand, we've seen situations where the vision comes from a single individual. Sam Walton at Wal-Mart and Henry Ford are examples.

So which is better, group process or individual drive? Neither. It depends on the situation and your personal style. The only thing that matters is that you catalyze a clear and shared vision for the company and secure a commitment to vigorous pursuit of that vision. If you do this, you'll be functioning as a leader.

Not Only for Charismatic Visionaries

We'd like to dispel the myth that setting a vision requires that you be somehow blessed with almost mystical or super-human charismatic visionary qualities. To believe this myth, every organization would need a CEO who is a cross between Churchill, Kennedy, and Martin Luther King. Indeed, many managers respond to the notion of vision by thinking, "It's not for me. I don't fit the stereotypical mold of a visionary."

But it is for you, no matter what your style or personal magnetism. Charisma's role in setting vision is vastly overrated. Some of the folks that have instilled extraordinary vision in their companies don't bowl you over with charisma. Phil Knight of NIKE, Kristine McDivitt of Patagonia, Bill Hannemann of Giro, Bob Miller of MIPS, Bill Hewlett of HP, Frank Wells of Disney—even Abraham Lincoln and Harry Truman—don't fit the stereotype of charismatic visionary. You don't have to be a member of some elusive group of people who call themselves visionary. You can just be yourself. As Ted Turner said:

> People don't call themselves visionaries. People get called visionary. All I am is Ted Turner.

The task before you is not to be a single charismatic individual with vision. The task is to build an organization with vision. Individuals die; great companies can live for centuries.

Chapter 3

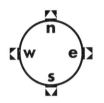

STRATEGY

Strategy is easy, but tactics—the day-to-day and month-to-month decisions required to manage a business—are hard.

Arthur Rock

"Strategy." The word sounds weighty, academic, scientific, ponderous.

To be a strategist, this momentous word implies, we would need the intelligence of a pure mathematician and the skills of a master chess player. High-priced strategy consultants would like us to believe that only the top 5% of academic performers from first-rate graduate schools can be virtuosos of strategic thinking. We're led to envision thoughtful experts of economic theory looking out on the world from lofty offices on the 45th floor of a tall building and applying the mysterious rigors of decision sciences to concoct strategies that dazzle the world with their brilliance.

Well, we've been on the 45th floor, and we can assure you that all these images of strategy are false.

Not that strategy is unimportant. It's very important. And not that strategy consultants are unhelpful. Their objectivity can be useful.

But strategy isn't difficult. Nor is setting strategy a complicated or purely scientific exercise.

The purpose of this chapter is to demystify the topic of strategy and provide a straightforward road map for setting a strategy. We will also address four key strategic issues commonly faced by small to mid-sized companies:

- How fast to grow

- Focus versus diversification

- Whether to go public

- Whether to lead a market or follow.

Overview of Strategy

Strategy is simply the basic methodology you intend to apply to attain your company's current mission. "This is how we will achieve our mission." That, in a nutshell, is strategy. There's no mystery to it. It's not a difficult concept.

A good strategy is *not* a thick, turgid plan that lays out every action of the company to the nth degree and requires six months of effort by a strategic planning staff. Business, like life, cannot be entirely planned. Nor should it be. There are far too many uncertainties and unexpected opportunities. Instead, it's better to simply have a clear, thoughtful, and uncomplicated methodology for attaining your mission—a methodology that leaves room for individual initiative, opportunities, changing conditions, experimentation, and innovation.

Four Basic Principles of Setting Effective Strategy

There are four key principles to keep in mind when setting company strategy.

1. The strategy must descend directly from your vision. Remember, it's impossible to set strategy unless you have a crystal clear idea of what you're trying to do in the first place. Vision first, *then* strategy!

2. The strategy must leverage off the strengths and unique capabilities of your company. Do what you're good at.

3. The strategy must be realistic. It must therefore take into account internal constraints and external factors. Confront reality, *even if reality is unpleasant.*

4. Strategy should be set with the participation of those who are going to be on the line to make it happen.

The Process

Setting strategy involves the following basic steps:

First, *review the vision* of the company. If you haven't clarified your vision, do so. In particular, ensure that the current mission is clear. As you recall from the previous chapter, your mission (which is the third component of vision, after core values and beliefs and purpose) is analogous to the specific mountain you are going to climb.

Next, *do an internal assessment* of the company's capabilities. This is analogous to examining the capabilities and resources of the expedition team.

Third, *do an external assessment* of the environment, markets, competitors, and trends. This is analogous to studying pictures of the mountain, examining weather reports, assessing new trends in technology that might help you in your ascent, and paying attention to competitors who seek to reach the summit ahead of you.

Finally, taking the internal and external assessments into account, *make key decisions* about how you intend to go about achieving your current mission. This is analogous to mapping out the route you are going to take up the side of the mountain.

Break the strategic decisions down into each of the key components of the business. We find the following categories work well:

- Products (or services); includes product line strategy and manufacturing strategy (or service delivery strategy)

- Customers (or market segments); includes who the customers are that you're serving and how you intend to reach them
- Cash Flow (financial strategy)
- People and Organization
- Infrastructure

Diagram of Vision, Strategy, Tactics

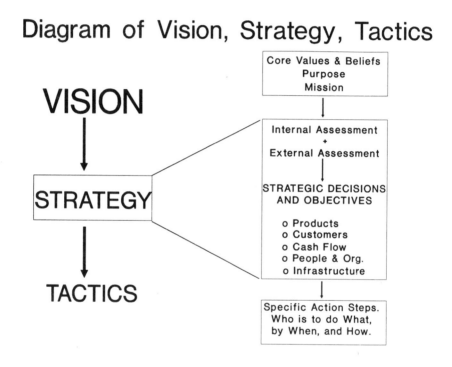

Figure 3-1

Internal Assessment

There are three components of a good internal assessment:

- Strengths and weaknesses
- Resources
- Innovations and new ideas

Strengths and Weaknesses

The first thing you need is a clear assessment of what your company is really good at and its blind spots. Remember, strategy should leverage off your strengths.

To get an objective reading on your strengths and weaknesses, we suggest asking a selection of employees and managers to list the top three strengths and the top three weaknesses of the company. To ensure candor, it's sometimes useful to have these submitted anonymously.

It's also valuable to get outside input on this question. Ask trusted advisors, investors, and board members what they see as your strengths and weaknesses. You might even ask a few key customer accounts (which has the additional benefit of developing a closer relationship with your customers.)

A particularly useful question is, "What are we better at than anyone else, and what are our unique capabilities that give us a competitive advantage?" The literature of strategic management ascribes a ponderous term to this notion ("Distinctive Competence"), but the idea is really pretty simple. It's also important. Simply put, smart firms stick to doing things they can do better than other firms.

Why should an endurance athlete try to compete in the 100 meter dash? Why should a football linebacker try to become an ice skating champion? Why should an engineering-driven firm try to compete primarily on marketing skills? Why should a company that's great at high-end, well-designed products try to compete in the low-price, commodity segment of a market? Why would Wal-Mart try to compete directly with Nordstrom?

This doesn't mean that you shouldn't try to eradicate crippling weaknesses. Any great company is continually working on its weaknesses, always seeking improvement and your basic strategy should play to your strengths. Do what you're good at.

Resources

Next you want to get a clear picture of your resources. Specific categories of resources to consider might include: cash flow, access to outside capital, scarce materials, production capacity, and people.

Innovations and New Ideas

A company can shape its market by innovation as much as a market can shape a company by its demands. Yet innovation is one of the most overlooked aspects of setting strategy.

Make sure that your company is responsive to its own internal creative output. Examine what innovations and new ideas are bubbling up in product development, research, design, and marketing. List all possible innovations that might come to fruition. Obtain estimates on how quickly the innovation could be made marketable, the level of resources required to complete its development, and the level of marketing required.

The last thing you want to do is to kill new ideas and innovations just because they're not planned. In fact, most great ideas are not planned, and if you introduce only products that are planned five years in advance, it's unlikely that you'll produce any break-through products.

Innovation is such an important part of corporate greatness that we devote all of Chapter 4 to it. Furthermore, innovation can have a dramatic effect on your strategic options.

The development of the tank, for example, was not part of the allied war strategy at the start of World War I. However, the invention of the tank altered the allied strategy at the end of the war. The generals didn't say, "Our strategy calls for a tank. Build us one." No, the tank was invented by a British War Department skunk-works and presented to the generals who then said, "Hey, we should change our strategy to use this thing."

The same phenomenon occurs in companies, as with HP's entry into pocket calculators, NIKE's "sock-racer" product strategy, Intel's entry into computer add-on boards, and literally hundreds of product strategies developed by 3M. Innovation should be able to influence strategy as much as your strategy should stimulate innovation. Innovation and strategy in a great company are inextricably linked.

External Assessment

There are seven components of a good external assessment:

- Industry/market trends
- Technology trends

- Competitor assessment
- Social and regulatory environment
- Macro-economy and demographics
- International threats and opportunities
- Overall threats and opportunities

Industry/Market Trends

Take a quick snapshot of your industry.

- How are your markets segmented, and in which segments do you compete?

- Roughly, how large are the market segments for your current product line and planned future products?

- Are the market segments for your products (services) growing, stable, or shrinking? How fast? Why?

- What are the dominant trends in your industry? What are the underlying forces behind those trends?

- *Most Importantly,* what are your customers telling you about their evolving needs? What are they telling you about how well your company is meeting their needs? How are customer demands changing? Direct input from your customers is an essential part of setting strategy. Get input directly from your customers regularly. They can tell you what's going on in your market because they *are* the market. They can also tell you about your competitors. It's wise to survey your customers at least once per year as an integral part of setting strategy.

- At what stage of evolution is your industry? What does this imply in terms of how the industry might change in the next five years? Use Figure 3-2, Stages of Industry Evolution, as a backdrop to this analysis. (Various versions of this chart are common in strategic management and marketing literature. A more detailed version can be found in *Competitive Strategy* by Michael Porter.)

Note: The stages of industry evolution analysis can be an enormously useful tool, but do not assume that all industries evolve the same exact way. See the note at the end of this chapter: "Caveats to Industry Evolution Analysis."

Stages of Industry Evolution

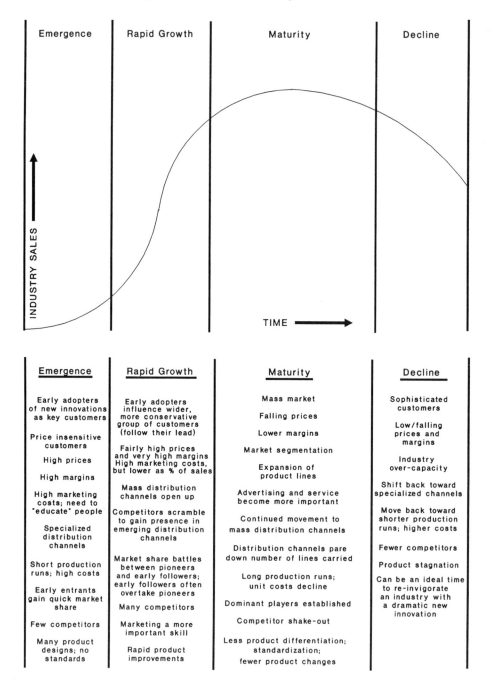

Emergence	Rapid Growth	Maturity	Decline
Early adopters of new innovations as key customers	Early adopters influence wider, more conservative group of customers (follow their lead)	Mass market	Sophisticated customers
Price insensitive customers	Fairly high prices and very high margins High marketing costs, but lower as % of sales	Falling prices	Low/falling prices and margins
High prices		Lower margins	
High margins		Market segmentation	Industry over-capacity
High marketing costs; need to "educate" people	Mass distribution channels open up	Expansion of product lines	Shift back toward specialized channels
Specialized distribution channels	Competitors scramble to gain presence in emerging distribution channels	Advertising and service become more important	Move back toward shorter production runs; higher costs
Short production runs; high costs	Market share battles between pioneers and early followers; early followers often overtake pioneers	Continued movement to mass distribution channels	Fewer competitors
Early entrants gain quick market share		Distribution channels pare down number of lines carried	Product stagnation
Few competitors	Many competitors	Long production runs; unit costs decline	Can be an ideal time to re-invigorate an industry with a dramatic new innovation
Many product designs; no standards	Marketing a more important skill	Dominant players established	
	Rapid product improvements	Competitor shake-out	
		Less product differentiation; standardization; fewer product changes	

Figure 3-2

Technology Trends

All industries, even "low tech" industries, have a technology component to their evolution, either in products or in process. Every industry is somehow affected by changes in technology.

For example, the banking industry, which has not historically been known as "high tech," was nonetheless dramatically changed by computer technology. In back-room processing, effective use of computers became a key strategic advantage for those who mastered their use quickly. In services to customers, adoption of ATMs became an essential part of banking services.

Examine the technology trends in your own industry and ask how you can best use them to your advantage. The question is not whether technology trends will affect your industry, but *how*.

Competitor Assessment

Never underestimate your competition. One of the biggest mistakes in mapping out a strategy is doing so in ignorance of the competition or, worse, with disdain for the competition.

- Who are your current competitors?

- Who are potential competitors?

- What are their strengths and weaknesses?

- What do you anticipate as being their future moves in the market? What are *their* visions and strategies?

- How do your strengths, weaknesses, and product line stack up against the competition? Where are they vulnerable? Where are you vulnerable?

- Do you have a clear, differentiated position with respect to your competitors? What is it?

Getting competitor information is fairly easy. Get on the mailing list for your competitors' press releases, publications, and promotional materials. Attend trade shows. Listen to your sales force. Listen to your suppliers. Listen to customers. Listen to technical employees who keep abreast of technology developments. Read trade and business journal articles about your industry and/or your competitors. Read the business section of newspapers published in towns where your competitors are located.

Be careful about how you gain competitor information. Under pressure, people can be easily tempted to misrepresent themselves to obtain competitor information on your behalf. This often happens with outside consultants who pose as "students doing a school project on your industry," or who call a competitor saying that they're "doing an internal audit." There are two problems with this. First, it's unethical. Second, it can leave you vulnerable to lawsuits.

For example, in the early 1980s, a prominent strategy consulting firm and one of its clients were sued—successfully— when a young researcher called into a competitor's manufacturing operations, posed as a member of the competitor's finance department, and asked for proprietary cost information.

Social and Regulatory Environment

All companies exist as integral parts of society-at-large, and are affected by powerful social, regulatory, and political forces. Keep abreast of these forces and assess how they might affect your company. Astute anticipation of governmental moves or regulatory-body decisions can create tremendous opportunities. Conversely, ignorance of the same can be disastrous.

Macroeconomy and Demographics

Examine the general macroeconomic climate and assess what impact the overall economy might have on your company.

Pay particular attention to demographic trends. Entire industries can be dramatically affected by demographic changes. For example, the United States "baby boom" (a gigantic bulge in the birth rate from 1945 to 1960) will continue to have a profound impact on a wide range of industries until at least the year 2020. This is only one of many demographic forces.

For companies doing business in the United States, a subscription to *American Demographics* magazine can be very useful. We also suggest scanning the *Statistical Abstract of The United States* each year to get a macro view of demographic trends.

International Threats and Opportunities

Factor international into your strategic thinking, even if you don't currently sell in foreign markets. International strategy is relevant for all companies; no matter what your size, there will probably be forces pulling you into the international arena. Small companies with good products are often approached by foreign distributors, retailers, resellers, and potential customers.

In an interesting and surprising study, David Birch analyzed the data from 34,000 exporters and found that those companies with between 50 and 500 employees were actually *more* likely to be exporters than larger companies.

When setting strategy, assume that participation in the international arena is a viable possibility and, furthermore, that international opportunities will present themselves unexpectedly. It may not make sense within the context of your vision to take advantage of these opportunities, but you should nonetheless make international an explicit part of your strategy, even if you decide to stay domestic.

Even if you decide not to compete in other countries, it's likely that at least one of your major competitors will be foreign. The days of purely domestic markets are gone forever, and competitor analysis should include a watchful eye on the international landscape.

Overall Threats and Opportunities

In preparing for a strategy session, ask a selected group of employees, managers, and objective outsiders to list the top three external opportunities and top three external threats facing the company. This is a quick and efficient way to tap the insights of a range of people as input to your external assessment.

Throughout the internal and external assessment process, it's absolutely paramount that you do everything possible to see reality—to see things as they really are and not the way you wish they were.

Indeed, one of the things that characterizes great companies is the willingness of their leaders and managers to relentlessly seek the truth, regardless of whether it's good news or bad news. Yet, we have observed that it's all too common for companies to behave just the opposite.

One of us (Jim) worked early in his career for a manager who was horrified at the idea of telling his superiors about problems with a soon-to-be-released product. "Upper management doesn't want to hear bad news," the manager counseled. "Just tell them what they want to hear and they'll be happy. If you give them reality, you'll be viewed as having a negative attitude."

The risk of this approach, of course, is that reality has a funny way of making itself known. You can't submerge it forever, and if you try, it usually comes back to nail you. In the above-mentioned case, the product weaknesses did indeed become apparent, but only *after* the product was on the market. If the company had confronted the problems directly and corrected them *before* going to market, a multimillion dollar catastrophe could have been avoided.

(Incidently, Jim decided to go against his manager's advice and he raised the issue with senior management. He discovered that his manager was right: they didn't want to hear reality, and they plowed ahead with a doomed product.)

Unfortunately, this is not an isolated incident. Most of us are familiar with situations where people are unwilling or afraid to present unpleasant truths. In many cases, who can blame them? The unspoken rule in all too many companies is: We don't want to see anything negative, even if it is true; we like our rose-colored glasses.

Ignoring facts, explaining away problems, and refusing to see the world as it really is doesn't change reality. It only invites catastrophe.

To illustrate this point, we like to use a vivid example from world history: the decade leading up to the World War II. In the 1930s, British, American, and French officials were confronted with an overwhelming series of unpleasant facts: Germany built military arms in violation of the Treaty of Versailles, German forces moved into the Rhineland, Hitler ordered military conscription, Germany devoured Austria and Czechoslovakia.

Yet, amazingly, these facts were not acted upon. Hitler was planning for a major war, but allied officials did not want to see this unpleasant (not to mention politically unpopular) truth. So, they behaved much as if the facts did not exist.

In his book *The Gathering Storm*, Winston Churchill described how Neville Chamberlain, Prime Minister of Britain 1937–40, deluded himself:

His all pervading hope was to go down to history as the great peacemaker, and for this he was prepared to strive continually in the teeth of facts. I begged the government to get these brutal truths into their heads. Had we responded to the facts as they became evident, war could have been averted without the loss of blood.

But these "brutal truths" didn't sink in until it was too late and a devastating war engulfed Europe.

Does this lesson from world history apply to setting business strategy? You bet it does. Whether leading a nation or managing a company, the lesson is the same: ignore reality and it will come back and smack you in the face. It's very important to prevent this from happening in your company.

There are a number of things you can do to ensure that you are not protected from reality.

First, surround yourself with people who tell it like it is. Strange as it seems, this is not an easy task. For one thing, most people know that telling the truth can be politically dangerous and many, like the manager mentioned earlier, are terrified of political fallout.

You need at least a few people around you who aren't afraid of you and who aren't concerned with politics. This is where detached and objective outsiders (consultants and directors) are invaluable. You also need honest people inside— people who are so honest and direct they are almost uncomfortable to have around. You don't have to like them. You just need to listen to them.

Churchill, for example, felt so strongly about this that he created a separate department whose sole responsibility was to root out and present the naked truth about pressing issues. Leaders of great companies never hesitate to reward what Thomas J. Watson, Jr. called "those sharp, scratchy, harsh, almost unpleasant individuals who see and tell you about things as they really are."

Second, personally stay in touch with what's happening. Don't rely solely on status reports, quarterly reviews, and other formal reporting methods for information. Use your company's products. Listen directly to employees at all levels. Talk to customers. Read consumer reports about your products. Personally answer customer complaints. In short, do whatever you can to keep in touch with reality.

Third, never punish people for telling the truth. We all know the story of how Peter the Great responded to the messenger who brought him news of defeat: he executed him.

None of us like to see reality when it's unpleasant or disappointing; all of us are guilty, at least to some degree, of wanting rose-colored glasses. This is no excuse for punishing those who tell us the truth and the tendency to do so must be vigorously resisted. If people raise a problem or an unpleasant issue, don't chastise them or treat them as if they have a bad attitude. Thank them.

The point here is not that your company should tolerate bellyaching, cynicism, and hopeless despair. None of us has time for that kind of nonsense. The point is that effective strategic decisions can only be made if you are not sheltered from reality, no matter how unpleasant that reality may be.

Making Strategic Decisions

Keep in mind the image of a balanced three legged stool; each leg should be strong in order for the stool to be stable. To make solid strategic decisions, you need *each* of the three legs: vision, internal assessment, and external assessment. Once you have done each of these, strategic decisions will, in most cases, be fairly obvious. (See Figure 3-3 on facing page.)

Be sure to pay as much attention to common sense, seasoned judgment, and intuition as to hard headed analysis. Don't overcomplicate the strategy. Keep it simple and straightforward.

On paper, the basic strategy should fit on *no more than three typed pages*. This may be shocking to those who think of strategic plans as thick, turgid documents. But keep in mind that no one reads thick, turgid documents. Instead think of creating a strategic guide that people at all levels can easily absorb. Specific tactical or implementation plans might be more than three pages, but the basic strategy should be short, clear, and elegant. (In fact, you should be able to capture the essence of the strategy in a few well-worded sentences.)

A useful approach is to take the five primary categories of a business—products (or services), customers (market segments), cash flow, people and organization, and infrastructure—and map out the key elements of your strategy in each

The Three Legs of Setting Strategy

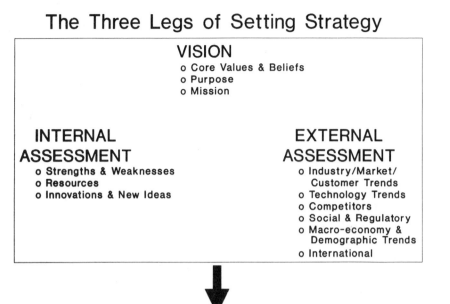

VISION
o Core Values & Beliefs
o Purpose
o Mission

**INTERNAL
ASSESSMENT**
o Strengths & Weaknesses
o Resources
o Innovations & New Ideas

**EXTERNAL
ASSESSMENT**
o Industry/Market/
  Customer Trends
o Technology Trends
o Competitors
o Social & Regulatory
o Macro-economy &
  Demographic Trends
o International

STRATEGIC DECISIONS

Figure 3-3

of them. An example of the output from such a strategy for-mulation is included at the end of this chapter.

What about all the boxes, bubbles, grids, and matrices that connote strategic planning? Some of these tools can be useful, but keep in mind that most of these were developed for use in large, multi-business companies. They are, in general, not as relevant in small to mid-sized companies. The best small company strategists don't use complicated matrices or bubble-boxes. Instead, they tend to use good old fashioned clear headed thinking.

The Multi-Year Rolling Strategy and Annual Strategic Priorities

It's seldom useful to lay out more than a five-year strategy. Some companies go no further than three years. We suggest having a three- to five-year strategy, revised annually. Think of strategy as dynamic, rather than static—as something that changes and evolves as your internal situation and the external environment changes.

It's also essential to set the top five strategic priorities for the coming year, with a specific person being responsible for each priority.

Try not to have any more than five strategic priorities for the year. If everything is a priority, then you have no priorities. Even the best companies can only concentrate on a few key issues at a time. (The example given at the end of this chapter also shows such a strategic priority formulation.)

The Annual Strategy Meeting

One of the most effective methods for setting and revising strategy is to schedule an off-site strategy meeting once per year. Attendees should include key people from each area of the company. The ideal group size is somewhere between five and ten people. Twenty should be the absolute maximum, although we would strongly encourage you to keep the size to under ten.

Some companies have found it useful to hire an outside consultant/facilitator to work with the group during the off-site meeting. Other companies prefer to keep the process entirely internal.

Prior to the meeting, each participant should be asked to prepare by answering a few questions. These questions should be circulated to the participants at least a week prior to the meeting. The content of the questions will vary from year to year, and from company to company, but should be related to the internal and external assessment.

To stimulate people to come to the meeting well prepared, we suggest asking each person to prepare a ten- to twenty-minute presentation on a specific topic. Few things capture people's attention better than knowing that they need to make a public presentation. Certain individuals might take on specific preparation tasks, such as industry/market trends, technology trends, new innovations, and competitor analysis.

We suggest using the following rough agenda:

- Review vision (core values and beliefs, purpose, and mission). Ensure that the vision is agreed upon and crystal clear.

- As a group, do an internal assessment.

- As a group, do an external assessment.

- As a group, decide upon/revise the basic strategy for reaching the current mission.

- As a group, decide on the top five strategic priorities for the coming year.

Someone should have responsibility for summarizing in writing the results of the meeting. This summary can be used as the strategic "guide" and should be distributed to all key people, referred to constantly, and used in setting individual goals and milestones (covered in Chapter 5).

Four Common Key Strategic Issues That Face Small to Mid-sized Companies

The following four key strategic issues commonly faced by small to mid-sized companies:

- How fast to grow
- Focus versus diversification
- Whether to go public
- Whether to lead a market or follow

How Fast to Grow

In an interview with Bill Hewlett and Dave Packard of HP, they were asked what one piece of advice they would give to people building companies. Hewlett responded:

> Don't grow too fast. You need to grow slow enough to develop good management. Venture capitalists often push these young companies too fast. But if you push too fast, you lose your values.

Growth is one of the most controversial and least understood strategic decisions. Notice that we said decision. How fast you want to grow should be an explicit strategic decision.

Growth is not *de facto* good (or bad for that matter), and rapid growth should not automatically be viewed as a desirable aim. This may sound like heresy to those who believe that a good manager should strive for as much growth as possible. However, the decision to grow rapidly should not be a foregone conclusion and, indeed, there may be reasons *not* to grow rapidly.

The question of growth should, as with all key decisions, tie back to the vision of the company. Do you even want to *be* a big company? Do you want the downsides that rapid growth brings?

Are there downsides to growth? Yes.

For one thing, rapid growth can create a perilous cash flow situation. A common pattern is that a company shells out cash to purchase materials and labor in anticipation of rapid sales increases. It then turns those materials into products and sales but, as you know, cash doesn't come in until months after the initial purchases. If the company doesn't hit its forecasts, cash is tied up in inventory. Cash is like blood or oxygen; without it, you die. And growth eats cash. This is why *roughly half of all bankruptcies occur after a year of record sales.*

There are many other downsides to rapid growth, including the following:

- Rapid growth can hide gross inefficiencies that don't show up until the growth slows.

- Rapid growth stretches a company's infrastructure, often past the breaking point.

- A rapid growth strategy can pressure your salesforce to commit to prices that severely cut your margins.

- There is tremendous human cost. The stress and strain on people during a rapid growth phase can be extreme.

- Rapid growth leads to increased organizational complexity and reduced communications.

- Large companies tend to be less fun, and rapid growth just brings about that largeness sooner.

- Rapid growth can quickly dilute the culture of your company, making it very difficult to develop management and reinforce your values.

The Warm Bodies Syndrome

This dilution of culture comes about largely by what we call the warm bodies syndrome. We've seen companies in a growth frenzy relax their hiring standards: "I don't care who you get. For heaven's sake, just get me a warm body. I need people!"

Warm bodies don't necessarily hold your values. And they might not live up to your standards of excellence. Rapid growth puts pressure on you to be much less discerning in whom you hire; and hiring is one place you want to be extremely careful.

Rapid growth can—and often does—evolve into a growth-for-growth's-sake mentality, which can then undercut the solidity of the company. For example, Osborne Computer priced its computers below cost in an effort to continue its heady growth. Of course, anyone can sell dollar bills for eighty cents—for awhile. And Osborne did, right up to the time that it went bankrupt.

Case Example: Lightcraft

One of us (Bill) was intimately involved with a classic situation where pushing for too much growth was a very poor strategic decision.

Lightcraft, a premier provider of lighting fixtures, competed on superior design, service, and excellent internal management (especially inventory management).

Lightcraft performed very well while it pursued a moderate growth strategy (10% to 15% annual growth rate). During this time, the company had profit margins far in excess of the industry average, and it was known throughout the industry as an outstanding company with a reputation for consistent tactical excellence.

Then the company was sold to Nu-Tone. The new owners decided to pursue a rapid growth strategy—50% the first year, which required an entirely different set of management skills than moderate growth. This put a strain on the company. Revenues in the prior year had been $6 million. Nu-tone pushed for $9 million in the next year. Bill tells the story best:

> The Nu-Tone salesforce , which replaced Lightcraft's sales reps, began giving discounts that cut deeply into our margins. We had built a big new facility to handle the increase in volume. The building, through

an unfortunate set of circumstances, developed structural defects resulting in chunks of concrete falling from the ceiling. Our inventory got out of control—we couldn't manage it as well as we used to, and we had a lot of cash tied up in it. At the rate we were going, we just couldn't provide the same level of customer service. Our whole infrastructure was pressed to the limit, and we began to lose the edge that made us so excellent in the first place.

Lightcraft grew to $7.2 million that year—which would have been high by past standards, but far short of the projected $9 million. Furthermore, since the products had short life cycles, excess inventory built for the $9 million had the possibility of becoming obsolete. The result was a severe deterioration of profitability. Lightcraft slowly lost its reputation and position in the market.

There's an additional downside to rapid growth that deserves special attention: rapid growth tends to create arrogance—a sense of invulnerability—that can lead to disaster. Both corporate and world history are peppered with examples of organizations whose confidence swelled to dangerous proportions, fueled by a string of unbroken successes or rapid expansion, only to blunder into catastrophe. In world history, notable examples include the French Army in 1812 (under Napoleon) and the German Third Reich in 1941 (under Hitler).

The corporate landscape is similarly littered with examples of companies whose rapid growth led them to believe they were unstoppable, only to have that belief dashed to bits. Osborne, Miniscribe, Televideo, Visicorp, Trilogy, and Magnuson Computer are all companies that went bankrupt shortly after a period of head-swelling success. In each of these cases, a sense of invulnerability led to poor decisions; arrogance contributed to disaster.

Growth feeds on itself; you may have a great product line in a growing market and be pulled into rapid growth. And once the growth pattern begins, it can be very difficult to slow down. The corresponding exhibit shows how growth feeds on itself.

THE RAPID GROWTH SPIRAL, AND ITS PITFALLS

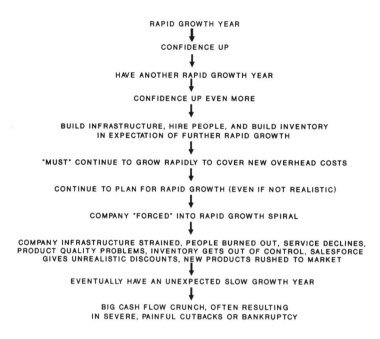

RAPID GROWTH YEAR
↓
CONFIDENCE UP
↓
HAVE ANOTHER RAPID GROWTH YEAR
↓
CONFIDENCE UP EVEN MORE
↓
BUILD INFRASTRUCTURE, HIRE PEOPLE, AND BUILD INVENTORY
IN EXPECTATION OF FURTHER RAPID GROWTH
↓
"MUST" CONTINUE TO GROW RAPIDLY TO COVER NEW OVERHEAD COSTS
↓
CONTINUE TO PLAN FOR RAPID GROWTH (EVEN IF NOT REALISTIC)
↓
COMPANY "FORCED" INTO RAPID GROWTH SPIRAL
↓
COMPANY INFRASTRUCTURE STRAINED, PEOPLE BURNED OUT, SERVICE DECLINES,
PRODUCT QUALITY PROBLEMS, INVENTORY GETS OUT OF CONTROL, SALESFORCE
GIVES UNREALISTIC DISCOUNTS, NEW PRODUCTS RUSHED TO MARKET
↓
EVENTUALLY HAVE AN UNEXPECTED SLOW GROWTH YEAR
↓
BIG CASH FLOW CRUNCH, OFTEN RESULTING
IN SEVERE, PAINFUL CUTBACKS OR BANKRUPTCY

Figure 3-4

Can Slow Growth Work?

You're probably wondering whether a slow growth strategy can work. Sure, there are significant downsides to rapid growth, but doesn't a company need to grow at a rapid clip to remain healthy, exciting, and vibrant? As one senior manager in an executive education program argued, "A company is like a shark; it has to keep swimming, or it dies. You either grow or die."

"Why do you say that?" we asked.

"Because you've got to give people room for advancement. If you're not growing fast, you'll have turnover. People need opportunities to grow into, and there just won't be the opportunities for new challenge. Without fast growth, a company is just not an appealing place to work. You'll also be limited in what you can provide your customers. Besides, who would invest in such a venture?"

He's got a point. Rapid growth makes room for advancement, and we admit there's something exciting about growth.

Nonetheless, there are companies with great people, low turnover (happy people), satisfied customers, superior financial performance, *and* a slow growth strategy.

Case Example:
University National Bank and Trust

Carl Schmitt, founder and Chairman of University National Bank and Trust Company, built his company on an explicit slow growth strategy. Founded in 1980, Schmitt believed that a slow-growth company can provide superior customer service and quality.

During the 1980s, when most banks were growing at a frenetic pace, Schmitt guided his bank along a methodical slow-growth path, gradually building a reputation for superior service. By the end of the 1980s, his bank boasted a return on assets 45% higher than the average return of other United States Banks, a 1.3% reserve ratio (very healthy), and virtually no non-performing loans. According to George Parker, a board member at University National Bank:

> The return on shareholder's equity at Carl's Bank far exceeds what shareholders could expect to receive by investing in other banks. The bank's slow growth allowed it to get the details right, and generate superior financial performance.

The key to UNB's slow-growth strategy lies in its ability to attract and retain good people. During a 1991 interview with us, Schmitt said:

> Do you know what the average teller turnover is at most banks? 50%. Do you know what we had last year? 0%. We didn't lose a single teller. And we've kept almost all of our top professional talent. People stay with us a long time, and they remain motivated.

How did UNB attract and retain good people without rapid growth? It offered freedom and fun. It hired "refugees" who had exhausted themselves in high-growth environments, and who knew first-hand the costs of growth. Schmitt made UNB a fun place to work. He let all employees—even tellers—have a wide range of decision making autonomy. As *Inc.* Magazine put it, Schmitt set " ... boundaries for growth while ensuring his employees feel boundless in making day-to-day decisions."

In contrast to University National Bank, however, there are instances where a rapid growth strategy is the only one that would work. If your mission is to become the dominant player in a rapidly expanding market, it would be unwise to let other competitors zoom too far ahead during the rapid growth phase of the market. For example, Compaq and Apple had no choice but to take a rapid growth strategy in the exploding personal computer market; no other strategy would have been viable.

So, where does all this leave us on the question of growth? Our main message is that growth rate should be part of your strategy formulation process, and that the pros and cons of various growth rates be thoughtfully considered. In general, the healthiest companies *do* grow, but at rates that allow them to put in place the pieces of greatness along the way. The question should not be, "How can we grow the fastest?" No, the question should be, "What growth rate is most consistent with our vision?"

Focus versus Diversification

One of the most effective strategies for a small to mid-sized company is to focus on one particular market or product line and, within that area of focus, be significantly better than the competition. A focused strategy ensures that your limited resources are concentrated to create the maximum advantage. This not only applies to financial resources, but also applies to a resource that is far more valuable: management time and energy.

Larry Ansin, former CEO of the highly successful Joan Fabrics Corporation of Lowell, Massachusetts, told us about his decision to focus:

> If you're diversified into five businesses, as we once were, the businesses that only make up 3% of your sales are going to take 20% of your time, energy, and attention. It's just not worth it. Focus. Do what you do better than anyone else. And the results will probably be very positive, as they were for us once we decided to concentrate all our efforts on one line of business.

Focus keeps you from being just another "also-ran" player. Also rans tend to fall in the worst possible strategic place: too small to take advantage of cost economies of scale, yet not differentiated enough to justify higher prices than the competition. To be stuck in the middle is deadly.

Of course, there are problems with a focused strategy. There is an inherent limit on growth, depending on the size of your target market. There is also the problem of cyclicality—being vulnerable to the ups and downs of any one market. In addition, a focused strategy provides less latitude for being opportunistic.

Nonetheless, we have seldom seen companies suffer because they were too focused, whereas we have seen quite a few companies flounder because they were not focused enough.

Case Example: GFP, Inc.

GFP was founded by Clem Atkins in the mid-1970s to bring to market his unique clock designs. His clocks were well received by a specific segment of customers: those who wanted highly functional clocks that were also viewed as works of art.

GFP grew to about $3 million, at which time Atkins decided to diversify into bicycle accessories. "I was interested in cycling, and I thought that my engineering and design skills could produce some excellent new and innovative products," explained Atkins.

And, indeed, the new bicycle products sold well, although Atkins noticed that sales of his clocks were beginning to slip. "All the more reason to diversify," he proclaimed. Atkins then got interested in the newly emerging personal computer market, and decided to produce accessories for personal computer users (special screens, keyboard holders, and other products).

This process of diversification continued—a ski resort, gardening products, recycled paper manufacturing—until the company began to lose money at alarming rates. Sales grew to $5 million and then declined precipitously.

Each of the GFP's markets were, in themselves, quite attractive. However, it was too much for GFP to spread itself across that many lines of business. The company never recovered and eventually failed.

Does this mean that a company should *never* diversify? No. Almost all companies eventually diversify. The question is when and how much.

Phased Diversification

Companies that pursue what we call phased diversification tend to be very successful in their diversifications. Phased diversification is a strategy whereby you focus on one line of business until you have reached your objectives in that market, *then* (and only then) move into a second arena. The exhibits shown in Figure 3-5 (page 120) illustrate this concept.

The Link Between Vision and Focus

Your vision should play a key role in determining how focused you are.

For example, Celtrix Laboratories, which you'll recall has the purpose, "To improve the quality of life through innovative human therapeutics" will produce only products that are innovative, and human therapeutics. Joan Fabrics set the mission, "To become the number one player in the upholstery fabrics industry." To pursue this mission, Joan de-diversified entirely out of all unrelated lines of business. To become the number one player in upholstery fabrics, CEO Larry Ansin believed it had to focus on that single line of business.

To become "the most respected and admired company in the worldwide bicycling industry by the year 2000," Giro Sport Design makes a concerted effort to remain focused on that goal. According to president Bill Hannemann:

> Our vision statement, and especially the mission part of it, helps us remain focused during strategic decisions. Every new product idea is put to the test: Will it help us become the most respected and admired company in the worldwide *bicycling* industry by the year 2000? We also put it against our purpose: Is it innovative, high quality, and the unquestioned best? If it doesn't pass the tests imposed by our vision, then we don't do it. Period.

Phased Diversification

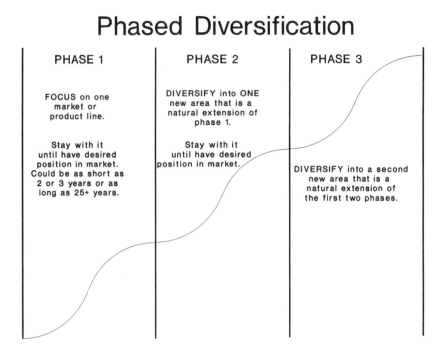

PHASE 1	PHASE 2	PHASE 3
FOCUS on one market or product line.	DIVERSIFY into ONE new area that is a natural extension of phase 1.	
Stay with it until have desired position in market. Could be as short as 2 or 3 years or as long as 25+ years.	Stay with it until have desired position in market.	DIVERSIFY into a second new area that is a natural extension of the first two phases.

Examples of Phased Diversification

PHASE 1	PHASE 2	PHASE 3
Running Shoes	Athletic Shoes	Sportswear
Rock Climbing Hardware	Mountaineering Hardware	Softgoods for Climbers
Electronic Test Equipment	Computers	Integrated Systems
Furniture Upholstery Fabric	Automotive Upholstery Fabric	Airline Upholstery Fabric

Figure 3-5

Whether to Go Public

Most outstanding companies eventually reach a stage where going public (raising cash by selling shares to the general public) is a possibility. For many, the glamour and liquidity (a chance to "cash out") of going public is alluring.

However, it's a common misconception that, once a company reaches a certain size or age, a public offering is always the next natural step. You don't have to go public. It's not pre-ordained.

For example, Minnesota-based Cargill, founded around the time of the American Civil War, grew to 1990 annual revenues of $42 billion (which would have put it ninth on the 1990 Forbes Sales 500 list of public companies) as a private company.

Before leaping into the realm of publicly traded corporations, we would urge you to think strategically about the pros and cons of a public offering. Perhaps no other strategic decision, once executed, has as significant or lasting an impact on a company.

Going public can be a helpful strategic step in working towards your vision, as it provides capital for expansion and investment in new products. It also provides liquidity for shareholders and can help solve some difficult estate-tax problems that occur with the death of a major shareholder.

But there are significant disadvantages to going public:

- It's a drain on management time, both before and after the offering. In the months leading up to an IPO (initial public offering) the top officers of the company are usually overwhelmed by the process. Road shows, "all hands" meetings, writing prospectuses, dealing with press, and other activities can (and usually do) turn into the primary use of management time. After the IPO, time must be spent dealing with the financial community, preparing quarterly and annual reports, and communicating with the press.

- It's expensive. Legal fees, accounting fees, printing costs, and filing fees will cost about half a million dollars right off the top. Underwriter's fees (a percentage that is paid to the investment banker who takes your stock to market) can be enormous; 7% of total proceeds is not uncommon.

You should assume that the total tab for an IPO will be well over a million dollars for most companies.

- You'll be managing in a fishbowl. You have to disclose financial information. You have to disclose salary information. Every move you make is scrutinized by investment analysts. Competitors can keep a better eye on what you are doing.

- You'll feel pressure to manage for the short term. Every public company feels pressure from the financial community to keep quarterly earnings as high as possible. There's a built-in disincentive to take short-term losses for the sake of long-term health.

- You may lose control of the company. If over 50% of the voting shares are in the hands of outsiders, the company can be bought by anyone who has the resources to acquire the stock.

- There may be a conflict of corporate purpose. Public shareholders view their stock holdings primarily as a *financial* investment. As long as the stock does well, they don't really care what the company is doing. Thus, if your purpose is not strictly to maximize shareholder wealth, you may be at odds with your shareholders. Public shareholders don't generally buy into a vision; they buy into the prospect of a capital gain.

Case Example:
Tensor Corporation

Tensor Corporation was founded in 1960 by Jay Monroe, a highly creative and intense man whose main purpose was to have a vehicle for bringing his ideas to market and to have fun. He had a vision for the company where it would make product decisions on aesthetic considerations as much as on short-term return on investment criteria. He felt the company should be able to produce products that might not produce the best short-term financial results, but that would ultimately be better and more interesting contributions to the market.

He made a fateful decision: he took the company public and left himself with less than 50% of the stock. The motivations of the public stockholders (short-term return on investment) came in direct conflict with Monroe's vision. Monroe was eventually faced with losing the company to a corporate raider or changing his vision—a loss either way.

In contrast to the Tensor case, L. L. Bean made the decision to remain a privately held company. A big part of the decision to remain private was a desire to maintain the exceptionally high Bean customer service standards, even if those standards at times affected profitability in the short term. In 1989, being private paid off when Bean decided to take $2 million right off the bottom line in a customer service improvement program.

Commenting on the decision, president Leon Gorman said in a *Wall Street Journal* interview, "It's a good thing we're not a publicly-owned company. We don't have to worry about earnings."

Related to the IPO decision is the strategic decision of outside investors. Certain types of investors, such as most venture capitalists, think primarily in terms of their "cash out" value. If you decide to seek venture capital—or capital from other investors whose primary motivation is to cash out within a few years—be aware that you are simultaneously making the strategic decision to go public or sell out.

In most venture-backed companies, going public (or becoming acquired) is *assumed*, and it's just a matter of *when*. Thus, if going public, for the reasons outlined above, does not fit with your vision for the company, then you probably should *not* seek venture capital or other "cash out" oriented investments.

To Lead a Market or Follow

In general, tremendous benefits accrue to market innovators—first movers or pioneers. Yet, a first mover advantage is by no means a guarantee of greatness and, indeed, there can be costs to being the market innovator.

The evidence shows that first movers generally acquire a market advantage:

Average Market Share*
Pioneers, Early Followers, and Late Followers

	Consumer Goods	Industrial Goods
Pioneers	29%	29%
Early followers	17%	21%
Late Followers	12%	15%

* Based on a sample of 1,853 businesses. Analyzed by W. T. Robinson and C. Fornell, *Journal of Marketing Research,* August, 1985.

This doesn't tell the whole story. There are many examples of first movers losing their advantage, usually due to a competitor introducing a better product, performing better marketing, or both. Indeed, early followers often ride the coattails of a pioneer, taking advantage of the fact that the market has already been primed and educated. The following examples, and many more, are provided in *Stanford Business School Research Paper #1084,* "To Pioneer or Follow?: Strategy of Entry Order," by Marvin B. Lieberman and David B. Montgomery.

- Bomar brought out the first hand-held calculators, and stimulated the market with extensive TV advertising. Bomar was then overrun by Texas Instruments and Hewlett-Packard.

- Visicorp, inventor of the market-shaping Visicalc spreadsheet software, was devastated when a well-marketed and vastly superior Lotus 1-2-3 came on the market.

- Docutel, pioneer of the automatic teller machine, lost its market position when competitors introduced ATMs with features not offered by Docutel.

- Osborne computer, pioneer of the portable computer market, was devastated when competitors introduced superior products, for which it had no answer.

- Ford was dethroned from the number one position in automobiles in the 1920s because it did not adjust quickly enough to the better, more differentiated cars offered by the then struggling General Motors Corporation. Ford never became number one in the auto industry again.

- British Air introduced the first commercial jet, but was overcome by Boeing's superior design in the 707. Boeing has dominated the commercial jet-craft market ever since.

Where does this leave us with respect to a market pioneer strategy versus a market follower strategy? It's clear that there are advantages to being a market leader. You can lock up customers. You can build early market share and gain a dominant trade name. You can get down the learning curve. You can sometimes gain patent protection. You can benefit from high margins, and use the resulting cash flow to fund further product development and marketing.

But—and this is key—taking a market pioneer strategy is not, in itself, enough. Being first will not protect you forever; you also have to *execute* well.

Although being first is a definite advantage, being the unquestioned best is a much more significant and sustainable advantage. If you have a choice between being first or being the best, be the best.

Of course, the ideal position—and the one pursued by many great companies—is to strive for being *both* first *and* best. If you're first and then continually work to improve your product, marketing, and service, you'll be in a very strong position.

This leads us right to the final two key parts of attaining corporate greatness: innovation and tactical excellence.

The thing you *don't* want to do with strategy is to invest all your time trying to plan and not enough time innovating or executing. Clear strategic thinking is essential for being on the right track, but, as Will Rogers said, "Even if you're on the right track, you'll get run over if you just sit there."

No business enterprise can be perfectly planned. Yes, it should have a clear overall vision, and a basic strategic guide for attaining the vision. It's impossible to rigidly plan every action down to the nth detail, and to do so would be an absurd waste of time. There needs to be some level of creative chaos in a great company. Most important, a company can't sit still. People in it have to act, move, do, try, fail, try again, struggle, push, scramble, innovate, and execute the details.

To return to a central theme of this book, it isn't any one thing that makes a company great. It isn't just strategy.

It isn't just leadership style. It isn't just vision. It isn't just innovation. It isn't just tactical excellence. It's *all* of these; and it's all of these done consistently for years.

The following pages contain a strategy formulation example for a small company. This example illustrates the flow from vision, internal assessment, and external assessment to strategy and a set of strategic priorities. The final page of this chapter gives some caveats to the stages of industry evolution analysis.

STRATEGY FORMULATION EXAMPLE
HARDROCK PRODUCTS, INC.

CORPORATE VISION

Core Values and Beliefs
We value high performance for its own sake.
We believe in being your best, maximizing your potential.
We value being in nice physical settings.
We only want to participate in markets where we can be outstanding; if we can't be number one or two, we don't want to play at all.
We value hard work.
We value having fun, and time away to play.

Purpose
To help outdoors sportspeople realize their full athletic potential, and to be a vehicle for making a living in a sport that we love.

Current Mission
To become the number-one supplier of rock-climbing hardware in the world by 1997.

INTERNAL ASSESSMENT

Strengths

Leading edge technology and hardware design skills

Knack for creating "core" products with
multiple spin-offs

Ability to generate lots of new ideas and innovations

Intimate knowledge of the rock-climbing world

Reputation for reliability, quality, and service

We know how to create great catalogs

Weaknesses

No finance or control skills

Design to production to market coordination is very poor

Cross-functional communication is very poor

Employee training is poor

Great products, but high manufacturing costs

Resources

Strong balance sheet

No debt; capacity to borrow if necessary

Philosophy of keeping close control; no outside investors

Innovations

New bolting technologies invented

New camming technology

Wildcat (code name)

EXTERNAL ASSESSMENT

Industry Trends
Market is approaching maturity with growth of 15% per year
Size is roughly 50,000 climbers U.S., 500,000 worldwide
Market is segmented into sport, traditional, and big wall
Sport-climbing segment is fastest growing
Driving forces of growth:
o new technology making climbing safer
o climbing competitions and television
o baby boom mid-life crises

Technology Trends
Camming devices
Bolting devices
Lighter, stronger raw materials

Competitors
Fragmented; no dominant player
Increasing competition from Europe
Primary direct competitor: Black Diamond

Social and Regulatory Environment
Park services restricting bolting because of effect on rock
Upcoming ISCC safety standards expected by 1993
Product liability insurance cost explosion

Macro Economy and Demographics
More leisure time
Baby boomers hitting mid-life and are seeking
new challenge

International
Market growth in Germany, France, Italy, and Australia

Top Three Opportunities	Top Three Threats
1. Sport Climbing	1. Not meeting ISCC standards
2. International markets	2. International competitors
3. Climbing competitions	3. Product liability costs

STRATEGY
1991–1993

Overview

To attain our mission of becoming the number one supplier of rock-climbing hardware in the world, we will pursue a strategy of focusing on hardware for rock climbing, with emphasis on the expanding sport-climbing segment. We will compete on superior innovation, design, quality, and service.

Products

We will only make hardware for rock climbing. Until we realize our mission, we will not make products for other sports, nor will we enter the "soft goods" market.

We will compete on superior technology, quality, and service, not on price. We will price at the upper end of the market.

We will develop groupings of "core" products that can be easily tailored to specific needs. This will keep our inventory costs low and our quality high.

We will take advantage of the trends towards sport climbing and speed climbing. We will therefore concentrate our product development efforts on these expanding markets.

We will make all of our products conform to the proposed ISCC safety standards, thus putting us in an excellent position once the safety standards are passed.

We will "over-engineer" our products for safety to protect against product liability lawsuits.

We will concentrate on new product innovation and will introduce two new products per year. We will capitalize on trends in bolting and camming technology.

Product Introductions:

1991: Ultra-light Bolt Drill, Quick Clips
1992: Hardcam, El Cap Pins
1993: Power Cam Unit, Wildcat (code name)

Customers

We will position ourselves, relative to our competition, as *the* supplier of *superior performance* products for the serious rock climber.

We will distribute our products primarily through our own mail order operations and through specialty retail outlets.

We will reach rock climbers through our own catalogue, advertising in specialized rock-climbing magazines, athlete endorsements, and sponsorship of climbing competitions.

We will seek as much "free advertising" as possible by getting the most high-profile climbers to use our gear.

We will seek to develop loyal customers through excellent customer service; 24 hour turnaround on orders; and making the process of ordering from us *enjoyable.*

We will introduce our products in at least three international markets over the next three years:

1991: France
1992: Germany
1993: Italy, Australia

Cash Flow

We will fund the business primarily through operations. We will therefore price our products to provide at least a 50% gross margin.

We will maintain banking relationships, and arrange credit lines (in the event we need them); but we will borrow as little as possible.

We will grow at a controlled rate; maximum of 15% per year.

Sales	Gross Margin	Profit After Tax
1991: 4.5 M	55%	10%
1992: 5.1 M	50%	8%
1993: 5.8 M	50%	10%

People & Organization

We will install a seasoned financial controller.

We will establish design-production-marketing teams responsible for each new product; eliminate the design to production to marketing problems we have had in the past.

We will continue to build our engineering and design staff.

We will continue to hire people who love the outdoors.

We will build up our specialty retail outlet rep force.

We will set up an international division.

We will develop an employee training program.

Infrastructure

We will locate and move into new facilities more conducive to cross-functional communication. We will buy our facilities, rather than rent. We will locate near the mountains.

1991 Strategic Priorities

1. Get Ultra-light Bolt Drill and Quick Clips introduced to market in time for summer season. (Primary responsibility: Joe).

2. Establish a foothold in Europe; sign up two super-star European climbers for endorsement contracts (one male, one female); set up mail order and hire reps in France; create French catalogue. (Primary responsibility: Beth).

3. Locate and hire a seasoned financial controller. (Primary responsibility: Bill).

4. Implement design-to-manufacturing-to-marketing product teams. (Primary responsibility: Sue).

5. Locate/acquire new facilities; be ready for move by 1992. (Primary responsibility: Bob).

Caveats to Stages of Industry Evolution Analysis

The following comments about the stages of industry evolution analysis come from our own observations and Michael Porter's *Competitive Strategy* (1980, Free Press).

The stages of industry evolution (emergence, rapid growth, maturity, decline) is probably the most common pattern of evolution, but it does not necessarily hold in all industries.

Porter offers four things to keep in mind when using the concept:

1. The duration of the stages varies widely from industry to industry, and it is often not easy to determine which stage the industry is in.

2. Industry growth does not always go through the S-shaped pattern. Industries can skip maturity, passing straight through to decline. Some industries seem to skip the emergence phase altogether.

3. Companies can *affect* the shape of the growth curve through product innovation and repositioning. If a company takes the stages of evolution as given, it becomes an undesirable self-fulfilling prophesy.

4. The nature of competition associated with each stage of evolution is different for different industries. Some industries remain concentrated. Some start fragmented and consolidate. Some remain fragmented.

To these four caveats, we would add a fifth. We believe that many industries are made up of multiple S curves. That is, because of product innovations, a single industry may progress through multiple S-shaped curves as new innovations are introduced and move from emergence to acceptance to decline. Note: this is known as the *Innovation-Adoption Cycle*. The Innovation-Adoption Cycle is well described in Everett M. Rogers' ground-breaking book *Diffusion of Innovations* (1983, Free Press). *Diffusion of Innovations* is, in our view, a must read for those interested in how new innovations are adopted by a population.

In sum, the stages of industry analysis is a very useful tool, but it should be used thoughtfully, and not taken blindly as gospel.

Chapter 4

INNOVATION

... all progress depends on the unreasonable
man.

George Bernard Shaw
Man and Superman

There's no shortage of good ideas.

Indeed, the biggest problem in building an innovative
organization is *not* stimulating creativity; the problem is how
to nurture the creativity that abounds all around us, and
how to get that creativity acted upon and turned into innovations.
(Think of an innovation as a done idea—an idea that has
been implemented.)

That's precisely what this chapter is about. To be an enduring, great company, we believe it must have the ability to innovate continually—to have a constant flow of new ideas, some of which are fully implemented. We say some are implemented (rather than all) because a great company will always have more good ideas than it can fund.

Most companies start with a creative founder. The challenge, however, is to become an innovative company, rather than a company dependent on an innovative founder.

We've identified six basic elements of what it takes to be an innovative company:

1. Receptivity to ideas from everywhere
2. "Being" the customer
3. Experimentation and mistakes
4. People being creative
5. Autonomy and decentralization
6. Rewards

We will guide you through each of these six elements, with specific examples and suggestions, and will conclude with some specific managerial techniques for stimulating creativity and innovation.

Corporate Innovation Element 1: Receptivity to Ideas from Everywhere

Highly innovative companies don't necessarily generate more ideas than their less innovative counterparts (good ideas are in plentiful supply for all companies). But highly innovative companies are often more receptive to ideas—and not only to their own ideas, but to ideas from everywhere. Furthermore, they do something about the ideas. Not that an innovative company executes every single idea, but it is much more likely to act quickly on a partly-baked idea than to spend countless hours deliberating about all the reasons it can't work.

Sadly, however, most of us have been trained to do just the opposite; we're well schooled in criticism, having learned that the way to show how smart we are is to cite all the reasons that something is a stupid idea or doomed to failure.

We've noticed many new MBAs, for example, are adept at finding all the flaws in a business idea, but they're much less practiced at coming up with ways to make the idea work. Many times we've stood facing a self-satisfied person who has just done a marvelous job of demolishing a new product idea during a discussion. Then we ask, "Yes, we know it's an imperfect idea. But then no idea is perfect. So, now how do you intend to make this idea successful in spite of its flaws?" Some people rise brilliantly to the challenge when they realize that the goal is no longer to show how bright they are by shooting holes in ideas. But, alas, others do not. They've been trained too well in the ethos of criticism, and to build a great company, they'll have to overcome this negative training.

Don't get us wrong. We don't mean to imply that every idea is a great idea, or that every new product idea will be a wild success. In fact, quite a few ideas will turn out to be failures. As we shall describe later, even those failures can pay handsome dividends in the long run.

It's essential to keep in mind that many great ideas were at first thought to be stupid ideas. Form 4-1 (shown on pages 138–39) provides a list of historically significant creations that were thought by so-called experts (we prefer to call them "wet blankets") to be dumb ideas.

We recommend that you circulate a copy of this list to everyone in your company. Put a copy on your own wall or above your desk. Keep it in front of you—and ask others to do the same. It's a helpful reminder about the importance of being receptive to ideas.

The first element in making your company creative and innovative is to seek ideas from everywhere and, most important, to create a climate of receptivity to new ideas. Let us reemphasize: *There is no shortage of good ideas; there is only a lack of receptivity to ideas.*

Ideas from Outside

Don't think that the only ideas worth doing come from within your company. Some of the most creative companies rely extensively on ideas generated outside their walls.

Form 4-1
Wet Blankets Through History

"This 'telephone' has too many shortcomings to be seriously considered as a means of communication. The device is inherently of no value to us."; Western Union internal memo in response to Bell's telephone, 1876.

"The concept is interesting and well formed, but in order to earn better than a 'C', the idea must be feasible."; a Yale University management professor in response to Fred Smith's paper proposing reliable overnight delivery service. Smith went on to found Federal Express Corporation.

"We don't tell you how to coach, so don't tell us how to make shoes."; a large sporting shoe manufacturer to Bill Bowerman, inventor of the "waffle" shoe and co-founder of NIKE, Inc.

"So we went to Atari and said, 'Hey, we've got this amazing thing, even built with some of your parts, and what do you think about funding us? Or we'll give it to you. We just want to do it. Pay our salary, we'll come work for you.' And they said, 'No'. So then we went to Hewlett-Packard and they said 'Hey, we don't need you. You haven't got through college yet.'"; Steve Jobs speaking about attempts to get Atari and HP interested in his and Wozniak's personal computer. Jobs and Wozniak founded Apple Computer Company.

"'You should franchise them,' I told them. 'I'll be your guinea pig.' Well, they just went straight up in the air! They couldn't see the philosophy. ... When they turned us down, that left Bud and me to swim on our own."; Sam Walton describing his efforts to get the Ben Franklin chain interested in his discount retailing concept in 1962. Walton went on to found Wal-Mart.

"Who the hell wants to hear actors talk?"; H. M. Warner, Warner Brothers, 1927.

"We don't like their sound and guitar music is on the way out."; Decca Recording Company rejecting The Beatles, 1962.

In 1884, John Henry Patterson was riduculed by his business friends for paying $6,500 for the rights to the cash register—a product with "limited" or no potential. Patterson went on to found National Cash Register (NCR) Corporation.

"What's all this computer nonsense you're trying to bring into medicine? I've got no confidence at all in computers and I want nothing whatsoever to do with them."; a medical professor in England to Dr. John Alfred Powell, about the CT scanner.

"Drill for oil? You mean drill into the ground to try and find oil? You're crazy."; any number of experienced drillers who Edwin L. Drake tried to enlist in his project to drill for oil 1859. He later became the first man to strike oil.

"That is good sport. But for the military, the airplane is useless."; Ferdinand Foch, Commander in Chief, allied forces on the western front, World War I.

"The television will never achieve popularity; it takes place in a semi-darkened room and demands continuous attention."; Harvard Professor Chester L. Dawes, 1940.

Apple Computer didn't create the basic ideas behind Macintosh; those ideas had been around for years, developed first on defense research projects and later at Xerox. A group of Apple executives attended a demonstration of mouse and icon technology at Xerox (which was an investor in Apple) and carried the basic ideas over to Apple.

The original McDonald's restaurant was created by the McDonald brothers in San Bernardino, California. Ray Kroc, who founded the company that transformed the McDonald brothers' concept into a chain, simply recognized the potential in what had already been created.

T/Maker Company didn't create the original prototype of *Personal Publisher* (the first desktop publishing package to hit the market); it came from an outside programmer who had initiated the effort on his own.

Johnson & Johnson didn't create Tylenol (a break-through non-aspirin pain reliever); the product came from McNeil Laboratories, which was acquired by J&J. Procter and Gamble didn't invent Oxydol or Lava Soap; it obtained them by acquiring William Waltke Soap Company. The 3M Company didn't invent its first landmark product (WETODRY waterproof sandpaper, brought to market in the early 1920s); Francis Oakie, a young Philadelphia ink maker, created the innovation and sold the rights to 3M.

Fight to prevent the NIH syndrome (i.e. If it's Not Invented Here, it can't be any good.) from taking hold at your company. With an open mind, look constantly outside your company for ideas. Let the entire world be part of your R&D lab. Make it possible for the thousands of great ideas swirling

around in the world to easily permeate the outer membrane
of your company.

Here are some specific activities you might consider:

- Make it everyone's responsibility to be receptive to new
  ideas submitted to the company from outsiders. Make
  it the responsibility of a particular individual to respond
  to ideas submitted by outside individuals. Granted, many
  ideas won't fit your mission or will be infeasible, but
  remember that Chester Carlson received icy receptions
  from over 20 companies to whom he offered his copying
  technology; frustrated, he founded Xerox.

- Arrange an employee swap with an admired company
  in another industry, in which one of your employees spends
  a few weeks at that company and one of theirs spends
  time at yours. This cross-breeding can stimulate wonderful
  insights.

- Hire outside designers. Some of the most creative designs
  come from outside designers (the outer design of the
  MacIntosh Computer, for example). Outside designers gain
  ideas from working with different product categories and
  different problems across a range of clients, and can
  therefore bring valuable and stimulating suggestions. (The
  same principle applies to other types of outside consultants
  as well.)

- Encourage people to join technical, industry, trade or
  other groups where they will come in contact with interesting people and ideas. Offer to pay their membership
  fees. Join some groups yourself.

- Allow people to travel to events or otherwise spend time
  out in the world exposing themselves to new ideas. NIKE,
  for example, allocates a portion of its design budget just
  for unrestricted travel. NIKE wants its designers to get
  out of the office and see things, just to spark new ideas.

- Pay for subscriptions to journals and publications that
  might have interesting new insights, ideas, technologies,
  and research results. Similarly, start a library and allow
  employees to purchase books, read them, and place them
  in the library.

- Invite leading edge idea people to give a talk or seminar. Encourage outsiders to attend and participate in lively discussion and debate.

- Pay for selected employees to attend education programs, seminars, and university-sponsored events; ask people to present to others in the company (perhaps at a staff meeting) "the most intriguing ideas" they encountered at the event.

- Encourage people to read nonfiction materials *unrelated* to their work, and to share insights gleaned. Bob Waterman, co-author of *In Search of Excellence,* told us that he gets many ideas via an "eclectic" reading list that ranges from architecture to world history. In fact, research on creativity shows that significant creative contributors have wide interests, a breadth of perspective, and a need for novelty and diversity. *Innovation often comes from seeing the relationship between unconnected ideas and melding them together.*

- Make it easy for customers to feed you thousands (and we do mean thousands) of ideas. At service outlets, make use of a customer suggestion box. Follow the example of Stew Leonard's Dairy (a single-unit, family-owned outlet that does $100 million in annual revenues, located in Norwalk, Connecticut). Stew Leonard's receives an average of 100 comments and suggestions *per day* in its suggestion box. To further stimulate customer ideas, each suggestion is followed up with a thank-you within 24 hours.

Ideas from Inside

Of course, good ideas don't come only from outside; many of the best ideas and innovations bubble up from inside. An organization is a natural incubator of great ideas and innovations.

Right now—the very moment you are reading this chapter—there are many creative ideas, some of them quite good, swirling about inside your company. Just as your company should be receptive to ideas from outside, it should be receptive to ideas from employees at all levels and all positions. Ideas can emerge from the furthest outposts, as with the Big Mac and the Egg McMuffin (invented by franchisees), or from the depths of scientific experimentation, as with the 3M™ Post-It notepads (created by a single researcher playing around with chemicals and discovering, quite by accident, the unique adhesive that made the product possible).

Remember the customer suggestion box? Well you should also have ways for employees to give suggestions on internal processes. Wal-Mart has a policy called *LTC* (Low Threshold for Change). Store managers regularly seek ideas for improvements and innovations from people working on the floor, and bonuses are sometimes paid for particularly good suggestions.

As a leader of your company, *you* can also be a major source of innovation. Indeed, we've noticed a significant number of new product innovations originating from the top of certain organizations.

- At Giro Sport Design, many new products are the brain-children of founder Jim Gentes and his design team. At one planning meeting, Gentes introduced over 30 new product possibilities for the company's consideration.

- Honorary Sony Chairman Masaru Ibuka originated the Sony Walkman.

- In its early days, numerous L. L. Bean innovations came directly from L. L. himself.

The point here is *not* that founders and CEOs are necessarily more creative than others, but that their push behind an idea vastly reduces (or completely eliminates) resistance to it. Could the Sony Walkman, which was thought by those in the tape and recording divisions to be a crazy idea, have survived had it not originated from Honorary Chairman Ibuka? Perhaps; but it certainly would have been less likely.

This returns us again to the central point of this section: the primary challenge you face is not in increasing creativity per se, but in *making your company receptive* to the vast amounts of creativity that already exist. The point is not to build a company that depends on you for its innovation, but to continually work towards an organization that is as receptive to new ideas *as if those ideas had come from you.*

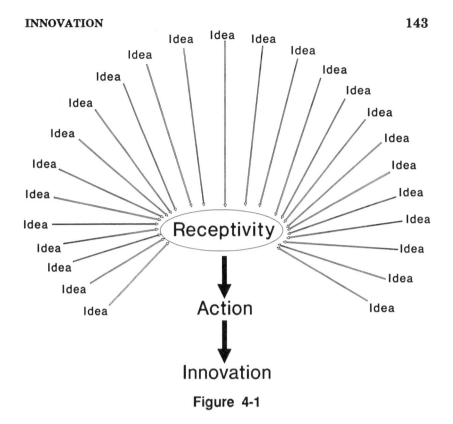

Figure 4-1

Idea-Push or Market-Pull?

Before moving on to the next section, we must address a vexing paradox.

On the one hand, classic business school dogma asserts that you should always define a market need first (via market research and other methods of analyzing customer benefit preferences, price sensitivities, etc.), and *then* develop innovations that meet that need (market-pull or, as it is sometimes called, market focus). This dogma appears sensible. After all, a business should create products or services that meet real customer needs. What better way to ensure this than to define those needs and then target your innovation efforts towards their fulfillment?

Yet, on the other hand, many market-successful innovations did not originate from market-pull, nor were they developed via classic market research techniques. Indeed, *many breakthrough products wouldn't even exist if the companies that created them had relied solely on a market-pull approach to innovation.*

- The fax machine is an American invention; yet, as of 1990, not one fax machine sold on the market is American-made. Why? Because, according to Peter Drucker, market research convinced the Americans that there was no demand for such a gadget.

- The experiment that led to the unique adhesive behind the 3-M Post-it™ notepad was not driven by pre-defined market demand. Spencer Silver (the scientist) didn't start with the idea in mind that there was a market for his unique adhesive. On the contrary, the adhesive was *a solution looking for a problem.* For over five years, Silver made a pilgrimage around 3M, asking people if they could think of any uses for the adhesive. According to Silver:

  > We really had to fight to get [the funding for] a patent, because there was no commercial product readily apparent. ... It's one of those things you look at and say, 'This has got to be useful.' ... At times I was angry because this stuff is so obviously unique. I said to myself, 'Why can't you think of a product?'.

  Furthermore, once the Post-it™ product had been conceived, it failed a four-city market research test! It was only after an intense period of *giving* the product away free— getting people addicted to the little note pads—that the product finally took hold.

- When Fred Smith conceived the idea for Federal Express (overnight nationwide delivery), UPS, Emery Air Freight, and the United States Postal Service, had all thought of the idea before. They had rejected it because they perceived no market need; no customers had ever *asked* for it.

- Debbie Fields, in launching her cookie store chain (Mrs. Fields Cookies), was warned that her ingenious ability to produce hot, soft, luscious cookies would fail; market research reports stated that people like *crispy* cookies, not soft cookies. Her store concept was, according to the market research experts, doomed to failure.

- When David Sarnoff tried to raise investment money to market the radio in the 1920s, he was repeatedly turned down because there was no market demand for the service of sending a message to no one in particular. It was only *after* the product was brought to market that people began to recognize its value; by making the radio available, Sarnoff created a market for its use.

- Windham Hill Record Company was told by distributors and record market experts that there was no market demand for a solo piano album. There was absolutely no indication from the market that such a concept could be successful. Yet the company introduced the innovative George Winston piano solo album anyway, and it sold over 500,000 copies.

- The first microwave oven was built in 1946, based on radar technology imported to the United States from Britain. There was no market demand for a microwave oven. In fact, according to Jack Kammerer, senior vice-president of marketing at Amana, who introduced the microwave:

> If this project had been given to a very highly structured company that had spent a year and hundreds of thousands of dollars in market research, they'd have probably thrown it in the wastebasket and never done it. It was only a gut feeling of a couple of individuals that this is the right product for the right time.

Furthermore, certain highly innovative companies are very clear that they consciously foster an idea-push approach to new product innovation. Akio Morita of Sony wrote:

> We seek to lead the public with new products, rather than ask them what they want. Instead of doing a lot of market research, we refine our product and try to create a market for it by educating the public.

This notion of leading a market—of *creating* a market—is essential to breakthrough innovations. With dramatic, new innovations, customers will often not tell you what they want (because they do not know what is possible) until you show them what they can have—as was the case with the 3M Post-it™ notes, the radio, and the fax machine.

This is very important to realize, or else your company might bypass tremendous opportunities. As seasoned French design expert Jean Pierre Vitrac put it, "Consumers, when confronted with something new and original, can be tempted by it, contradicting all the criteria previously applied to them."

In a study of sixteen commercial breakthroughs, P. Ranganath Nayak and John M. Ketteringham, concluded in their outstanding book *Break-throughs* that "It is flatly wrong to say that the bulk of successful commercial innovation results from 'market pull' rather than 'technology push.'" In *not one* of the 16 cases did classic market research play a major role in stimulating the original idea behind the breakthrough. According to Nayak and Ketteringham, the original motivation came from the curiosity or problem-solving drive of a single inventor:

> Certainly, the search for a market often followed quickly on the heels of the problem solver's drive. In some cases, it was a parallel phenomenon. *But we found no instance of the market demanding a breakthrough before the inventor had found it lurking in the depths of his semi-consciousness.*

But wait a minute! Surely there is a place for market input into products. We don't want to toss the entire discipline of market research out the window, do we? What about being close to the customer—about listening to customer input into products? What about the great consumer marketing companies, like Procter & Gamble, that attribute much of their success to their ability to identify customer needs and then develop products to meet them?

What about companies like Tensor Corporation, whose Tensor Lamp lost its position in the marketplace because inventor Jay Monroe refused to listen to customer input? What about Visicorp, who failed to respond rapidly enough to customer requests for more powerful features in their best- selling Visicalc Spreadsheet package, and was subsequently destroyed by upstart Lotus Development Corporation? What about Ford's being surpassed by GM in the late 1920s because Henry Ford turned a deaf ear to customer clamorings for more styles and colors, responding with "They can have any color they want, as long as it's black."?

To resolve this dilemma, we must first cut through the clutter and clarify the question.

The question is not whether innovations should meet a genuine human need (to be commercially successful, they had better meet a need). The question is: How should innovation be generated in the first place? What should your company *do* to ensure a continual flow of innovations, including some breakthroughs, that meet genuine human needs?

We will address this question throughout this chapter. But the first step is to recognize that you need both idea-push and market-pull in your company. The classic business school market-pull dogma shouldn't be mindlessly worshipped. Yet, at the same time, there certainly is a place for market input, as ignoring customer input can lead to missed opportunities or disaster. Think of original breakthroughs as coming primarily (although not exclusively) from idea-push, and subsequent incremental innovations coming from customer input. The total amount of innovation is higher by using both approaches, rather than relying exclusively on one.

Reject the extremists. Reject those who say, "*Always* go ask the market what it wants first." Remember, just because customers haven't been asking for the innovation doesn't necessarily mean that they won't be thrilled when it's offered to them. Also reject extremists at the other end of the spectrum who say, "We're so good we *never* need to pay attention to the market; we always know what's best." Be receptive to ideas from everywhere, no matter what their origin.

There is an additional answer to the paradox: what appears to be purely idea-push is often just the opposite. Even though the inventor hasn't done a general market analysis, he is often as close to the customer as he can get: he *is* the customer! This brings us to our second major element of making your company highly innovative.

Corporate Innovation Element 2: Being the Customer

> In the end, we make clothes to satisfy us. We wear them.
>
> *Patagonia Catalog, 1989*

One of the best ways to make and keep your company innovative is to have people invent solutions to their own problems or needs. In other words, be your own customer and satisfy yourself. If that is not possible—if you are in a business where you cannot be your own customer—then figure out a way to experience the world as a customer experiences it.

Solve Your Own Problems
and Meet Your Own Needs

The idea here is simple. If someone in your company creates an innovation to solve her own problem or meet her own desire, there are probably other people in the world that would benefit from her invention.

Returning to our example of T/Maker and the *Personal Publisher* product, the innovation was stimulated by President and CEO Heidi Roizen's personal need to create a party invitation at her computer. She preferred to use an IBM PC (because she was accustomed to it), yet the lack of IBM graphics software forced her to use a MacIntosh. "Too bad it's not possible to do something graphically oriented on an IBM PC," she mused. Out of this personal experience grew the *Personal Publisher* project, which generated the first desktop publishing package to be offered on the IBM PC.

Jim Gentes at Giro comes up with his great ideas not by sitting in an office and staring out the window, but by going out on his bicycle at lunchtime and hammering away against the wind. "On a bike, on the road, is my best laboratory. I'm always trying to figure out ways to make myself go faster with less effort," says Gentes.

Even the original personal computer itself was invented to meet a *personal* need. When asked how he and Steve Wozniak got the idea for the personal computer, Steve Jobs responded:

> Like most great ideas, it came from something right in front of us. We designed this computer because we couldn't afford to buy one; we just wanted to educate ourselves about computers. So *we* were the initial market. Our secondary market was all our friends. Gradually as the number of people that it was neat for expanded, we got more and more excited. We didn't sit in a chair and think, "My God, 10 years from now the survey says that everyone is going to be using personal computers." It didn't happen that way. It was more of a gradual process.

In 1920, the band-aid™ was invented by Earle Dickson, an employee of the fledgling Johnson & Johnson company, whose wife was constantly cutting herself in the kitchen. The accidents occurred frequently enough that he finally decided to make a ready-to-use bandage that she could apply to herself. Laying out a long strip of surgical tape, he placed small pieces of gauze on it at intervals, and to keep the adhesive from sticking, he covered it with a piece of cotton crinoline. Dickson mentioned his invention to colleagues at work, and thus sparked one of the most successful commercial products in history.

The Woodwork Factor

Think of it as the woodwork factor; by solving your own problem, other people who have the same problem (but who would not be easily identified via classic market research techniques) come out of the woodwork.

The woodwork factor was originally articulated by the team behind the invention of Tagamet, one of the most successful prescription drugs in history. (Tagamet is a drug that heals ulcers without surgery, and changed forever the way people cope with ulcers.) Thomas Collins, the head of Tagamet's United States effort, described:

> In my age group, I can remember all sorts of people with ulcers. But they weren't under active treatment. They did whatever they had to. So, from my point of view, I always said, I don't think anybody knows what the hell the size of this market is. This is the woodwork factor. They're all my friends. I had a vision of patients coming out of the woodwork.

Heidi Roizen, Jim Gentes, Steve Jobs, and Earle Dickson also experienced the woodwork factor. In fact, this is what HP meant by its famous next bench syndrome.

Here are some specific things you might do to stimulate people in your company to be the customer and to replicate the woodwork factor:

- Hire customers. NIKE, for instance, has lots of athletes as employees. We visited NIKE during a product development session, and found Marketing Manager Tom Hartge—an avid runner—working with the design team to create shoes that he used on his own runs. NIKE hires elite athletes as product testing consultants who are expected to test new products under the most severe circumstances and report back with ideas and problems.

- Allow employees to take time to field test products or services. At L. L. Bean, for example, any Bean executive can get an extra week's vacation to do product testing, even if that means a fly-fishing trip in Alaska, going to Ontario for the opening of the duck and goose season, or checking out enormous Danner Yukon cold-weather hunting boots in British Columbia.

- Distribute an annual blank "personal idea journal" to all employees, wherein they are encouraged to make notes about problems and ideas they personally confront in their work and personal lives.

- Communicate the woodwork factor by writing up specific stories in the employee magazine or newsletter about how individuals or teams invented successful products by meeting their own needs. People learn through stories. Make the woodwork theory part of the mythology of the company.

What if you are in a business that makes products or delivers services that you and your employees don't extensively use? Can the woodwork factor work here as well? Yes, but the process is different.

Simulate Being the Customer

If your business is such that you can't literally *be* a customer of your own products, then simulate a way of being the customer. There are two basic approaches.

One approach is to solve the specific problem or fill the specific need of an individual customer—not an individual customer *group*, but a *single, solitary individual customer*. The idea here is the same as above: if you invent a solution to the problem of a single customer, chances are there are other potential customers hidden in the woodwork that would also be interested in the innovation.

For example, baby powder was invented one day in 1890 when a physician wrote Fred Kilmer at Johnson & Johnson Laboratories that one of his patients complained of skin irritation from using a medicated plaster. To solve the problem, Kilmer sent the customer a small container of Italian talc. J&J then decided to include the talc with its plaster products. Soon thereafter hundreds of customers came out of the woodwork, asking for more of the powder, and Johnson's Baby Powder was born.

A second approach is to get so close to the customer that you experience what the customer experiences. Don't work simply to know who your customers are; but to know them. The key is not to assemble reams of market data sheets, which are then analyzed, sorted, and interpreted. No, the key is to directly observe customer experience in the field, in real time. It's much better to actually be there when the customer is wrestling with a certain problem, or attempting to use one of your products or services, than it is to ask him to later recall his experience. We call this the "touch and feel" approach.

Case Example of Touch and Feel: Ballard Medical Products

Ballard Medical Products, with sales of about $10 million in 1987, set a strategy to develop and dominate niches that big companies neglected, and to do so by prolific new-product innovation.

The first premise at Ballard, as described in an *Inc.* magazine article, is that customers themselves are an integral part of the product innovation process. The second premise is that salespeople—people actually out dealing directly with customers —are also part of the process. Salespeople are expected to go on-site and interact directly with the customer *as* he goes about his activities. A salesman for Ballard described:

> You can't just ask the director of respiratory therapy or the head nurse if there are problems. You've got to walk through yourself ... and ask the nurses whether *they've* got problems.

The third premise at Ballard is that R&D must respond to product ideas from salespeople. In one instance, the vice-president of sales proposed his own product idea, helped design it, and worked with R&D to get it out the door. The entire product innovation cycle—from concept to delivery—was only a few months.

This real-time touch and feel approach to customer input is practiced by the very best product innovators. An even further step you can take is to rotate R&D people into actual sales roles for a period of time or, at minimum, to send them out to the field to interact directly with customers. (Incidentally, we think it's a good idea for you as a leader of the enterprise to spend part of *your* time touching and feeling customer problems.)

NIKE, Herman Miller, Bang and Olufson, BMW, Olivetti, and Patagonia expect their designers to be in close personal contact with the final users of their products. As design manager Paulo Viti of Olivetti puts it:

> Of course, this is a somewhat unscientific form of marketing, but it often gets the designers' insight and intuition working much better than boring written reports.

But is it really unscientific? It certainly appears to be. But think for a minute; what's the essence of being scientific? What do scientists do? Do they just read boring written reports assembled by other people? No. They figure out ways to touch and feel the world, so that they can make precise observations about it. They go out and look at things for themselves.

And they experiment.

Corporate Innovation Element 3: Experimentation and Mistakes

> What's important is experimentation. I only plan to succeed 10 to 20 percent of the time. I try a lot of different things, and by sheer dumb luck some of them work.
>
> *Vinod Khosla, co-founder,*
> *Sun Microsystems*

By now, we hope you're inspired to be receptive to new ideas from everywhere, to have both idea-push and market-pull, and to be the customer. However, there is probably a nagging question: how do you know if an idea is a good one? Are all of the examples we've given simply examples of luck? What about all the idea-pushes and single-customer solutions that didn't create a woodwork factor? Can you eliminate all risk and determine if an idea is good before acting on it?

Sadly, the nature of innovation is that it is fraught with the unknown. The best way to find out if something is a good idea is to experiment, to give it a try. This, of course, leads to mistakes—ideas that aren't good—but they are part of the process. Innovation requires experimentation and mistakes. You can't have one without the other two, period.

Thomas Edison persisted through over 9,000 iterations before he successfully invented the light bulb. Finally one of his associates asked, "Why do you persist in this folly? You've failed more than 9,000 times." Edison looked at him incredulously and said, "I haven't even failed once; 9,000 times I've learned what doesn't work." Edison's philosophy of experimentation, mistakes, and correction, is the heartbeat of innovation.

We've always enjoyed John Cleese's (co-founder of Video Arts) vignette of "Gordon the Guided Missile," which so vividly captures this idea:

> Gordon the guided missile sets off in pursuit of its target. It immediately sends out signals to discover if it is on course to hit that target. And signals come back—'No, you are not on course. So change it—up a bit and slightly to the left.'

> And Gordon changes course and then, rational little fellow that he is, sends out another signal. 'Am I on course now?' And back comes the answer, 'No. But if you adjust your present course a bit further to the left, you will be.' And the missile adjusts its course again and sends out another request for information. Back comes the answer, 'No Gordon, you've still got it wrong. Now you must come down a bit and a foot to the right.'

> And the guided missile, its rationality and persistence a lesson to us all, goes on and on making mistakes, and on and on listening to feedback and on and on

correcting its behavior in the light of that feedback, until it blows up the Nasty Enemy Thing.

And we then applaud the missile for its skill. And if, then, some critic says, 'Well, it certainly made a lot of mistakes on the way,' and we reply, 'Yes but that didn't matter did it? It got there in the end. All its mistakes were little ones, in the sense that they could be immediately corrected. And as a result of making many hundreds of mistakes, eventually the missile succeeded in avoiding the one mistake which really would have mattered—missing the target.'

Sometimes the mistake-driven innovation process happens quite by accident. For example, the Reebok soft-style "crinkle" shoe leather that fueled demand for its exercise shoes in the 1980s was not planned. It came from a production mistake.

Indeed, many innovations have as their root source some form of just doing it—giving something a try, experimenting, just to see if it will work. Returning to the example of the 3M Post-it™ Notes, Spencer Silver described the original genesis of the adhesive:

> The key to the Post-it™ adhesive was doing the experiment. If I had sat down and thought about it, I wouldn't have done the experiment. If I had really seriously cracked the books and gone through the literature, I would have stopped. The literature was full of examples that said you can't do this.
>
> People like myself get excited about looking for new properties in materials. I find that very satisfying, to perturb the structure slightly and just see what happens. I have a hard time talking people into doing that. It's been my experience that people are reluctant to just *try*, to experiment—just to see what will happen.

The idea of using microwave for cooking came about through a simple experiment. Les Vandt, an engineer working on microwave technology, bought some popcorn and held it in front of a microwave power tube. Another engineer commented about the experiment:

> It [the popcorn] began to jump all over hell. It didn't involve the board of directors and all that kind of stuff; just Les Vandt and the bag of popcorn.

One of our favorite examples of innovation via experimentation comes from a small California company, Powerfood, Inc. Powerfood invented a revolutionary energy bar that athletes—runners, climbers, cyclists, swimmers, etc.—could eat immediately prior to or even *during* exercise to raise their energy levels without upsetting their stomachs. Athletes had suffered for years with the rule, "Don't eat at least three hours before workout." But with Powerbars, this problem vanished, which has changed the lives of thousands of athletes around the world.

The Powerbar invention illustrates many of the ideas presented thus far. The idea came from Brian Maxwell, an Olympic marathoner who chronically suffered from "hitting the wall" during races due to lack of energy (being the customer, solving his own problem). Maxwell founded the company because the big companies approached with the idea said, "It's impossible to make such a bar, and the market for such a bar is too small, even if we could do it. We're not interested." (Note again the importance of receptivity to ideas from everywhere.) And, finally, the product solution came about via massive experimentation, as described by Maxwell:

> I see Jennifer, Bill, and me in our Berkeley kitchen littered with bags of white powder and bottles of brownish liquids. A balance scale dominates the dining room table and on first glance, visitors conclude that we're the kingpins of some illegal drug empire. Then they notice baking sheets and pie tins, lined with wax paper and numbered, strewn on every flat surface. Closer inspection reveals sticky-looking patches of strange colored dough in each one. The visitors don't escape without tasting at least four or five and recording their comments on file cards. Those who exercise regularly leave with a baggie of cellophane-wrapped samples to "try before your next workout."

These images of Maxwell and his friends concocting hundreds of experimental samples, Vandt exploding popcorn all over the microwave tubes, Silver mixing chemicals in the lab, and Edison's 9,000 light bulbs are essential to keep in mind when thinking about how to keep your company innovative.

We've even found with our own teaching that our best innovations come from experimentation in the classroom. We just try stuff all the time. Some of the experiments work, and become permanent parts of our course. Others fail and are discarded immediately after the first attempt. We've come up with a number of teaching innovations because we are willing to throw things against the wall and see what sticks. You've got to be willing to do this, even if it means periodically falling on your face (and we've fallen on our faces plenty of times).

Just Do It

We've found the simple phrase "Just Do It" to be immensely helpful in our own efforts to remain creative, and we have tried to pass this along to companies. At one company, we obtained a whole stack of "Just Do It" stickers, note-pads, and key chains and had them distributed to people throughout the company. People need reminders that it's ok to "Just Do It"—to act without fifteen layers of approval. In fact, we always try to point out to people that it's far easier to ask for forgiveness than permission. Just Do It.

Don't Make It Big Before You Have To

Successful experimentation requires easy endings. That is, you've got to be willing to try lots of different things, keep those that work, and put a quick, painless death to those that don't.

Keep projects small as long as possible, thus making it easier to say, "Well, *that* didn't work. Let's try something else." If a project becomes too big too quickly, it'll begin to fight for its own life, even though it might be wiser to end the experiment and start a new one: "Hey, we've assigned seventeen people and spent a year on this thing. We *can't* end it."

For example, Novellus Systems, a small semi-conductor equipment company, consistently outmaneuvers competitors 10 times its size by using this "less is more" approach to new product development. The company uses three or four key engineers in the early stage of product design, and adds people only when it is clear the machine will work.

The Role of Product Failures

How far should you take experimentation? Should you take it all the way to the marketplace? It's acceptable to experiment in the lab, but what about the process of bringing products to market, which is much more expensive if the experiment fails?

This is a difficult dilemma, for if you never put out a product unless you have 100% rational certainty that the product will be a success, then you'll never put an innovative product on the market (and you'll be left in the dust by those that do). On the other hand, of course, product failures cost money, time, prestige, and can hurt confidence. There are two basic answers to this dilemma.

First, you can sometimes do small market-test experiments before making a full-blown product introduction. Put it out in a certain geographic area and see how it does. Or thoroughly test the product with a subset of your customers, and learn from their reactions. The idea here is to continue the process of lots of small experiments, mistakes, learning, and correction—just like our friend Gordon the Guided Missile, who self-corrects through thousands of "mistakes," but ultimately hits The Nasty Enemy Thing.

Second, highly innovative companies are not afraid of product failures. Not that they enjoy product failures, but they are willing to risk market failures and then learn from them.

For example, Apple Computer's first two follow-on products to the Apple II (the Apple III and the Lisa) were horrendous failures. But Apple applied all the information learned from those failures to create the incredibly successful Macintosh. Henry Ford introduced numerous products—including some notable failures, such as his original Model B—leading up the famous Model T. Ford learned from each product introduction (and product failure) in designing the revolutionary Model T. Motorola had a string of valuable product failures from which it learned: the Model 55 radio (1933), the first push-button car radio (1937), a gasoline heater (1947), its first color TV (1957)—these were *all* product failures for Motorola.

Ok, you say, but these are *big* companies; they can afford to have some product failures. What if you're a smaller company? Good point; but look again. In each of the above instances,

Product Innovation Cycle
Apple Computer

Figure 4-2

Break-Through Innovation Cycle

Figure 4-3

the product failures occurred early in the company's history, when the company was much more vulnerable. Indeed, one of the reasons they got through the early stages to a place of greatness is partly because they had product failures early on.

The aim is to have multiple product cycles—putting products on the market, learning quickly where they fall short, and continuing to innovate and improve based on market input. (Note: this also applies to new services as well.) The Japanese, who are not as good at breakthroughs as Americans, have mastered the incremental improvement process, which has contributed significantly to their dominance in certain industries, such as cars.

Figures 4-2 and 4-3 show how the break-through/incremental-innovation cycle works, and how it played itself out in the early days of Apple Computer.

[Note: Given the management turmoil at Apple since 1985, we found ourselves wondering whether we should include Apple examples in this book. Apple has displayed three of the four elements of greatness (performance, impact, and reputation), but we're skeptical about the fourth (longevity). Will Apple be a great company in the year 2040? Given the fact that between 1984—the year the MacIntosh was introduced—and 1991 there were no new major breakthrough innovations, and given the abhorrent behavior of Apple top management (CEO John Scully earned $16 million in 1990 and then laid off 10% of Apple's workforce because of his poor planning), we're concerned about Apple's long-term prospects for greatness.

Nonetheless, we believe that the phenomenal impact on the world achieved by the company from the late 1970s through the mid 1980s makes it attractive to use a handful of examples from its early history. You'll notice that each of the Apple examples in this book come from before 1985.]

Good Mistakes and Bad Mistakes

Should you be tolerant of all mistakes? Are all mistakes good?

A good mistake comes from an honest effort to try something combined with a diligent attempt to execute it well. A bad mistake is one where an idea fails primarily because of sloppy, inattentive, or indifferent effort. Saying "mistakes are valuable" should not be interpreted as, "we don't have to try to do our best." It's one thing to put the wrong product on the market, it's another to do a sloppy job of putting the product on the market.

The worst mistakes, however, are those that are repeated over and over again. It is the lesson learned from a mistake that makes it valuable, not the mistake itself.

The Popcorn Image

We like to think of an innovative company as having a *popcorn image*. Think of your organization as the popcorn popper, and think of unpopped corn as the seeds of good ideas. An innovative organization has the same feel as popping corn—lots of good ideas placed in a conducive environment, "popping" into experiments all over the place. Next time you go to the movies, observe the popcorn popper in action and keep the image in mind.

During a visit to Patagonia's main facilities (where design, production, research, marketing, and finance all reside), we felt like we were in the middle of just such a popcorn popper. The level of activity—people moving, trying things, talking, walking, designing, drawing, writing, meeting, deciding—was phenomenal. There was no post-lunch lull. There were no dreary, boring meetings. There were no frustrated people sitting around waiting for approval to act. There were no clocks, much less anyone watching those clocks. People moved just as quickly at 4:30 P.M. as they did at 8:00 A.M.. People spoke in a rapid-fire "let's make this quick, because I've got a project I'm working on that I want to get back to ..." style.

One way to stimulate the popcorn image is to have an explicit policy of allowing people to spend up to ten or fifteen percent of their time tinkering on unofficial projects or ideas of interest. 3M, for example, has had a policy like this for its scientists and engineers since it was a small company.

Another way is to set aside some uncommitted funds for internally generated ideas. Set aside a certain amount each year as internal venture financing, which can be tapped by people inside the company who want to develop an idea. Someone—or a group—would serve as internal venture capitalist and make decisions about which projects to fund.

Let Persistence Win

A colleague of ours asked Andy Grove, CEO of Intel Corporation, how his company chooses from the large number of new product ideas generated by its entrepreneurial engineers. Grove responded: "No one is ever told to shut up, but you are asked to come up with better arguments. People are allowed to be persistent."

The phrase, "People are allowed to be persistent," is perfect. It captures the notion of a "Darwinian" or free-market style environment where ideas are never killed outright, but where the fittest ideas survive.

In one instance at Intel, a group of middle managers wanted to develop add-on boards for personal computers, but the idea was initially not included in Intel's product strategy. The middle managers received funding from Intel's internal corporate venturing program, and turned the boards into a separate business.

A Company of Experimenters and Tinkerers

To remain innovative, you've got to have people at all levels doing lots of experimenting, tinkering, and doing—creating the popcorn effect. How do you do this? How can you create the environment where this happens? There are three basic answers, which we shall now discuss in detail:

- Employ creative people

- Get out of their way

- Reward them for being innovative

Corporate Innovation Element 4: People Being Creative

To remain innovative, a company must have people within it who are being creative.

Wait! Before you stop reading because you think this is so completely obvious that it's not worth reading about, please read on. This point is not as obvious as it first appears.

Indeed, most of the literature on corporate innovation has focused primarily or solely on *structural* solutions. Although we agree that there are structural components to remaining innovative (discussed in the next section), innovation ultimately comes because people are being creative within those structures.

Unfortunately, there is a common belief that creative people belong to a special, unique subset of the human race, and that creativity is a trait that belongs *only* to that subset. In other words, the common belief tells us, there are creative people and uncreative people, and uncreative people are forever doomed to remain uncreative.

Garbage.

All people have the capacity to be creative. There is no such thing as an inherently uncreative person; creativity is a capability that resides inside each and every one of us. There is no special breed of person somehow ordained from God with the gift of creativity. Nor is it true that most of us were born deprived of that blessing.

The first step in having people at all levels be innovative is to believe in their inherent creative capability. After all, how can you possibly expect people to innovate if you don't fundamentally believe that they can?

Help People Develop Their Creative Capabilities

The second step is to help people develop their personal creativity. Consider the following steps:

- Provide educational training in the creative process. Training sessions and seminars on personal creativity can be very effective in getting people to see that they are creative and how they can be more creative. Some of the most innovative companies, such as NIKE, make extensive use of such training.

  Prior to a creativity seminar at NIKE, we asked, "Why do you want us to come and teach you about innovation? It seems a little odd; teaching NIKE about creativity feels a bit like teaching Jessie Owens about track and field." NIKE training director Pete Schmidt responded:

  > Innovation is the most important aspect of this company and we must preserve it as we grow larger.

As we bring in more and more people, we want them to understand the importance of innovation, and we want to back it up by helping them to be more creative. You can't take it for granted that people will have tapped their full creative talents; we've got to keep stimulating them in that direction.

- Provide educational materials on the creative process. When people are hired, give them a book on personal creativity. Purchase and circulate reading materials on creativity; you might even consider selecting one book per year that the company buys for each person and gives as a gift. Some readings on the creative process that we recommend are:

  —*Creativity in Business,* by Michael Ray and Rochelle Myers.

  —*Conceptual Blockbusting* by James Adams

  —*The Art of Problem Solving* by Russell Ackoff

  —*Lateral Thinking* by Edward deBono

  —*A Whack on the Side of the Head* by Richard Van Oech.

- Write your own "Innovation Manifesto." Develop your own ideas about corporate innovation. Draw on ideas from this book, your own experiences, and from other authors. Create a one-page innovation statement that every employee gets. It might be a simple list of 10 key points, like:

  1. We shall never say, "That is a stupid idea."

  2. We shall experiment first, evaluate later.

  3. We shall take 1,000 ideas from our customers.

  4. We shall produce 25% of our revenues in any year from new products introduced in the past five years.

  5. We shall listen to anyone who has an idea.

  6. We shall never do a "me too" product; every product we do must be innovative in some way.

  7. etc...

Write your own list. It's fun. And valuable.

Hire and Nurture Unusual People

Seek people who have done creative things. Look for people who have done different and interesting activities—people who have started little businesses while in college, people who have had a diverse set of experiences, people who have shown initiative throughout their life, people who don't exactly fit in any pre-defined mold.

The Case of the Mish-Mash Resume

Bill Wraith invented some highly innovative financial securities, including something called a *dual issue option,* which involved solving a long-standing finance problem that had been deemed by most finance experts as unsolvable." Who, you ask, is Bill Wraith? Suffice it to say that he's a very creative financial designer.

The fascinating part of this story is how Wraith got the opportunity to create these innovations. His resume read like a completely unfocused collection of items; he'd been a designer, a marketing manager, and a salesman, and he'd jumped from integrated circuits to personal computers to engineering work stations—all before the age of 30. Says Wraith, "Recruiters would look at my resume and think, 'Oh what a mish-mash. Nothing here fits. You're just jumping around with no coherent focus.'" But Wraith had a common thread running through his work: he had a knack for coming up with creative solutions to tough problems.

So he was hired by an investment bank. The bank saw that Bill was very bright and very creative, so they just hired him and turned him loose on tough problems.

Not only do you need to hire a few creative "misfits," you also need to tolerate their sometimes bizarre behavior. Some of the most creative people simply don't fit into typical well-behaved molds. They're often rebels, irritating and somewhat out-of-control.

Jim worked at McKinsey & Company early in his career. McKinsey is a very conservative organization, full of gray-suited, serious people. Yet, at the same time, McKinsey consistently produced some significant innovative contributions—including the book *In Search of Excellence*. Jim tells the story of encountering co-author Tom Peters in the office:

> His office, which was right across the hall from me, was chaotic and covered with all kinds oï funny hats: fire hats, World War I helmets, baseball caps, etc. The place did *not* look like a McKinsey office. And then, in the middle of a normal workday, this whirlwind flew by my office in baggy shorts, blown-out tennis shoes, and a t-shirt that had an inscription along the lines of, "Don't ask me any questions, because I really couldn't give a ...." It was Tom, rushing into his office to pick up a few papers.

Obviously, Peters never entirely fit into the McKinsey mold. Yet the firm tolerated him, letting him run wild while he and Bob Waterman finished the book.

Vinod Khosla, co-founder of Sun Microsystems, spoke on trying to keep Sun innovative:

> You have to balance the "flakes" with the organization. You have to be willing to put up with some unusual people because some of the most creative people are very unusual. I had one engineer (a man) who came to work in a big dress-like gown—sort of like a pregnant lady's dress, something that was real loose and comfortable. And by the way this is not atypical. The point is that these people had the ability to create things we needed to compete.

Do all creative innovations come from weird people? No, of course not. In fact, some of the most creative people we know come in fairly conservative packages. Yet, to have an innovative company, it's also wise to have tolerance for a few unruly crazies. As Max Depree of Herman Miller puts it, "If you want the best things to happen in corporate life, you have to find ways to be hospitable to the unusual person."

As your company grows, be aware that the type of people attracted to your company will tend to change—there will be more stability conscious types, fewer innovators. Fight this tendency by always hiring a few wild ducks.

Size/Innovation Evolution Pattern

Small Company

↓

Attract Innovators

↓

Success and Growth

↓

Become Large

↓

Attract Risk Averse and
Stability Conscious People

↓

Install Bureaucracy

↓

Highly Innovative People Leave

↓

Reduced Innovation

Figure 4-4

Hire Diverse Talents, But Not Divergent Values

Breadth and diversity breed creative insight. People with different experiences and backgrounds working on the same problem will usually produce more creative—and usually better—answers than people with similar experiences. We urge you to hire an eclectic bunch of folks.

At Giro Sport Design, president Bill Hannemann has been adamant about building the senior management team with an incredible diversity of backgrounds—an ex-teacher, an ex-advertising executive, an ex-academic dean, an ex-video game design manager, an ex-Xerox designer. Yet, at the same time, Giro has taken care to screen a very narrow range of core values.

Follow the Giro example; seek diversity in your company. Yet keep the core values tight.

[<===================================>]

DIVERSITY OF BACKGROUNDS

[<==>]

DIVERSITY OF CORE VALUES

Hire People Who Don't Know Much

Daniel Boorstin in his landmark work, *The Discoverers* (a detailed history of human discovery and invention), observed that many significant contributions came about because people were naive. In describing Ben Franklin's electricity discoveries, for example, Boorstin explained:

> In fact his (Franklin's) achievement illustrated the triumph of naivete over learning... His amateur and non-academic frame of mind was his greatest advantage; like many another discovering American, he saw more because he knew much less about what he was supposed to see.

The same thing happens in business. When people become fat with conventional wisdom, they're dangerous. A lot of being innovative in business is being willing to give something a try because you don't know it flies in the face of conventional wisdom. As Debi Coleman, Apple VP of information systems and technology, puts it: "The single biggest roadblock to creativity and innovation I've encountered in business is conventional wisdom."

Returning to our example of Bill Wraith (Mr. Mish-Mash resume), he solved the unsolvable dual issue option pricing problem by purposely *not* learning what other people had done. His boss said, "We have some academic experts on contract you can talk with, and you can obtain any journal or publication you want to work on the problem."

"No thanks," said Wraith. "I'd rather look at the problem totally naive. I'm afraid that seeing the blind alleys they took would just get in my way."

So Wraith went off to a dark room for a few days and just thought about the problem on his own. He reached an innovative solution by framing the problem in a way never before conceived. "If I'd known the traditional way to frame the problem, I never would have solved it," says Wraith.

The point here is not that every person you hire should be naive or know nothing about your industry. Knowledge and experience are valuable. But they can also be a liability. The point is to have a balance of experienced, knowledgeable experts, *and* naive clean minds. Just because someone doesn't come from your industry or comes straight from college (or didn't even go to college, for that matter) isn't a reason to turn him away.

Hire Designers

Design talent is one of the most underutilized creative resources in industry. By design talent we mean those who are trained and talented in the craft of design. There are two basic categories of design relevant to most businesses: graphic design and product design. Designers are trained to be highly creative and, most important, to apply that creativity to practical problems.

Think for a minute about great products: BMW cars, the MacIntosh Computer, Bang and Olufson turntables, Herman Miller furniture. Notice that design is a critical variable in the differentiation of these products—they have extraordinary elegance, beauty, and function.

Design can be a crucial differentiating factor even in mundane industries. For example, Joan Fabrics Corporation attributes much of its success in dominating the furniture upholstery market to the quality of its designs. According to former CEO Larry Ansin:

> Don't underestimate the importance of style—which we achieved through excellent design talent. There's a tendency to think that design is unimportant in traditional,

old-line businesses. Not true. We succeeded in large part *because* of our design talent.

Hire designers. Hire graphic designers to help with logos, marketing materials, catalogues, packaging, and the like. Hire product designers to be integrally involved in the product development process, not as simply an adjunct to make the product "pretty," but from the very early conceptions of the product development cycle.

Some companies, such as Braun, Giro Sport Design, Patagonia, and Joan Fabrics, actually hire designers as employees. Whereas others (Herman Miller, Olivetti, Bang and Olufson, and Yamaha, to name a few) make extensive use of outside design consultants and design firms. Whichever path you take, we urge you to "think design" in every aspect of your business, from product development to marketing. Good design should permeate your company—buildings, processes, structures, products, the whole works.

Corporate Innovation Element 5: Autonomy And Decentralization

Freedom, inefficiency, and prosperity are not infrequently found together.

Samuel Eliot Morison

In 1988, K. C. Jones, then coach of the Boston Celtics, mentioned to a CBS Sports interviewer, "I give the players a lot of leeway on the court, so they can use their imagination and creativity."

"Doesn't that cause problems?" the interviewer asked.

"No," responded Jones. "We've been in the championship four of the past five years, and won it twice."

Jones' approach to coaching illustrates a central truth about creativity: it *requires* autonomy.

Trust, Respect, and Courage

Stanford Business School has a reputation as one of the most innovative educational institutions in the world. We have

had the chance to experience how it works firsthand, which
is captured in Jim's description of his first year at Stanford.

> I was 30 years old with no track record teaching at
> the University level. Dean Roberts made me the offer
> to teach, and then said simply, "Let us know what
> time slots you want. Good luck." That's all the direction
> I got. No one asked me what I was going to do in
> the classroom. No one gave me specific directions. No
> one even looked at my syllabus. I was given free rein
> to do pretty much whatever I wanted. Of course, I
> had seasoned colleagues to consult, and there were some
> course materials already developed. But I was basically
> left on my own to just do it.

Two years later, sitting at a luncheon celebrating an hon-
orable mention for his teaching performance, Jim said to Dean
Roberts, "You sure took a big risk on me. Why did you do
that?"

"That's the way we do things around here," Roberts responded. "I didn't really view it as a risk, but more of an
opportunity. See, by letting you go all out we believed that
you would do your best work, and produce some good stuff.
Of course, it doesn't always work out that way with people,
but the innovation and performance we generally get by that
approach is worth it."

Given how little Jim knew about what he was doing,
we don't fully agree that the proposition was risk-free. But
Roberts demonstrated the key element: trust and courage. He
was willing to take a chance, and believed that Jim would
rise to the occasion.

The basic message is to hire good people, create the environment for them to work, and get out of their way.

This is the magic that Tracy Kidder captured in his wonderful book, *The Soul of a New Machine,* wherein he described
the design team's motivations behind the birth of a new computer:

> ... they did the work, both with uncommon spirit and
> for reasons that, in a most frankly commercial setting,
> seemed remarkably pure. ... more than two dozen people
> worked on it overtime, without any real hope of material
> rewards, for a year and a half; and afterwards most
> of them felt glad. That happened because West and
> the other managers gave them enough freedom to invent,
> while at the same time guiding them toward success.

This need for freedom and autonomy is well recognized by companies that remain innovative. Herman Miller allows its designers to work away from central facilities, in whatever environment they find conducive to work. Merck & Company, one of the most innovative pharmaceutical firms, hires the best scientists it can find, lets *them* select targets for basic research (not marketing or corporate), and stays out of their way.

This applies at all levels of human endeavor, from a five-person basketball team to entire societies. Indeed, freedom of action—room to experiment—is the primary factor behind the relative strength of Western economies compared to their centralized, eastern-bloc counterparts. In their book, *How the West Grew Rich*, Nathan Rosenberg and L. E. Birdzell, show that the underlying source of the West's economic advancement is the large number of innovations that come about via autonomous experimentation. This experimentation, in turn, comes about because people *can* act, because there are few restrictions holding them back from giving something a try. Just imagine what the United States economy would be like if every new business had to get formal government approval from a ministry of central business control. (Actually, we don't need to imagine; just look at the Soviet economy.)

Yet the tendency of human organization is to move in the opposite direction—to seek control and order, to minimize unexpected surprises. To remain innovative, this tendency must be resisted, and resisted with crushing vigilance.

The oppressive desire to exchange life and soul for sterility and order is like a persistent vine, constantly creeping up the sides of an organization and wrapping itself around its limbs until it can no longer move swiftly and nimbly. Eventually, if left unchecked, the vine will wrap itself around the organization's throat, tighten its vice-grip, and strangle away the company's life spirit.

Indeed, one of the great ironies of corporate evolution is that nearly all new companies begin as highly innovative entities. Yet many of these same companies lose their innovative capabilities as they grow and age—the spirit that was responsible for early development becomes ensnarled in the twisted, suffocating vine of bureaucracy and centralized efforts to control.

DON'T LET THIS HAPPEN TO YOUR COMPANY!

But how? What can be done to prevent this from happening as a company grows larger?

Decentralization: Slicing up the Diamond

The basic solution is decentralization, or as we call it, slicing up the diamond. This is the basic solution pursued by companies that managed to keep an innovative spark alive while becoming much larger, such as Johnson & Johnson and 3M.

The idea is simple: by continually breaking the enterprise into small, semi-autonomous chunks, you can become larger overall, yet retain many of the advantages of being small. People within each small sub-unit can then have a sense of personal ownership, responsibility, autonomy, and accountability that simulates being an entrepreneurial business within the overall corporate umbrella.

George Hatsopoulus, CEO of Thermo Electron Corporation, described in an interview with *Inc.* magazine how this can work:

> You have to find a new structure for U.S. industry that combines the advantages of small companies and the support of large companies. My own answer is to have a bunch of small companies in a family, which gives them financial and management support and strategic direction. But at the same time they are acting as though they are independent companies. Right now [in 1988, with $400 million in revenues] we have 17 business units.

Raychem is another company that has managed to remain highly innovative by continually slicing up the diamond. As the company grew, it continually subdivided, "to keep the company a series of small groups," according to founder Paul Cook:

> If you are going to have literally hundreds of products being developed, ... that calls for a rather loose, unstructured type of company as compared to a tightly controlled one. We are a *very* tough company to compete against.

When to Decentralize

When should a company decentralize? You should always be heading in that direction—giving people autonomy and room to initiate and act. A good rule of thumb is that when you reach somewhere between 100 and 200 people it's time to think seriously about formally slicing up the diamond.

Making Decentralization and Autonomy Work

We don't have the space here to cover in immense detail all the specifics of a decentralized structure. Nonetheless, there are some general principles about making a decentralized structure work:

- Link to vision. If your vision (values, purpose, and mission) is clear, people or groups operating autonomously can self-regulate themselves relative to the shared overall vision. They can all sight on the same guiding star, yet be in separate vehicles heading toward that star. *Shared vision is the crucial link in making decentralization work.*

- Overcome lack of centralized control with increased communication and informal coordination. People need to know what other decentralized sub-units are doing so that they can act in concert with them. At Patagonia, for example, Product Line Directors meet at least once per month to coordinate. Another way to gain increased communication and coordination without the burden of increased bureaucracy is to use electronic communications—electronic mail, voice mail, computer networks, tele-conferencing, etc.

- Facilitate the transferring of valuable knowledge between sub-units. Hold internal seminars where members from different sub-units share ideas, present papers, and learn from each other's experiences. Grant prestigious awards to those who contribute a significant idea, invention, or other valuable assistance to another sub-unit.

- Have an open system. People operating autonomously can make good decisions only if they have good information. One of the best ways to achieve this is to make lots of information available to people—even traditionally sensitive information. At NeXT, for example, any employee can get access to any piece of information—even people's salary levels and internal financial information. Although you may not feel comfortable going to this extreme, we urge you to head in this direction. Again, compare centralized, secretive societies like the Soviet Union (and how terribly inefficient they are) with open systems like the United States. The same principle applies to companies.

- Avoid matrix structures. In an attempt to have the best of both worlds, some companies make the mistake of creating matrix organizations. Don't do this. Matrix structures remove the fire of personal ownership, not to mention accountability.

Making Decentralization Work
Purpose, Mission, Philosophy

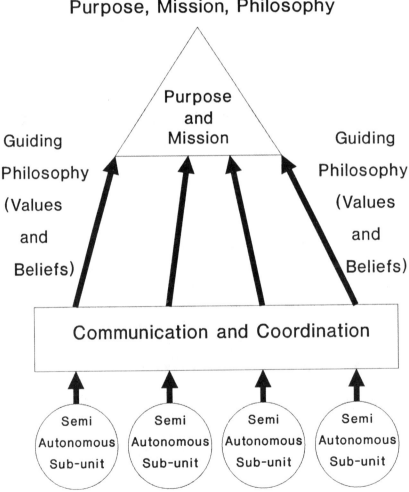

Figure 4-5

You might be wondering, "What about the duplication of effort that can take place in a decentralized environment? Don't you need centralized control to ensure that there's not too much overlap, which would be a waste of resources?"

Good question. But think again of the centralized Soviet-style economy versus the decentralized market-based economy. At first glance, a market-based economy would appear to be less desirable. After all, isn't it inefficient to have 36 separate computer companies all participating in the same industry, each with its own overhead, marketing effort, and product development effort? Wouldn't it be more attractive to have one National Computer Company and centralize all these functions? Well, of course, we all know that it would be less desirable. There's immense duplication of effort in an industry with 36 companies, but it nonetheless generates more economic wealth and innovation than if there were only one company.

We're not necessarily suggesting that you pit all of your divisions against each other in a complete laissez faire free-for-all (although both IBM and P&G have made conscious decisions during their evolution to promote spirited internal competition between groups). We ask you to rethink the notion that decentralization, replete with duplication of effort, is less efficient than the alternative.

This brings us to a central truth about organizations: *they are inherently messy.* There are no panaceas, no structures that solve all problems. Any attempts to completely eliminate the mess are doomed to failure. Yes, there are costly inefficiencies in decentralization, but the fire of personal ownership—of being our own little business—elevates human motivation and stimulates innovation in powerful, albeit somewhat chaotic, ways.

"Democracy sure is a chaotic, inefficient system," observed Harry S. Truman, "but it's better than anything else around."

That's precisely the case with decentralization and autonomy; it seems uncontrollable and inefficient. And, in some ways, it is. There is repetition of effort. It can be confusing to customers. There is difficulty in sharing technology. It just seems so unwieldy. However, like freedom and democracy, it's better than the alternative. Much better.

If you want the lightning bolt of innovation to strike again and again, you have to live with the inefficiencies. You've got to make a basic philosophical choice that the inefficiencies and disorder are worth the benefits.

It's impossible to have an organization with all the fire and zeal of decentralization and the complete efficiency of centralized control. Pick decentralization, fully implement it, and live with its difficulties as best you can. If you try to go halfway, it'll be like having a country shift from driving on the right side of the road to driving on the left side of the road, but only implementing it part way.

Corporate Innovation Element 6: Rewards

We listened patiently one day while the CEO of a medium-sized software development company lamented that he couldn't get his people to be more innovative and entrepreneurial. "I really want them to come up with new product ideas and new businesses and to take the initiative to make that happen. But they spend all their time managing their current divisions, and no time developing new things."

"How are they compensated?" we asked.

"Base salary, plus a bonus based on the annual revenues of their division," he responded.

"Would it detract from their current annual revenues to work on something new?" we asked.

"Yes, it would," he conceded. It took only a moment for the inconsistency to sink in.

In another situation, we were asked by an electronics company to examine the question of why many of its most talented engineers and scientists were leaving for other companies. We interviewed the best of those who had left, and received comments like this:

> The only upward path for me was to move into management. But I don't want to be a manager! I'm really happy being a designer, and making creative contributions. It's what I do best, and it's what I love doing. They told me that the only way I could move to a new level of pay (and, I might add, corresponding prestige) was to take a management job. So I left for this start-up where I'll be rewarded handsomely if my contributions are successful in the market, and where I'll be a hero.

These two examples illustrate a simple point: Your reward structure should explicitly recognize the importance of creative contribution.

We don't mean to suggest that people being creative are motivated solely by money, or power, or prestige. In fact, they're often motivated by the desire for interesting work, the challenge of a tough problem, the joy of contribution, or the satisfaction of doing something new. Nonetheless, innovation should be explicitly rewarded. All people, no matter how pure their motivations, are influenced by the reward systems of their organizations. Rewards matter. And if you want to remain innovative, you've got to reward innovation.

Some specific things you might consider:

- Make heroes of creative contributors through awards, honors, and recognition. Establish prestigious awards for extraordinary creative contribution—technical or new business ideas. When possible, give awards to *teams* as well as to individuals. Consider having a new product or business award *and* an internal process innovation award. Write articles in the company newsletter or magazine about people who've done something creative. Even have a "great try" award to recognize people for helpful, heroic failures as well as successes.

- Set measurable innovation goals and evaluate based on those. One of the best is to set the goal that a certain percentage of revenues (25% is a good number) in any given year—both for the company and for any given division—must come from new products or services introduced in the previous five years.

- Have a separate career track for creative contributors who don't want to go into management. Make this career track as potentially lucrative as top management positions. Why should the Vice President of Finance receive three to four times the compensation of the top creative designer? That makes no sense to us, yet it's exactly what most companies do. In contrast, Herman Miller, has one of its top designers on a $100,000 per year retainer for 10 years; other Herman Miller designers have grown wealthy on royalties. Designers are heroes within the Herman Miller culture, and are accorded the same prestige and respect as any corporate Vice President.

- Compensate people for specific valuable creative contributions. If someone comes up with an innovative idea about how to reduce production costs and that idea is adopted, why not give a bonus for that contribution? If a team invents a valuable new product, why not reward them specifically for that invention? Perhaps pay royalties or allow them to share in the profits of a new innovation.

- Let people play "pinball." Certain creative people are motivated more than anything else by the desire to pursue their work, the chance to do interesting and challenging things. When an individual or team makes a creative contribution, one of the best rewards is the opportunity to turn their attention to something else new, exciting, and important. Tom West, in Kidder's *Soul of a New Machine,* called this "playing pinball":

> 'You win one game, you get to play another. You win with this machine, you get to build the next.' Pinball was what counted. ... 'I will do this, I want to do it. I recognize from the beginning it's gonna be a tough job. I'll have to work hard, and if we do a good job, we get to do it again.'

The crucial thing to realize is that truly creative people aren't primarily motivated by the opportunity to rest and take it easy. That's the last thing in the world they want. They want the chance to continue to create, innovate, take on new challenges, learn, and to be valued for their work.

Not Just Products but Processes

We've spent the bulk of this chapter on new product or service innovation, but we also want to emphasize the importance of creativity in all aspects of a business—in marketing, production, organization, the works.

Creative marketing is also important to the success of a company. With the myriad of products and immense noise in the market, you need to invent ways to pierce the customer's screening system and leave a vivid imprint on his mind. This is particularly true for small to mid-sized enterprises that do not have the resources to compete dollar for advertising dollar with large behemoths. We call it *guerrilla marketing*—ways of making a huge impact with few resources.

Patagonia avoided the expense of large advertising budgets by creating a spectacular catalogue, complete with authentic adventure photos and riveting text. For years, the catalogue was so beautiful that people looked forward to reading it. Patagonia also struck close relationships with magazine photographers who influence what people wear for photo shoots. You can't place an ad on the cover of Outside Magazine, no matter what your budget, yet numerous times adventurers have appeared on the cover wearing Patagonia clothing. Patagonia spends only a paltry 1/3% of sales on print advertising.

Bob Moog, CEO of University Games, raises awareness of his game products by hosting a radio game show, wherein the audience calls in to play games over the air. People have fun, remember Moog, and buy games.

Even if you have a good-sized budget for marketing, keep in mind that creativity is still more important than volume.

Think back to the introduction of the MacIntosh Computer. Those who were watching the Super Bowl on January 25, 1984, will never forget seeing the surrealistic, eerie, grayish image of hundreds of passive people with vacant faces listening to "Big Brother" drone on and on. The famous "1984" commercial reached out from our TV screens and grabbed our full attention. Jolly football fans fell silent, drawn uncontrollably to the spectacle unfolding in their living rooms and bars. The commercial was shown only once, yet left an unforgettable impression. Does anyone remember any other commercials run that day?

Innovative products + Creative marketing = Magic

Don't stop there. Even in supposedly uncreative areas like finance, there is tremendous opportunity for creativity (and we mean legal creativity here). For example, Ben & Jerry's ice cream company circumvented the traditional hassles of full blown public offerings by doing their own personal-style offering. They avoided expensive Wall Street underwriters by offering stock through the slogan "Get a scoop of the action" (printed on the lids of their ice cream cartons, along with an 800 number). Local folks (mainly customers) snapped up the offering.

Innovation is equally important in day-to-day manufacturing and operations. There is a wonderful example of creativity applied to operations at Federal Express. At one point, packages were getting backed up at its main sorting hub in Memphis, and no control system solved the problem. Then someone noticed that part-time workers were slowing the system down so that they could work (and be paid for) more hours.

Now, think for a moment; what would you do?

The obvious answer would be to set speed standards, and to enforce the standards with elaborate measurement and reward systems. Federal Express, however, did something simpler and more creative: it simply gave the workers a minimum daily financial guarantee, and announced that those who got done early could leave early. Within forty-five days, the problems were entirely cleared up.

The basic elements of organizational creativity described throughout this chapter—receptivity to ideas, solving your own problems, experimentation and mistakes, having creative people, granting autonomy, and rewarding innovation—apply to all areas of the business. Use them. Educate everyone about them. Stimulate innovation everywhere. There's no shortage of good ideas.

Eight Management Techniques for Stimulating Creativity

We've spent most of this chapter describing the traits of companies that remain innovative. We'd now like to discuss things individual managers can do to stimulate creativity.

1. *Encourage; don't nitpick.* Keep in mind that there's no shortage of good, workable ideas, but that there's a tremendous shortage of receptivity to ideas. Don't be like one of those "wet blankets" that shot down the radio, the telephone, Federal Express, the personal computer, and NIKE shoes as "dumb ideas."

   William McKnight, the man who more than anyone else shaped the innovation capabilities of 3M in its early days, lived by the maxim, "Encourage; don't nit-pick." McKnight himself set a precedent of listening to anybody who had an idea. When one of his young inventors would come up with a "screwy idea," McKnight would listen, and usually respond by saying, "Sounds interesting. Give it a try. Get to work, and quick."

Don't shoot down an idea by pointing out all its flaws and warts before the idea gets tested. The world is full of critics—critics who never stimulate anything truly great. Don't be one of them.

2. *Be Not Judgemental.* Harshly critical people destroy creativity and initiative. The fear of being criticized or being made to look and feel stupid is the biggest impediment to people experimenting, initiating, trying new things. The problem is not that people are inherently uncreative, it's that people are *afraid* to be creative—afraid of being laughed at, ridiculed, personally attacked, or otherwise psychologically abused. It's the deep-rooted fear we all carry around of the seventh-grade math teacher making an example of us in front of our peers.

The key word, again, is *respect*. Show respect for people's psyches. Don't make people feel stupid or worthless. If someone makes an honest mistake, never attack the person, address the event (review "Hard/Soft People Skills" in Chapter 1).

How you deal with mistakes and failures greatly influences people's creativity. Always ask yourself, "How would *I* want to be dealt with if I made that mistake or had that failure? How could *I* be dealt with so that I'd learn and, at the same time, maintain my desire to try?"

3. *Help Shy People.* Some good ideas never go anywhere because the people who have them are too shy to speak up. In fact, some of the best ideas come from quiet people. Quiet people tend to be excellent observers and thinkers; like cats, they're watchful and attentive, and often intensely curious. Yet they're also often fearful of voicing their ideas.

We have found some of the most insightful comments come from quieter students. When reticent students feel safe to share their points of view, some tremendous ideas emerge. It's not uncommon for a quiet student to finally raise his or her hand and speak with a slight quiver, yet deliver a stunning insight. Other students are left thinking, "Wow, where did that come from?"

To tap this resource—to make it easy for the shy people to contribute—you might need to do more than simply encourage. Something as simple as a suggestion box, or making it clear that anyone can submit an idea in writing (anonymously if they like), can work. When you get a good idea, share it with everyone, perhaps saying at a staff meeting, "I got a really great idea in the suggestion box that I wanted to share with everyone."

4. *Stimulate Curiosity.* Relentless curiosity, the pure desire to know things, to test them, to see if something will work, fosters creativity. The most creative people ask many questions; it's as if they never outgrew that naive childlike desire to ask why. Create an environment where it's ok to ask questions. Ask questions yourself—not critical questions (again, don't be a wet blanket), but open ended questions in the spirit of inquiry. A favorite question of ours is, "What did you learn from that experience?"

Regis McKenna, whose firm formulated the highly creative marketing campaigns of companies like Apple and Intel, believes that a creative organization is a questioning organization: "I try to get my people to write out at least two pages of questions before they go to any meeting. Actually have the questions written out. You rarely get through the first page. You find that those questions lead to other questions."

Never respond to a question by saying, "That's a dumb question." Don't show disdain for a question. Respond openly, "That's a good question" or "I'm glad you asked that" or "Hmmm, that's intriguing, what do you think?" Do not under any circumstances make people feel stupid for asking questions.

5. *Create Necessity.* Human beings have an amazing ability to innovate their way out of seemingly impossible situations. "Necessity," as the cliche goes, "is the mother of invention." But cliche or not, it's true. In fact, many great ideas have emerged precisely *because* a company lacked the resources to do what it ideally would have liked.

Case Example: Giro Sport Design

In 1985, Jim Gentes, founder of Giro Sport Design, knew he had invented a bicycle helmet that could revolutionize the bicycle helmet industry. It was extremely light (only 7.5 ounces), yet passed all safety standards. The helmet, made of expanded polystyrene foam, had no hard plastic shell.

However, Gentes was confronted with a problem. Without a decorative shell, the product was ugly—like riding a bike with a styrofoam beer cooler on your head. On the other hand, with a standard hard shell, the product lost its weight advantages. Gentes devised a solution: a covering of extremely thin, very light plastic.

A great solution, right? Yes and no. There was one remaining problem: it cost nearly $100,000 for the tooling to make the thin, light shells—an amount far beyond what the then tiny company could afford. Gentes solved the problem by creating colorful lycra fabric caps that fit snugly over the helmet. The caps could be removed and washed, or exchanged for other colors. Fashion-conscious riders could thus match the lycra helmet covering to their outfits, and teams could get custom covers made to display their team emblem and sponsor names.

The helmet was a tremendous success and did indeed revolutionize the helmet industry, due in large part to the innovative lycra coverings. According to Gentes:

> The lycra covering was a great idea. It really helped the product and caught everybody's attention. And the irony is that, if we would have had the money for the tooling, we might not have ever invented the lycra cover solution.

(As an aside, Giro's lycra helmets were so successful that the company was able to fund development of the thin-shell technology and introduce it to the market three years later.)

You can replicate the Giro experience in any number of ways. In some instances, you might consciously limit resources. In fact, we believe in running lean even when you have the resources to do otherwise. We've noticed that Silicon Valley companies that've raised too much venture capital money tend to lose the innovative fire necessary for greatness. Gavilan Computers, which burned almost $40 million in venture funding, yet never got a product out the door, is a good example.

Setting stiff, almost impossible, targets also creates necessity. For example, when Motorola was a small, struggling company, founder Paul Galvin would force invention by setting ludicrous targets. In one instance, he told his people to engineer $20 of cost out of a product. They told him it was impossible. He responded that he was sure they could find a way—and that they *had* to find a way. Ten days later, his son Bob (who'd been working on the project) sheepishly reported that they'd accomplished the reduction.

6. *Allow Time Away from the Fray.* Certain highly creative individuals need solitary time to do their best thinking, time away, time to think in silence. Phil Knight, founder of NIKE, believes that people get their best ideas away from the office, at the beach, or running, which is one reason why NIKE has a wide ranging campus with running trails, tennis courts, basketball courts, weight rooms, and aerobics studios. Herman Miller lets its designers choose their venue for creativity—and some choose to do much of their work at home or somewhere else off site.

Let people have some "at home" work days. Allow people to sneak off into a quiet room and work undisturbed for a period of time. Follow the example of Claude Rosenberg, founder of Rosenberg Capital Management, who set up two quiet rooms in the office "... that I keep trying to get people to use, because I really do believe that your most creative moments will not come in your normal occupation when sitting at your desk." Rosenberg has a corollary to this belief: *require* vacations. "I happen to think vacations should be real breaks from work—I'm really upset with my partners when they go on vacation and they call the office. If you clear your mind, you're probably going to be much more creative."

At Patagonia, the pattern-making group (part of the design department) has a little sign posted near its area:

PLEASE OBSERVE QUIET TIME.
Closed from 8:00 to 12:00.

---

7. *Catalyze Group Problem Solving.* "Quiet time" is not the whole story at Patagonia. In addition to letting people have quiet, solitary incubation and thinking time, it's essential to capture the creativity of multiple minds thrashing about together. Brainstorming and other group activities produce extraordinary ideas.

Desks at Patagonia are jumbled together in large, open bullpen-style pits (called "Bangladesk"). People are expected to work closely with others—both spontaneously and scheduled—in coming up with new ideas and solutions to problems.

We've found in our own work, both in business and academics, that the most creative answers come with a combination of time away from the fray *plus* time spent tossing ideas around in group sessions. One plus one is often much greater than two when it comes to generating creative ideas.

A caveat: *The group must not have any wet blankets.* Group creativity sessions can work *only* if there are no members who nit-pick ideas to death. Even just one person who prematurely critiques ideas will devastate any chance of a group being creative. Get rid of the nit-pickers!

8. *Require Fun.* "As far as I'm concerned, the most important thing is having fun," explains Ted Nierenburg, founder of Dansk International Designs. "If you're not having fun in what you do, lock it up and try something else."

We're serious about fun. Fun leads to creativity. Ask people, "Are you having fun?" Ask yourself. Set enjoyment as an absolute requirement of work; if there's no joy, there will be little creativity. Have you ever noticed that some of the most creative people are a lot like little kids? They like to play, and, to them, work *is* play.

This doesn't preclude hard work. Creativity is hard work, but it should also be fun.

Faith in the Creative Process

We've given you a comprehensive view of corporate innovation, but there's one more element: faith in the creative process.

No one knows exactly how the creative process works. It's often a painful process, fraught with uncertainty. Creative insight comes in unpredictable flashes, usually after extended periods of hard work, frustration, and incubation. We can't say, "Tomorrow at 10 A.M. I will have a great idea." Well, we can say it all we want, but it probably won't happen. It just doesn't work that way. The lightening bolt of creative inspiration usually takes us by surprise, striking while we're in the shower, on the freeway, working in the garden, sweating at the gym, hiking in the hills, swinging a golf club, reading a book, waking up, or in any of a thousand other settings.

The really wild thing about creativity is that, given helpful conditions (spelled out earlier in the chapter), it's *certain* to emerge; we may not know how, when, or in what form, but it *will* come.

To keep a company innovative requires this leap of faith—faith that all people have the capacity to be creative, faith that there are lots of good ideas, faith in the woodwork factor, faith in experimentation, and faith in giving people the freedom to act. Man is by nature an inventor, discoverer, and explorer; we're endowed with a powerful urge to create, and a commensurate ability to do so.

It's exciting to create new things. We feel euphoria with each new "Eureka!" By inventing new products or better ways of doing things we get to feel a small slice of what Columbus must have felt when he discovered the New World or Galileo felt when he invented the telescope.

Indeed, not only does innovation keep a company healthy and prosperous, it satisfies the basic human drive to create and, at the same time, moves humankind forward. What could be more satisfying?

Chapter 5

TACTICAL EXCELLENCE

God is in the details.

Mies van der Rohe

Think for a moment of building a great company as analogous to creating a new climbing route up the sheer face of El Capitan. All elements discussed thus far are necessary: clarity of goal (shared vision), ability to keep the team going (leadership style), an assault plan (strategy), and creative solutions to a myriad of challenges along the way (innovation). However, there is another crucial element: physically doing the climb. If you don't execute the small details (like tying your knots right) or pay close attention to your hands and feet, you just might end up dead. The same is true of companies.

Think about another analogy. Building a great company is similar to writing a great novel—you need an overall conception (vision), a plot (strategy), and creative ideas to move the plot along. You also must sweat over each sentence, executing the book word-by-word, line-by-line, page-by-page. Hemingway was once asked why he'd rewritten the last page of *A Farewell to Arms* 39 times. He responded simply, "Getting the words right."

This notion of paying attention to the actual tactical execution of your vision and strategy, of "tying your knots right" or "getting the words right", is crucial to corporate greatness. You can have the most inspirational leader, the most profound vision, a brilliant strategy, and a thousand great ideas, but if you don't execute well, you'll never be great. Think of Olympic diver Greg Lougainis hitting a consistent string of beautiful dives, and that's what you should be working for. Or think of Hemingway and his 39 revisions.

In fact, many outstanding businesses have been successful *primarily* because of outstanding execution. An *Inc.* magazine survey of its *Inc.* 500 (fastest growing private companies) showed that 88% of CEOs attributed their company's success primarily to extraordinary *execution* of an idea versus only 12% who attributed success primarily to the idea itself.

Jim Gentes, founder of Giro Sport Design, likes to point out that he believes in vision and creativity, but that he just as fervently believes in "getting the helmets right." He's fond of saying, "Hey, I'm not that special. I had an idea, and I just executed that idea really well."

Bill Hannemann, who was hired by Gentes to be President and Chief Operating Officer of Giro, explained that this commitment to tactical excellence convinced him to take the risk of joining Giro when it was a tiny, unproven company with a single product:

> Giro's product was the first of its type on the market. But you always have to ask, "What's being first worth?" If you're not committed to tactical excellence, your first-mover advantage will evaporate. That's what impressed me about Jim; he would never cut corners in the execution of his ideas.

Think about Compaq Computer Corporation, one of the top three personal computer makers (along with IBM and Apple). The astounding thing is that Compaq is a *clone* maker (it copies IBM's architecture); it succeeds because it executed the IBM compatible strategy better even than IBM. (Compaq, by the way, doesn't price lower than IBM, it just makes the same products much better.) It's interesting to note that in 1990 Compaq had the highest pre-tax profit per employee in the computer industry, at $62,579 compared with $53,608 for Apple and $26,955 for IBM.

Think about Wal-Mart. Sam Walton didn't invent discount retailing; in fact, there were many other companies trying to do the same thing in the early sixties, when Wal-Mart was just getting off the ground. As Vance Trimble put it in his historical analysis of Wal Mart:

> The key ingredient turned out to be Sam's masterful execution of the idea ... Other retailers were out there trying to do just what he was doing. Only he did it better.

Conversely, there's the example of a West Coast chain of restaurants with a wonderful concept: fast Mexican food that is also good for you (low fat, healthy ingredients). We were excited by this (we love Mexican food, and yet we don't like to eat too much fat, and we're always pressed for time). But, alas, we don't eat there any more.

Why not? Because of little things. The cashiers had trouble with the computerized order system, thus creating long lines. We got exactly what we ordered only 50% of the time. The food was hot and spicy sometimes, cold and tasteless at others. If you happened to be eating near closing time, they'd put chairs on the tables and glare at you for not eating fast enough. At the time of this writing, one of the two outlets in our area had closed and the other had much slower traffic than when it first opened.

In short,

Great concept + poor execution = death.

Ok, perhaps that's a bit strong. But the best that could be hoped for is bleak mediocrity.

From Vision and Strategy to Tactics

Once you have your vision and strategy, it's necessary to translate them into solid tactical execution.

The first step is to make sure that all key people have a copy of the vision, strategy, and the current year's strategic priorities in front of them at all times. They should be brought to every staff meeting. They should be referred to constantly.

Bill Hannemann of Giro keeps a copy of the strategic priorities with him at all times. Not a staff meeting goes by without his referring to it. "I always try to make sure that our priorities are always being worked on in some specific way," he says.

Milestone Management

Most important, each strategic priority must be broken down into "bite-sized," discrete chunks—milestones. Think back to the analogy of climbing the sheer face of El Capitan. You don't think about all 3,500 feet of rock at once; you break the climb up into manageable 100 foot sections (called pitches). It is the concentration on one pitch at a time that gets you up all 3,500 feet of granite.

Each milestone should have a person responsible for its attainment plus—and THIS IS EXTREMELY IMPORTANT—a specific completion date.

Dates and milestones, however, should not be unilaterally imposed. People are always more committed to objectives and timetables that they have a hand in shaping. We suggest a process whereby individuals and their manager develop the milestone mutually and, whenever possible, the individual picks the date for its completion (one that the manager can live with, of course). We then suggest that the individual (not the manager) put to paper the agreed-upon milestone and date. This process of "signing up" tends to create significant psychological commitment.

Indeed, the transfer of broad vision and strategy to specific milestones owned by specific people who have committed to specific dates is crucial to getting things done.

VISION
↓
STRATEGY
↓
ANNUAL
STRATEGIC
PRIORITIES
↓
SPECIFIC MILESTONES
SPECIFIC DATES
SPECIFIC PEOPLE

Figure 5-1

Of course, getting things done is not enough; things have to get done well. And, to be a great company, they've got to get done *consistently* well, and with continual improvement. This requires building the right environment.

Creating an Environment Where People Attain Consistent Tactical Excellence

> The bulk of the causes of low quality and low productivity belong to the system [created by management] and thus lie beyond the power of the workforce.
>
> *W. Edwards Deming*

We ran across a wonderful little article in the *Wall Street Journal*, entitled "How L. L. Bean Restored My Soles—and Warmed My Soul," by A. Richard Barber. In it, he wrote about how Bean employees went to heroic efforts to resole a pair of 30-year-old Feather Weight Lounger Boots in a size

Bean no longer carried, and for which there was no standard
resoling process.

Barber described how each Bean employee took personal
responsibility for his situation, giving him their first names
(Maggie, Ann, and Steve) and making themselves personally
accountable: "My name is Steve Graham at extension 4445,
just so you have someone accountable at our end." He wrote
about the "clear, crisp un-world-weary" tones of their voices,
and how they were genuinely apologetic about unexpected delays.
"It was comforting to know," wrote Barber, "that so many
people cared about [my boots]."

Barber concluded the article:

> Thirty years from now I hope I'm speaking to Maggie
> and Steve and Ann. They gave me a wonderful lift.
> On this anniversary of our happy encounter, I wish
> them as happy a holiday as they gave me last year.

Barber's article raises the question: are the people who
work at L. L. Bean different from other people? Is there something
unusual about Freeport, Maine?

We think not. L. L. Bean doesn't have special access to
dedicated, conscientious people—at least not any more than
your company does. No, Bean has simply created an environment
where people throughout execute well.

This leads us to a central tenet of tactical excellence: If
your people aren't executing well, it's not their fault.

It's yours.

Leaders of great companies have faith in the ability of
ordinary people to perform extraordinarily well. They know
that there are very few lazy, uncaring people and that, given
the right environment, most people will deliver outstanding
performance. Poor performance is usually the result of poor
hiring decisions, poor training, lack of clear expectations, poor
leadership, inadequate appreciation, poor job design, or some
other failing of the company, not the employee.

There are five basic conditions under which people tend
to execute well:

1. *People execute well if they're clear on what they need to
   do.* How can people possibly do well if they don't have
   a clear idea of what "doing well" means—if they don't
   have clear goals, benchmarks, and expectations?

2. *People execute well if they have the right skills for the job.* The right skills come from talents, temperament, and proper training.

3. *People execute well if they're given freedom and support.* No one does a good job with people looking over his shoulder; when people are treated like children, they'll lower themselves to those expectations. Also, people need the tools and support to do their job well. To use an extreme illustration, imagine how difficult it would be for Federal Express employees to make on-time delivery without reliable trucks.

4. *People execute well if they're appreciated for their efforts.* All people want their efforts to be appreciated. We've consciously chosen the term appreciated rather than rewarded because it more accurately captures that excellent performers value respect and appreciation as much as, and often even more than, money.

5. *People execute well if they see the importance of their work.*

This last condition is so important that we'd like to expand on it.

While waiting for a flight out of San Francisco Airport, we stopped for a shoeshine. We noticed that the shoeshine expert paid great attention to getting our shoes just right, and inspected every angle to ensure the quality of his workmanship.

"Are you guys in a hurry?" he asked. "I'd like to spend a couple of extra minutes to let this scuff mark set and then give your shoes a second coating." We had plenty of time, so we agreed.

While he applied himself to his task, he talked about his work. "It's really important that I get people's shoes done right," he said. "My customers are traveling to important meetings. The last thing they need is for their shoes to look bad. When they go into that meeting, I want their shoes to look wonderful. It's sometimes the details—like poorly shined shoes—that can make people look bad."

And therein lies the essence of tactical excellence: people caring about their work *because they see its importance.*

A powerful example of this is the experience of an airplane parts manufacturer during the World War II. The company, according to Peter Drucker (to whom we owe the example), was experiencing terrible problems with its work force—absenteeism, strikes, slowdowns, and slipshod work.

So what to do? Press people harder? No. Fire the bad apples? No. Increase wages? No. None of these solved the basic problem.

The workers had never been shown the importance of their work! They'd never seen a finished bomber, much less seen where the part they made fitted, or how important that part was to the bomber's performance, or how important the bomber was to the war effort. So the company brought a finished bomber to the factory facilities, along with crew members who told them how important the bombers were to the war effort and how important the part was to the bombers. And, according to Drucker, "the bad morale and unrest disappeared at once."

There's an interesting aspect of the above example: the presence of crew members. No longer were the workers responsible merely for a part in a bomber, they were responsible for specific people—for George, and John, and Sam—whose lives would depend on the performance of the bomber. The same is true of the shoeshine expert at the airport; he has a sense of direct, personal responsibility for each customer.

People see the importance of their work—and thereby tend to be committed to doing a good job—when they know other people are depending on them.

John Gardner, former Secretary of Health, Education, and Welfare and founder of Common Cause, told us of a fascinating study on heroism he was involved with. The study asked the question: what motivates people to heroic behavior? The overwhelming answer was not glory, or country, or patriotism, or anything like that. It was primarily a person's belief that comrades were depending on him, and he couldn't let them down.

If you can create an atmosphere where people are dependent on each other—where people think, "I can't let these people down"—you'll get extraordinary performance.

Have you ever wondered how Federal Express managed to grow fast and, at the same time, execute the "absolutely, positively overnight" promise so well? Federal's founders did it by creating an organization where people depend on each other. (As an aside, we think Federal Express is a good example of success due primarily to the quality of execution, rather than the brilliance of the idea. The concept of nationwide overnight delivery was nothing new; other firms had thought of it. Doing it—and doing it well—was the challenge.)

Founder Fred Smith was heavily influenced by his experiences in the Vietnam War, where he was a company commander and reconnaissance flyer. There he observed that the "average person" would do extraordinary things when platoonmates depended on him. He wanted to build a company that would be built on this basic truth.

Smith told Bill Moyers in an interview:

> Federal Express is a creature of Vietnam. I don't think I would have done anything like this [without that experience]. People will rise to the occasion if you give them a chance. Give people the challenge and they've got the basic intelligence and outlook to do it.

Art Bass, an early chief operating officer at Federal Express, explained the ethos:

> We brought together people who were proud of what they were doing, people who had very few other opportunities in their whole lives to be proud of anything. Whether you were in a truck or a plane or in the hub, you were all alone out there, but everybody was depending on you. You had to come through.

The statement "You had to come through" is perfect. It captures the essence of what you want to create, people depending on other people.

That's exactly how L. L. Bean warmed Richard Barber's soul. Maggie and Steve and Ann at Bean believed they had to come through for Richard. Richard wasn't a consumer. Richard wasn't order number 3365. Richard wasn't that guy with the damned boot problem. He was *Richard,* and he wanted—needed—his boots resoled, and they *couldn't let him down.*

You, as a leader of the company, have a responsibility to make sure that every single person is doing something important and that the person knows *why* her work is important.

The Link to Vision

As described earlier, one of the primary functions of corporate vision is to add meaning, to be a source of motivation for extraordinary human effort. A clear and compelling vision is essential to people seeing the importance of their work. If you haven't yet read Chapter 2 on vision, read it. If you haven't set a vision, do so.

Also, remember that one of the components of a good vision is a set of core values and beliefs, a set of guiding principles and precepts. This underlying set of core values plays an essential role in guiding people's daily behavior and standards. In fact, there is a direct link between values and tactical execution. For example, if one of your core values is "treat customers like human beings" and if it is well inculcated throughout your organization (as it is at L. L. Bean), people are going to treat customers like human beings.

A Mentality of Continual Improvement

Tactical excellence isn't an end point; it's a path. It's the path of continual improvement.

Think for a moment about the Japanese miracle. "Made in Japan" used to mean "Poor quality." Not anymore. The Japanese have established a worldwide reputation for quality. They are masters of consistent tactical excellence. What happened? How did the Japanese make this extraordinary transformation?

Part of the answer lies in the influence of Dr. W. Edwards Deming, who educated Japanese management in quality control techniques. (Deming's influence on the Japanese was so great that he was awarded the Japanese Second Order of the Sacred Treasure—the first American to ever receive such an honor. The famous Deming Prize, a prestigious and much sought after award for total quality control, is named after Deming.) The central tenet of Deming's work, put forth in his book *Out of the Crisis,* is constant improvement.

Improvement is not a one-time effort. The whole idea is to measure where you are today, evaluate what you can do better, set a plan in place to improve, implement it, measure again, and repeat the process. Infinitely.

The game is to never stand still, to never be good enough. What passes for excellent this year should be mediocre compared to what you're doing five years from now, which should be mediocre compared with 10 years from now, and so on. Forever. There's no end. There's no stopping point. There's no "having made it."

A Six-Part Process

Creating the environment where people throughout achieve consistent tactical excellence involves a six-part, never-ending process:

- Hiring
- Inculturating
- Training
- Goal-setting
- Measuring
- Appreciating.

CREATING AN ENVIRONMENT FOR TACTICAL EXCELLENCE
A SIX-PART PROCESS

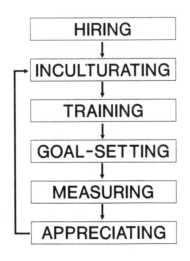

Figure 5-2

1: Hiring

It all starts with hiring decisions. Good people attract good people, who, in turn, attract more good people, and so on. Hiring good people requires a substantial investment of time. We've seen numerous companies get themselves into trouble because they didn't invest properly in the hiring process.

It's more expensive to "un-hire" a poor choice (and then find a new person) than it is to find and hire a good choice in the first place.

What is a good choice? Good shouldn't be defined primarily in terms of education, skills, or specific prior experience (although these will certainly factor into the choice). The *primary* assessment of good should be, "Does this person fit with our values? Is this person willing to buy into what we're all about? Is this person likely to live with our precepts?" As Kristine McDivitt of Patagonia put it:

> I've hired a lot of people who have lacked traditional credentials, and they've worked out great. I've also hired people with awesome credentials who didn't fare so well. I look primarily for a values-fit—especially a love of the outdoors—and an attitude about doing good work. We're fanatical about the quality of what we make, and we want equal fanaticism in the people we hire.

Giro Sport screens rigorously for people who are concerned about quality, innovation, and a solid work ethic. Home Depot looks for home-fix-it do-it-yourselfers who enjoy helping people. Williams-Sonoma, a supplier of cooking devices, searches for people who have a personal interest in fine cooking. Our friends up in Freeport at L. L. Bean seek people who use Bean products and exhibit a generally positive attitude about people; "We look for people who like to help people."

Finding good fits requires looking at a large number of applicants and spending extensive time before making a hiring decision. Stew Leonard's Dairy, for example, hires only one person for every twenty-five applicants. (Roughly half of the company's employees have a relative who also works for the company—a further reinforcement of screening on values.) Marriott, which places great emphasis on finding people who fit, interviewed 40,000 applicants for 1,200 jobs at a newly minted hotel.

Applicants should never be hired on one interview alone; they should be interviewed by at least two people before an offer is made.

Do reference checks. THIS IS IMPORTANT. If we had to pick one place where companies consistently trip up in the hiring process, it's that they don't do reference checks. Check references with former bosses, subordinates, peers, and others. An employee should never be hired without at least two reference checks, and we recommend five or more.

Finally, avoid hiring outside people for senior positions; hire from within whenever possible. There are two reasons. First, hiring outsiders can devastate morale: "Why should I work hard when they'll just bring in someone above me? I'll never really have a shot at getting promoted." Second, people need to be inculturated into the company, and this is easier if people come in at lower levels and work their way up.

2: Inculturating

Even if you make good hiring decisions, people need to be inculturated into the organization. By "inculturating" we mean instilling and reinforcing the vision, especially the core values. You can't just assume that people fully understand the precepts of your organization when they walk in the door. You need to educate them. And you need to educate them *early*.

In fact, inculturation should begin in the hiring process. Give applicants materials that describe your philosophy; have company representatives talk about the vision during job interviews.

Early in his career, when interviewing for a job with Russell Reynolds Associates, one of us (Jim) was flown out to New York from California to meet personally with founder Russ Reynolds. The entire interview centered on personal and company philosophy. Reynolds sent Jim away with a package of sensitive documents to better understand the company philosophy. No new professional is hired without a personal "philosophy meeting" with Reynolds or another senior officer of the firm.

New hires should be further educated in company values soon after starting work. Some specific steps to consider:

- Give a "starter kit" of written materials to every new hire, and make it clear he or she ought to read it. Obviously, this should include your vision statement, with special emphasis on the core values. Anne Bakar at Telecare Corporation, for example, gives copies of the company's values to all new hires.

  John Mackey, founder and CEO of Whole Foods Market, a chain of health food supermarkets headquartered in Austin, wrote the "Whole Foods General Information Handbook," which tells the company's history and values. It advises people on how to advance their careers and what to expect from co-workers and supervisors. At a few stores, new hires are given quizzes to show they understand the philosophy.

- Write! Write! Write! Never underestimate the power of the written word. Few company leaders make good use of the most powerful human tool—the pen. Use it. People will read what you write because you're the leader, and they'll be influenced by it. Think of how much weaker the United States would be if the Constitution had never been written down.

  It's a good idea to personally write a letter or article that has a touch of the company's philosophy a few times per year. It can be circulated on its own (to all employees, not an exclusive group) or printed in the employee newsletter or magazine. Leon Gorman, CEO of L. L. Bean, for instance, makes extensive use of the "Bean Scene."

  Use writing as a way to continually reinforce the importance of people's work. Tell stories of how people came through for others who were depending on them. Give examples of how a specific employee made a difference in the life of a customer. Never miss an opportunity to heighten the sense of noble purpose that people at all levels can (and have a right to) feel about their work.

- Write a history of the company that every new employee will receive upon joining. The history should trace the roots of the firm, its phases of evolution, and the origin of its values. Marvin Bower, co-founder and architect of McKinsey & Company, wrote a marvelous book, *Perspective on McKinsey,* which has chapters like:

"Years of Shaping Purpose"

"The Firm's Early Years"

"Building a Distinctive National Firm"

"Professionalism: The Firm's Secret Strength"

"Developing Our Managing Philosophy and System"

Three very important points about such a book:

1. You (if you are a founder, president, or CEO) should write it. The words should come directly from you, not the PR department or an outside writer. Make every new employee feel that you are personally communicating directly with him or her through the pages of your book. Bower's book is an excellent example of this.

2. Write for employees, not the outside world. Write it as a very personal connection between you and employees. Bower's book, for instance, contains the following inscription: "Written privately and printed for readership by only the Personnel of McKinsey & Company, Inc."

3. Don't wait too long. If yours is a young company, you may be wondering if such a history makes sense. We agree that it's awkward to write a history of something that's only a year old. However, by the time the company is five years old, you should be drafting a short corporate history. It needn't be hardbound; it could be reproduced at the copy center. You can then easily update and revise it as the company grows.

• Give a company philosophy talk to all new employees. If possible, do it in person, either in groups or individually. If it is not possible (because of geographic constraints or if your company is too big) then perhaps use video.

We point you to the example of Jim Miller, president of Miller Business Systems, a 300+ person provider of office services. Miller meets one-on-one with every new employee, during which time he describes the company philosophy and gives the employee a bottle of green liquid labeled "enthusiasm" and an "I believe in myself" mirror. Miller Business Systems won the Office Products Dealer magazine Award of Excellence for customer service in 1987.

- Use a buddy program. Assign each new hire to a buddy who takes him under her wing and personally educates and role models the values, as well as teaches specific skills.

- Send new employees to training seminars that instill values, in addition to teaching specific skills. One of the keys to IBM's successful inculturation of hundreds of thousands of people is that its training programs have always emphasized IBM values and beliefs more than managerial techniques.

3: Training

Even though training programs should have a good dose of inculturation, people also need specific skills training. After all, people can't do a great job unless they know how to.

Train people at all levels, not just managers. Keep in mind that training isn't a perk; it's a tremendous business advantage. Returning to our friends in Freeport, new L. L. Bean front-line employees receive a full week of training on the computerized phone ordering system, telephone skills, and product knowledge. The use of personal names ("this is Steve") doesn't happen randomly; people are taught to do it.

Another example of front-line training comes from Parisan, a retail chain that boasts two times the average national sales volume per square foot. Parisan attributes this success in large part to the fact that front-line employees receive 45 hours of training before they're allowed to deal with customers, plus a 12-hour refresher course after 90 days.

You can use a variety of training methods.

- You can use written materials, such as the Russell Reynolds Associates "Practice Guide," a manual of standards and tactics for the executive search process.

- You can use video and audio. Dominos Pizza, for example, has a VCR in every store on which employees watch videotaped training programs.

- You can use apprenticeship programs, where seasoned, successful employees educate new people. This is used at Dansk Designs and at legendary Goldman Sachs.

- You can use outside training courses for teaching specific skills. At Stew Leonard's Dairy, for example, some front-line workers are sent to $600 Dale Carnegie programs. Home Depot offers handyman skills classes each week. Many of the best high technology firms take advantage of advanced technical training offered at universities.

- You can develop your own courses. NIKE has an entire internal training program with multi-day sessions for managers. McKinsey started extensive consulting training back in the forties, when it was a tiny firm.

- You can even create your own "university." There's the famous McDonald's Hamburger University; Lenscrafters has three "campuses" for its management training school, known as Precision Lenscrafters University; Apple has an entire group called Apple University. These universities create educational programs attended by company employees.

But whatever you do, don't wait too long. Many smaller companies complain that they don't have the resources to do training. We ask them: how can you possibly expect to develop into a great company without it?

4: Goal-Setting

"How do you get your runners to go so fast?" a second-tier track coach asked the championship track coach.

"They work hard," she responded.

"So do mine," said the second-tier coach. "I make them run all the time. And I tell them I want them to run *fast*. I'm out there yelling and pushing at every practice."

"Not me," said the championship coach. "I never yell at my athletes. I don't even tell them to run fast."

"What do you do?" asked the incredulous second-tier coach.

"It's simple. I sit down with each athlete at the beginning of the season and talk about her ambitions, what I think she's capable of, the team's goals, and where I think she can best help the team. We then mutually develop her goals for the season, and I provide advice to help her reach them."

"So do I," said the second-tier coach.

"Do you? Give me a specific example."

"Well, you know, I just want them to run fast. I want them to win."

"Ah, I see," said the championship coach. "Perhaps you might do better to define the goals more precisely. For example, Jane over there just ran a 5:28 mile at the State meet. Her goal for the season—which she developed with my help—was to break 5:30. I didn't have to yell, push, or anything like that. The 5:30 pulled her forward every day."

Stop. Think for a minute. Does every employee in your company have specific goals? Did he take the primary role in creating them? Does he believe they're achievable? Does he want to achieve them? Has he translated these goals into quarterly goals, weekly tasks, and daily activities? Do the goals dovetail with the company's vision and strategy? Do the goals fit with his personal ambitions in life?

If so, you can move on to point number 5.

We suspect, however, that you've not skipped to point 5. Most leaders, if they're honest with themselves, can't answer yes to all of the above questions. Yet they ought to be able to.

Goal-setting is one of the most neglected parts of tactical execution. It's hard work, for both the employee and his coach. It takes time, thought, discussion, and negotiation. Yet, on the other hand, once the goals are clear, you can give much more free rein to people; you don't need to look over their shoulders and "direct" their activities.

If goals are set well, the traditional annual review process shouldn't be much of a "review" process at all. The employee should be able to see for himself whether he'd attained his goals—did I run 5:30 or not? He shouldn't need his manager to tell him that.

Does this mean annual performance reviews are superfluous? Not exactly. Instead of the traditional "here's how you did" review, time should be spent largely on goal-setting. Feedback ("you did well on that project" or "you could have done better; let's figure out how") should be ongoing and continuous throughout the year. The primary purpose of a well-constructed review, on the other hand, is to *set next year's goals.*

Most review processes are ineffective. They're either tied specifically to raises, which tends to suppress serious goal setting and evaluation, or they're viewed as a piece of administrative trivia.

Toss out the traditional annual review process and replace it with a goal-setting and review process. Consider doing it on a quarterly basis. Yes, quarterly.

Don Lyle, an outstanding manager we've observed in a number of situations and who was architect of a particularly difficult turnaround at DEI Corporation, uses just such a quarterly goal-setting process. He starts with the long term company vision and strategy, then breaks that into a set of annual goals. Then he works with his people to break those into their personal annual goals. Then he asks each of them to draw up a list of four or five quarterly goals for each quarter. They discuss them, negotiate, and reach an agreement, which they both sign.

At the end of each quarter, Lyle sits down again with each person to make a mutual assessment on performance versus goals and to update goals for the next quarter. He expects each of his people to do a similar process with their people, who do it with their people, and so on down the line. According to Lyle:

> This process makes sure that we don't let the urgent preempt the important. It keeps us focused on priorities. And it gives people a concrete sense of how they're doing. People crave to know how they're doing, and this gives them an objective, consistent method for knowing. It's very powerful.

The goals should be specific. For example:

"Open 35 new customer accounts by July 31."

"Get our European office up and running by November 30."

"Have the new bolt-cam product ready for manufacturing by December 31."

"Create a new product introduction process by August 1."

"Write three articles for publication by December 31."

Ideally, the process should merge the individual's personal vision and the company's vision, and then cascade down to quarterly goals, weekly tasks, and daily activities.

Personal	Individual Annual	Corporate
Vision ============>	Goals	<============ Vision

Quarterly
Goals

Weekly
Tasks

What am I going
to do today?

We recognize that life is chaotic and unpredictable. A perfectly linear process from corporate vision and strategy to individual annual goals, quarterly goals, weekly tasks, and daily activities is improbable. However, that's not a reason to avoid personalized goal-setting. There are lots of things that can affect that runner trying to break 5:30 in the mile. But setting 5:30 as a goal is nonetheless a valuable step.

In a classic study on motivation, Professor Frederick Herzberg found that the number one factor contributing to extreme job satisfaction was personal achievement (number two was recognition). People want to achieve. They want to set goals and reach them. Tap into this natural wellspring of motivation.

5: Measuring

Let's suppose you're a track coach, and your objective is to take the team to a new level of performance. Further suppose that we've taken away your stopwatch and closed the quarter-mile track.

What would you do? You'd probably go out in your car and measure miles on the street and go buy a stopwatch.

Just as a track coach needs to define "fast" and measure speed, a company needs to *define* tactical excellence, *measure* it, and *post* the results.

L. L. Bean measures the percentage of flawless shipments (99.89% in 1987). All packers (not just managers) receive daily updates on percentage of correct orders. Bean has a battery of measurements carefully tracked, ranging from customer wait times to number of defects.

The reason for Bean's extraordinary record is not that it has a standard, or that it has quotas. Rather, the key lies in the fact that Bean tracks its performance, identifies barriers to perfect performance, and continually seeks to improve.

And Bean is not alone in its fetish for measurement. When Marriott was a small company, founder J. Willard Marriott began a tradition of benchmarking and measuring its tactical execution. (Marriott himself would read and tabulate results from customer comment cards.) That tradition carries forth even today, to the point where it's difficult to stay at a Marriott without being inundated with opportunities to fill out rating forms, which are then collected, collated, dissected, and reassembled into something called the GSI, or Guest Service Index. The Guest Service Index for a given site is analyzed, tracked, and posted at the site for every employee to see. And, most important, the GSI is used as a basis for benchmarking and a guide for continual improvement.

Like Bean and Marriott, great companies have a tradition of defining and measuring tactical excellence. Jim Miller of Miller Business Systems tracks and posts how well the company is doing relative to its standard of completing 95% of customer orders within 24 hours. In 1936, W.R. Hotchkiss, founder of Deluxe Corporation (which prints roughly half of all checks used in the United States), set the goal of continual improvement towards zero-printing defects and two-day turnaround. Of course, Deluxe measures, tracks, posts the results, identifies deficiencies, and continually seeks improvement towards perfection.

Have you ever eaten at a Bob Evans Restaurant? The chain of coffee-shop restaurants, founded in the 1940s, has developed a reputation for tactical excellence, culminating in multiple first-place rankings in industry surveys for service, quality, and value.

Bob Evans sets tough standards for itself. A customer should receive water and a pleasant "hello" within 60 seconds of being seated. Hot food should arrive within 10 minutes after ordering. Tables should be ready for the next guest within five minutes. No customer should wait for a table longer than 15 minutes, even at the busiest times. And, you guessed it, Bob Evans constantly measures itself against these standards and tracks its performance. (The Miller Business Systems, Bob Evans, and Deluxe examples are described in the book *The Service Edge* by Ron Zemke and Dick Schaaf, which presents 101 case studies of companies that attain tactical excellence in services.)

People pay attention to that which is measured. Why do people love to participate in sports? Because its one of the few areas of life where you can objectively see how you're doing, where you can objectively track improvement.

Try an experiment with yourself. Identify a household chore that you really hate to do—taking out the garbage, mowing the lawn, or doing the dishes. Measure yourself on your next chore day. Suppose it takes you 14 minutes to take out the garbage. Now, set a benchmark—say, 10 minutes with zero mistakes. Measure yourself and track your performance. Two things will probably happen. First, you'll probably figure out a way to get better and better. Second, it'll be more fun, like a game.

The same applies to tactical execution. Figure out a way to define tactical excellence, measure it, track it, post it, learn from it, and use it as a way to continually improve. Make it fun. Make it the great game of business.

The link between measurement and continual improvement is captured in "The Shewhart Cycle," (see Figure 5-3) originally articulated by Walter A. Shewhart. The Shewhart Cycle is used extensively by the Japanese in their quest for consistent tactical excellence. It's a helpful framework for improvement of any process.

The Shewhart Cycle for Continual Improvement

What could be the most important accomplishments of this group? What changes might be desirable? What data are available? What measurements are needed? Plan a change or test.

Carry out the change or test, preferably on a small scale.

STEP 1 ———————→ STEP 2

STEP 4 ←——————— STEP 3

Study the results. What did we learn? What, if anything, should be implemented system-wide?

Measure and observe the effects of the change or test.

Repeat steps 1 to 4 infinitely.

Figure 5-3

6: Appreciating

Stimulated by Richard Barber's warmed soul (see article referred to earlier in this chapter), we made a phone call to L. L. Bean to place an order—and to ask a question.

"Welcome to L. L. Bean, this is Terri."

After placing our order and having a friendly chat with Terri about the coming of spring (it was early March), we asked, "What makes you folks at Bean take such care with a customer? Why do you, Terri, put so much of yourself into your work?"

At first, the question struck her as odd; we might as well have asked her, "Why do you breathe?" But she responded with characteristic cheer:

> It starts with our president. From him on down, I just know that I'm appreciated. They don't take me for granted. It's the little things—the juice and cookies during the Christmas rush, the pat on the back, the thank you's, the visits from our president. I got this job out of the want ads, just like any other job. But its not just any other job. They actually care about how I feel. I know I'm important.

If you want mediocrity, take people for granted, show no appreciation, and treat them like peons.

But if you want consistent tactical excellence, make sure people feel respected and appreciated. There's nothing mysterious about it. It's not conceptually difficult. It doesn't require a Ph.D. to figure this out. Simple, honest, genuine appreciation—what could be more obvious and straightforward?

An important question: If we called some of your employees at random and asked them to talk about their relationship with your company, would they give an answer like Terri's at L. L. Bean?

Appreciation should come in all three basic forms: informal, awards and recognition, and financial.

- *Informal appreciation.* Leaders throughout your company should practice the personal touch and hard/soft people skills described in the leadership style chapter. Remember, you set the example; they'll be influenced by your style.

Informal appreciation should be continuous and timely. People should be shown that they're appreciated throughout the year, not just at review time or at the annual awards ceremony. Do you wait until Valentine's day or a birthday to let your loved one know that he or she is something special? Do you tell your kids they're great only once a year? Of course not. And just like a healthy family, a healthy employee relationship is built on the same day-in and day-out respect and appreciation.

* *Awards and Recognition.* Never underestimate the power of non-financial awards and recognition. Keep in mind that the Herzberg study showed recognition as the second most important factor leading to extreme job satisfaction (behind achievement). Furthermore, what better way to highlight the importance of someone's work than to recognize it publicly, or to give an award?

Establish awards for customer service heroism, product quality, sales success, or other categories you deem important to being a great company.

You can have rare, highly prestigious awards, like the "Golden Falcon" award at Federal Express, given for dramatic or heroic achievements. Only a handful of people in any year receive a Golden Falcon, which comes with a personal phone call from the Chief Operating Officer. Combined with these, you can also have awards given more commonly. Federal Express has the "Bravo Zulu," given to hundreds of employees each year for a job well done.

Award special, well-designed pins or other visible badges of honor. For example, at Lenscrafters, if a customer commends the company's service in a letter, and mentions the employee by name, the employee receives a special lapel pin. Next time you watch an Ohio State football game, observe how the players have highly visible "buckeyes" for good plays on their helmets.

We also encourage you to give public recognition to people. Write about them in the newsletter or company magazine. Comment on them at staff meetings, or at company meetings. Look for opportunities to say, "This person did something excellent. This person's work is important."

- *Financial.* Use financial rewards as a way to further reinforce your appreciation for someone's efforts.

Make it possible for managers at all levels to grant small bonuses or other financial awards throughout the year. "Throughout the year" is a crucial part of this. People generally expect to receive a raise or bonus on an annual basis. Thus, the traditional annual "compensation increase" does very little, if anything, to express appreciation. In fact, it can often send just the opposite message if people receive less than they expect.

Suppose a dedicated employee is sifting through her mail and finds a note:

> "We're well aware of the tremendous strain on your family during the Christmas rush when you had to work so many extra hours. We appreciate your efforts. Please take your husband and children out for a nice dinner at a restaurant of your choice, and give us the bill. Bravo Zulu."

Or suppose a young engineer picks up his phone and hears the voice of the company president:

> "I just wanted to let you know that you did a great job getting the bugs out of that software in time for the trade show. It really made our product look good. I've had 100 shares of stock options allocated to your account. Keep up the good work."

Or suppose a salesperson who set and exceeded significant goals is told:

> "Congratulations. You set high goals, and made them. I have the honor to tell you that you've earned a spot in the 'Pacesetters' club. You'll receive your own personalized 'Pacesetter' business cards; you and a guest get a night out on the town at our expense; and for the next year, your merchandise discount will be increased from 20% to 33%."

The financial impact of these actions is minimal, yet the psychological impact is enormous. Why? Because these people are getting specific attention that shows personal appreciation for a job well done. The financial rewards are being used in a way to say: *you* did a good job; *you* are appreciated; *your* work is important.

Technology and Information Systems

We've dwelt primarily on the human and motivation side of attaining tactical excellence. And this is proper, as people ultimately get the job done. But we'd like to briefly digress into an additional component of attaining tactical excellence: use of technology and information systems.

We tend to think of computers, information systems, and reams of data as somehow cold, impersonal, and antithetical to the warm, human side of enterprise that we've emphasized in this book. Not true. Information technology is a powerful tool that should be used.

Outstanding companies, like Wal-Mart with its advanced check-out stands and vast databases, are constantly looking for ways to leverage technology and use information systems. L. L. Bean makes extensive use of technological systems to better aid its customers. According to Bean's senior vice president of operations, "I don't see how we can get too much technology out there." Both Bean and Wal-Mart are "people" companies, yet they're heavy users of information technology. Technology and people fit together perfectly, just as a stopwatch is a powerful aid to a track coach.

A Timely Flow of Data

Next time you take an airline flight, glance into the cockpit and notice all the dials, screens, and digital read-outs. The flight crew relies heavily on these instruments, monitoring them constantly while guiding the aircraft safely to its destination.

Keep that image in mind while running your company. Just like the flight crew, you want a constant flow of timely information. What altitude are we flying at? What's our speed? How much fuel do we have? Are our engines doing ok? Are we on schedule? What turbulence might we expect up ahead?

In a small to mid-sized company, you should have a similar body of information. And you should have it fast. You don't want to run out of fuel and, later (after you've crashed), get a delayed report that you're about to run out of fuel. Furthermore, it should be well-summarized and easily accessible. Again, keep in mind the simple digital readout in a cockpit.

The five most critical types of information to track are:

- Cash flow, both current and projected. Cash is like fuel to an airplane; you want to anticipate a fuel shortage long before the panel display flashes: "WARNING! You're almost out of fuel." Related to cash flow is accounts payable and receivable information, with the age of those accounts. Many companies run into serious cash problems because they mismanage their payables and receivables during a period of rapid growth.

- Financial accounting information (balance sheet and income statement) and financial ratios. It's particularly useful to have comparative statements (this period compared with last period, compared with last year). A list of useful ratios is given in Form 5-1 on page 214.

- Cost information. Many companies make the mistake of continuing unprofitable product lines because they have no idea that they're losing money on those lines. Put in place systems for determining costs and profitability by product line (or service line). Know your costs.

- Sales information. Track sales trends in each product or service category, which can be sorted or analyzed along dimensions relevant to your company (geography, price points, by distribution channels, etc.)

- Customer information. Customers are one of your best sources of information; they'll tell you what's good and bad about your products, how you stack up against the competition, why they buy your products, what suggestions they have for improvements and new products, what they use your products for, and just about anything else you ask. They'll even tell you who they are, what they do, how much they make, and where they live. Most important, they'll tell you when you're missing major trends or market needs.

There are many ways of getting customer information in a systematic, consistent, timely, and continuous way, such as:

—Customer response cards. Have customers send in warranty response cards that ask information about them, what they bought, and why. Use these to keep

FINANCIAL ANALYSIS RATIOS

Use these ratios to track the financial health of your company. Track the ratios over time, keeping an eye for negative trends. It's also useful to compare your ratios with the average ratios for your industry. Industry average ratios can be found in the publication "Key Business Ratios" in *Dun's Review* published by Dun & Bradstreet Publications Corporation.

return on assets: profit-after-tax/total-assets
 quick assessment of how efficiently the firm uses its assets

return on sales: profit-after-tax/net-sales
 quick assessment of profitability of total operations

return on equity: profit-after-tax/stockholder's-equity
 quick assessment of return on stockholder's investment

gross margin: gross-profit/net-sales
 indicates core profitability of product lines

working capital: current-assets less current-liabilities
 indicates basic liquidity of the firm

current ratio: current-assets/current-liabilities
 indicates basic liquidity of the firm

acid test ratio: (current-assets less inventory)/current-liabilities
 removing inventory gives a more clear picture of liquidity

debt to equity: (current-liabilities + long-term-debt)/stockholder's-equity
 indicates how much the firm relies on debt versus equity for funding

receivables collection period: (avg-receivables-for-the-year X 365)/annual-credit-sales
 indicates how many days it takes for the firm to collect receivables

payables period: (avg-accts-payable X 365)/materials purchases
 indicates how many days it takes for a firm to pay its payables.

inventory turnover ratio: COGS/avg-inventory-for-the-year
 indicates how many times the firm turns over its inventory

continual track of who is buying your products or services and why.

—Customer service reports. If your company has customer service reps, either in the field or via phone, institute a method by which comments made from customers get tabulated, tracked, and shared throughout the company. Each time a customer calls for service, you can gain information.

—Customer surveys. If you know who your customers are, you can go back to them and ask questions. People love to tell you what they think of your product or service. People love to share their ideas, suggestions, and frustrations. Do a customer survey regularly, and track how well you're doing in the customers' eyes. The customer is the most important link in the production process—it's ultimately only the customer's satisfaction that really matters.

—Focus groups. A focus group is a simple technique where you bring together a group of customers in a group setting and have them respond to questions and products. This can be a rich of source of information.

Information systems is a gigantic subject—too large for us to deal with it adequately here. Our purpose is not to delve into the myriad of details about these systems, but only to earmark their importance. You probably already have technology and information systems, and perhaps very good ones. We therefore leave you with two questions to consider:

1. Are you using technology to the fullest extent possible? We live in a rapidly advancing technological age, and companies that don't constantly seek ways to use technology to their advantage, will be put behind those that do.

2. Is the information *useful*? Don't let the "information experts" determine how your information is packaged. In fact, the problem in many companies isn't the lack of information, it's the poor packaging of that information. Keep working on it until it comes to you in a easily digestible and useful form.

Trust

You'll notice that we've spent no time in this chapter on "control"—on ways of making sure people do the right things, of preventing employees from taking advantage of your company. That's because control" doesn't work.

Remember the terribly destructive "micro-manager" described in the leadership style chapter, and how he devastated people's morale? (See "Personal Touch" section in the leadership chapter.) Neither you, nor your company, can afford to micromanage" if you want to attain consistent tactical excellence.

People need freedom to act. Motivated, trained, and well-inculturated people don't need to be "controlled." Adults don't need to be treated like children. People tend not to do their best work with someone looking over their shoulders.

Do people in your company—*all* people—have the authority (i.e. without approval from anyone) to make decisions that cost money? They ought to.

Whoa! We bet that got your attention. Are we serious?

Yes. We're very serious. Of course, we don't mean that all people should have the authority to commit the company to million dollar contracts, or that front-line clerks should be able to authorize the purchase of a new building. But people should have wide discretionary power to take responsibility to make sure something gets done fast, and done right.

It cost L. L. Bean money, in time and labor, to resole Richard Barber's 30-year-old boots. Bean employees didn't have to get approval to do all the back-flips; they just *did* it. No one sat around and figured the cost versus benefit analysis of spending all that time resoling his boots.

Think about it for a minute. Suppose you had to seek approval for every expense from your banker—every time you wanted to buy a personal computer or install a phone. How well could you run the company? The company would bog down in a morass of paperwork and approval, rather than attaining consistent tactical excellence.

The same principle applies right on down the line. Granted, someone on the front line shouldn't have the same spending authority as you, but the principle is the same. This simple phrase should apply all up and down your organization: "I trust you to do your best to do the right thing."

Rigorous Standards

Trust is only one side of the coin. The other side is rigorous standards.

There are two parts to this: values standards and performance standards.

Values standards are the most rigid. If someone disregards the core values of your company, they should be asked to leave. At first you might see if they just don't understand the values. However, if they understand and then disregard any of your sacred tenets, then they don't belong. It's impossible to inculcate a set of values into an institution if its leadership refuses to weed out people who don't adhere to those values.

Thomas J. Watson of IBM had a simple tenet: If an employee does something unethical, he should be fired—no matter how valuable that person is to the company. Period. No ifs or buts. No penalty box. No second chance. Out. Finished.

Performance standards should be less rigid, but nonetheless very high. Good performers lose respect for companies that tolerate poor performance. There's nothing inconsistent between having a close-knit "family" feeling and weeding out poor performers. Bill Hannemann, president Giro Sport Design, described how this works at Giro:

> We go to great lengths to build a family environment around here. But we also expect outstanding performance. We try our best to provide job security, but that *doesn't* mean keeping people around who don't perform.

Keep in mind, however, that there may be many causes for poor performance. The person might not have been properly trained. The person might not have been given crystal-clear guidance about what is expected. The person might be in a job that doesn't fit his strengths, but might do well in another position (which might even mean a gentle transition to a position outside the company). Explore these possibilities first.

Unfortunately, however, there are some people who just don't care—and perhaps never will care—about doing a good job. There are some who will consistently miss their milestones, targets, and goals. There are some people who will take personal advantage of every situation. There are some people in whom the dark side wins. Your company should rigorously weed these people out. You can do it with compassion (remember, it was your mistake to hire them in the first place); but it should be done.

Fortunately, these people are rare. And we don't base this claim solely on a personal faith in human nature. A variety of studies on worker motivation reach the same conclusion:

- A 1980 Gallup study conducted for the U.S. Chamber of Commerce concluded that 88% of all working Americans believe it is personally important to them to work hard and do their best on the job. The Gallup study also concluded that a poor work ethic was not responsible for declines in U.S. productivity.

- A study conducted for Connecticut Mutual Insurance Company found that 76% of all Americans frequently feel a sense of dedication to their work.

- A Public Agenda Foundation study asked a wide cross-section of American workers to pick one of the following four descriptions of how they view work:

  1. Work is simply a business transaction; the more I do, the more I get paid.

  2. Work is one of life's unpleasant necessities; I would not work if I did not have to.

  3. I find my work interesting, but I would not let it interfere with the rest of my life.

  4. I have an inner need to do the very best job I can, regardless of pay.

Eighty percent chose "I have an inner need to do the very best job I can, regardless of pay" as the first or second best description of their attitude about work, and the majority (52%) chose it as their first choice. Only 20% chose options one or two as even their second choice.

The vast majority of people (albeit not all people) want to do a good job. They want to be part of something they can be proud of. They want challenge and an opportunity to show what they're capable of. They'll rise to the occasion when other people are depending on them. They'll do extraordinary work when they're respected.

The Final "Secret"—Respect

There's nothing mysterious about building a great company. The builders of outstanding companies that we've had the privilege to observe personally, many of whom we've used as examples throughout this book, are not superhuman. They're not smarter than everyone else. Nor do they belong to a rare breed of charismatic entrepreneur.

Many of them are baffled by the question: "What is the secret of your success?" "Secret? There is no secret," is the most common response. They refer back to the basics covered in this book: having a vision, making good strategic decisions, being innovative, and—they always emphasize this—executing well.

If it's not mysterious, then why do only a fraction of companies become extraordinary? None of this is rocket science. It doesn't require hard-to-grasp concepts. Is there something we're missing?

Then we listened closely to what Fred Smith said in his Bill Moyers interview:

> Most people who run companies ... look down on the people who are working on the factory floor. They have a disdain for the average person, even though that person may be the one who is making them zillions of dollars.

Then the theme behind almost everything we've observed came to the front: respect.

We've always been moved by the story of Jaime Escalante, the high school teacher in Los Angeles on whom the movie "Stand and Deliver" was based. He took a bunch of high school kids from a poor ethnic neighborhood and taught them advanced, college-level calculus. His students consistently passed the advanced placement calculus exam at a rate higher than students in almost any school in the country.

Why did Escalante succeed when most people thought his students had no chance of passing something like the advanced placement calculus exam? During a talk at Stanford, he mentioned two simple words: love and respect. He loved his students and he respected them. He respected them enough to demand more of them than anyone else thought possible.

Therein lies the secret, if there is one. Great companies are built on a foundation of respect. They respect their customers, they respect themselves, they respect their relationships. Most important, they respect their people—people at all levels, and from all backgrounds.

They respect their people, and therefore they trust them. They respect their people, and therefore they're open and honest with them. They respect their people, and therefore they give them freedom to act and make decisions. They respect their people, and therefore believe in their inherent creativity, intelligence, and ability to solve problems.

They respect their people, and therefore *expect* high performance. They set high standards and stiff challenges because they believe their people can meet the standard and rise to the challenge. Ultimately, employees in outstanding companies attain consistent tactical excellence because someone believes they *can*.

Out of this respect grows a company that itself is respected—a company that rises to the stature of role model and makes a positive impact on the world, not only through its products, services, and employment, but also as a guide for other companies to follow.

You too can build a company that stands for something, that sets a standard, not only of performance, but also of values. You too can build an organization that rises above the fray and shows by its success that greatness and fundamental human decency and respect go hand in hand. You too can build a company that you can look back on at the end of your life, and say, "I'm proud of what I'm leaving behind, and I respect myself for the way I've gone about doing it. My life has been well spent."

NOTES TO CHAPTERS

Chapter 1: Leadership Style

Page 1 "The key to a leader's impact": William Manchester, *The Last Lion, Alone* (Boston, MA, Little, Brown, and Company, 1988) p. 210. Throughout our book, we use Churchill as an example. For an excellent insight into the life and leadership style of Churchill, we refer the reader to Manchester's *The Last Lion* series.

Page 7 Within a few weeks after John F. Kennedy came to office: William Manchester, *Portrait of a President: John F. Kennedy in Profile* (Boston, MA, Little, Brown, and Company, 1962).

Page 7–8 Walton examples: Vance H. Trimble, *Sam Walton* (New York, NY, Dutton, a division of Penguin Books, 1990) pp. 141–155. Vance Trimble's book on Sam Walton is an excellent biographical account of Walton and historical profile of Wal-Mart.

Page 9–10 George C. Marshall: Merle Miller, *Plain Speaking: An Oral Biography of Harry S. Truman* (New York, NY: Berkley Publishing Group, 1984) p. 406.

Page 10–11 "When all the evidence seems to be in": Michael Ray and Rochelle Myers, *Creativity in Business* (New York, NY, Doubleday, 1986) p. 157.

Page 11 "Strangely enough": Ray and Myers, *Creativity in Business,* p. 163.

Page 13 "The only thing I learned": Miller, *Plain Speaking,* p. 313.

Page 14 "Do not fear mistakes": Harry Mark Petrakis, *The Founder's Touch: the Life of Paul Galvin of Motorola* (New York, NY, McGraw-Hill Book Company, 1965) p. 226.

Page 14 Continuum of decision-making styles: An interesting discussion of management decision making styles is described in *Managing for Excellence* by David L. Bradford and Allan R. Cohen, *Managing for Excellence* (New York, NY, John Wiley & Sons, 1984) p. 185. Although we have adapted and evolved the concepts presented in their book, we were influenced by their description of decision-making styles.

Page 15 "The best decisions": C. Krenz, "MIPS Computer Systems," *Stanford Case Study* S-SB-112.

Page 16 "The fact that": Robert F. Kennedy, *Thirteen Days* (New York, W.W. Norton & Company, 1969) p. 111.

Page 18 "Do first things first": Peter F. Drucker, *The Effective Executive* (New York, Harper & Row, 1967) p. 24.

Page 19 "Most people get killed": Bob Bright, talk given at Stanford Business School, May 1, 1987.

Page 20 "If your work is successful": Kenneth Atchity, *A Writer's Time* (New York, W.W. Norton & Company, 1986) pp. 29–31.

Page 20 Marriott: Robert O'Brian, *Marriott: The J. Willard Marriott Story* (Salt Lake City, UT: Deseret Book Company, 1987) pp. 265–267.

Page 20–21 Churchill: Manchester, *The Last Lion, Alone,* pp. 3–37.

Page 22 L. L. Bean: Arthur Bartlett, "The Discovery of L. L. Bean," *The Saturday Evening Post,* December 14, 1946.

Page 25 "The open door policy": Thomas J. Watson, Jr., *Father, Son & Co.* (New York, NY, Bantam Books, 1990) pp. 308-309.

Page 25–26 Sam Walton: Trimble, *Sam Walton,* pp. 141–155.

Page 26 "They were flat": Debbi Fields, *One Smart Cookie,* (New York, NY, Simon And Schuster, 1987) p. 132.

Page 29 Psychologists: Thomas J. Peters and Robert H. Waterman, *In Search of Excellence* (New York, NY: Warner Books, Inc., 1982) pp. 55–60.

Page 29 Psychologists: Russell A. Jones, *Self-Fulfilling Prophecies: Social, Psychological and Physiological Effects of Expectancies* (Hillsdale, NJ: Lawrence Erlbaum Associates, 1977) p. 167.

Page 30 "Happy people": "The Business Secrets of Tommy Lasorda," *Fortune Magazine,* July 3, 1989, pp. 129–135.

Page 30 "End practice on a happy note": John Wooden, *They Call Me Coach* (Chicago, IL, Contemporary Books, 1988) p. 108.

Page 30 San Francisco 49ers: Bill Walsh, *Building a Champion* (New York, St. Martin's Press, 1990) p. 147.

Page 30–31 Wooden: Wooden, *They Call Me Coach,* p. 60.

Page 31 "The stylish": Walsh, *Building a Champion,* p. 97.

Page 34 "I remember": Robert Sobel, *Trammell Crow: Master Builder* (New York, NY, John Wiley & Sons, 1990) p. 234.

Page 35 Jim Burke: Warren Bennis, *On Becoming a Leader* (Reading, MA, Addison-Wesley Publishing Company, 1989) p. 192.

Page 36 "Suppose my neighbor's house": William Manchester, *The Glory and the Dream,* (New York, NY, Bantam Books, 1990) pp. 229–230.

Page 37 "[Apple] is based on": Steven P. Jobs, talk given at Stanford Business School, May, 1980.

Page 44 Paul Galvin: Petrakis, *Founder's Touch*, p. viii.

Page 44 William McKnight: Mildred Comfort, *William L. McKnight, Industrialist* (Minneapolis, MN: T.S. Denison & Company, Inc. 1962), p. 179.

Page 45 Henry Ford: Robert Lacey, *FORD: The Men and the Machine* (New York, NY: Ballantine Books, 1989), p. 141.

Chapter 2: Vision

Page 47 "The basic question": Edward Hoffman, *The Right to be Human: A Biography of Abraham Maslow* (Los Angeles, CA: Jeremy P. Tarcher, Inc., 1988), p. 280.

Page 49 "Consider any great organization": Thomas J. Watson, Jr., *A Business and Its Beliefs* (New York, NY: McGraw-Hill Book Company, Inc., 1963), pp. 4–5. This short book is a landmark contribution, and we'd recommend it highly.

Page 49–50 3M: Minnesota, Mining, and Manufacturing Company, *Our Story So Far: Notes from the first 75 Years of 3M Company* (St. Paul, MN: Minnesota, Mining, and Manufacturing Company, 1977).

Page 50 "Any organization in order to survive": Watson, *A Business and Its Beliefs*, pp. 4–5.

Page 50 Watson's father: Thomas J. Watson, Jr., *Father, Son & Co.* (New York, NY, Bantam Books, 1990), p. 51.

Page 51 Johnson & Johnson Credo: Lawrence G. Foster, *A Company that Cares: One Hundred Year Illustrated History of Johnson & Johnson* (New Brunswick, NJ: Johnson & Johnson Company, 1986), p. 108.

Page 51 McKinsey: Marvin Bower, *Perspective on McKinsey* (New York, NY: McKinsey & Company, Inc., 1979). This is not a book in general circulation; it was written and privately printed for readership by only personnel of McKinsey & Company. Jim worked at McKinsey early in his career where he read and was impressed by the book.

Page 54 "With all its problems, Israel": Barbara W. Tuchman, *Practicing History* (New York, NY: Ballantine Books, 1982), p. 134.

Page 55–56 MIPS Computer: C. Krenz, "MIPS Computer Systems," *Stanford Case Study* S-SB-112.

Page 57 "You know, you never defeated us": Harry G. Summers, Jr., *On Strategy: A Critical Analysis of the Vietnam War* (New York, NY: Bantam Doubleday Dell Publishing Group, Inc., 1982), p. 21.

Page 57 In terms of tactics and logistics: Summers, *On Strategy,* pp. 21–22.

Page 57 "This confusion over objectives": Summers, *On Strategy,* p. 149.

Page 58 "The principals never defined": William Manchester, *The Glory and the Dream,* (New York, NY, Bantam Books, 1990) p. 1054.

Page 60 "I picked Willamsburg": Watson, *Father, Son & Co.,* pp. 285–289.

Page 60–61 Vermont Castings: C. Hartman, "Keeper of the Flame," *Inc.,* March, 1989, pp. 66–76.

Page 62 Collins-Porras framework: J. Collins and J. Porras, "Organizational Vision and Visionary Organizations," *California Management Review,* Fall, 1991.

Page 64 "Sell good merchandise": Arthur Bartlett, "The Discovery of L. L. Bean," *The Saturday Evening Post,* December 14, 1946.

Page 64 L. L. Bean actions: "L .L. Bean, Inc. (B)," *Harvard Business School Case* 9-676-014.

Page 65 Herman Miller: Max DePree, *Leadership is an Art* (New York, NY: Doubleday Dell Publishing Group, Inc. 1989), pp. 4–80.

Page 65 Telecare Corporation: Interview with Anne Bakar, CEO.

Page 66 Johnson & Johnson Credo: Foster, *A Company that Cares,* p. 108.

Page 66 Dave Packard: "Interview with Bill Hewlett and Dave Packard," *HP Lab Notes Journal,* March 6, 1989.

Page 66 Bill Hewlett: Interview with Jim Collins and Jerry Porras, November, 1990.

Page 67 Merck & Company: Merck & Company, "Statement of Corporate Purpose," 1989.

Page 68 "Business cannot be defined": Peter F. Drucker, *Management: Tasks, Responsibilities, Practices* (New York, NY: Harper & Row, 1974), pp. 59–61.

Page 68 "Quantitative goals can't invest": T. Richman, "Identity Crisis," *Inc.,* October 1989, p. 100.

Page 68–69 L. L. Bean: "L. L. Bean, Inc. (B)," *Harvard Business School Case* 9-676-014.

Page 69 "I don't feel that I'll ever be done": Steve Jobs, talk given at Stanford Business School, March, 1989.

Page 70 Merck: Merck & Company, "Statement of Corporate Purpose," 1989.

Page 70 Schlage Lock Company: Corporate Vision Statement, 1990.

Page 70 Celtrix: Bruce Pharriss, Interview with authors, July, 1991.

Page 70 Lost Arrow/Patagonia: J. Collins, "Lost Arrow Corporation (C)," *Stanford Business School Case* S-SB-117C.

Page 70 Pioneer Hi-Bred: Ron Zemke and Dick Schaaf, *The Service Edge: 101 Companies that Profit from Customer Care* (Markham, Ontario: Penguin Books, 1989), p. 462.

Page 70 Telecare Corporation: Anne Bakar, Interview with Authors, July, 1991.

Page 70 Mary Kay Cosmetics: Mary Kay Ash, *Mary Kay on People Management* (Newport Beach, CA: Books on Tape, Inc, 1984), cassette 1, side 1.

Page 71 Kennedy-Jenks: David Kennedy, Interview with Authors, July, 1991.

Page 71 Advanced Decision Systems: Mike Kaul, Interview with Authors, July, 1991.

Page 74 "This nation": Daniel J. Boorstin, *The Americans: The Democratic Experience* (New York, NY: Vintage Books, 1974), p. 596.

Page 75 Examples of ineffective mission statements: F. David, "How Companies Define Their Mission," *Long Range Planning*, Volume 22, #1, February, 1989, pp. 90-92.

Page 76 "Make the MIPS architecture": C. Krenz, "MIPS Computer Systems," *Stanford Case Study* S-SB-112-TN.

Page 76 Democratize the automobile: Boorstin, *The Americans: The Democratic Experience*, p. 548.

Page 76 "Our whole people": Winston S. Churchill, *Blood, Sweat, and Tears* (New York, NY: G.P. Putnam's Sons, 1941), p. 403.

Page 77 IBM 360: Watson, *Father, Son & Co.*, pp. 346-351.

Page 77 Boeing: Harold Mansfield, *Vision: Saga of the Sky* (New York, NY: Madison Publishing Associates, 1986), pp. 329–339.

Page 77 Procter & Gamble sets up direct sales: Oscar Schisgall, *Eyes on Tomorrow: The Evolution of Procter & Gamble* (Chicago, IL: J.G. Ferguson Publishing Company, 1981), pp. 87–98.

Page 78 "We like to try the impractical": Schisgall, *Eyes on Tomorrow*, p. 200.

Page 78 50/50 chance of success: Boorstin, *The Americans: The Democratic Experience*, p. 595.

Page 79 Merck mission: P. Gibson, "Being Good Isn't Enough Anymore," *Forbes*, November 26, 1979, p. 40.

Page 79 Coors mission: C. Poole, "Shirtsleeves to Shirtsleeves," *Forbes*, March 4, 1991, p. 56.

Page 79–80: Tokyo Tsushin Kogyo: Akio Morita, *Made in Japan* (New York, NY: E.P. Dutton, 1986), pp. 63–74.

Page 80 Home Depot: C. Hawkins, "Will Home Depot be 'The Wal-Mart' of the '90s'?," *Business Week*, March 19, 1990, p. 124.

Page 80 Wal-Mart: Vance H. Trimble, *Sam Walton* (New York, NY, Dutton, a division of Penguin Books, 1990) p. 168.

Page 80 "Our goals are always based": "Being the Boss," *Inc.,* October, 1989, p. 49.

Page 81 "We always believed": John Sculley, *Odyssey* (New York, NY: Harper & Row Publishers, 1987), pp. 4–5.

Page 81 "Yamaha wo tsubusu!": G. Stalk, Jr., "Time —The Next Source of Competitive Advantage," *Harvard Business Review,* July-August, 1988, p. 44.

Page 81 Phil Knight: "Sneaker Wars," *ABC's 20/20,* August 19, 1988.

Page 82 Parkinson: J. Collins, "Passion Can Provide a Propelling Purpose," *San Jose Mercury News,* August 7, 1988, p. PC 1.

Page 83 Trammell Crow: N. Aldrich, "The Real Art of the Deal," *Inc.,* November, 1988, p. 82.

Page 83 Norwest: S. Weiner, "The Wal-Mart of Banking," *Forbes,* March 4, 1991, p. 65.

Page 83 Wal-Mart: Trimble, *Sam Walton,* pp. 33-34.

Page 83 "We are committed": General Electric Company, *The General Electric Story* (Schenectady, NY: General Electric Company, 1989), p. 128.

Page 84 "We had a dream": "The Art of Loving," *Inc.,* May, 1989, p. 46.

Page 90 "You have to get [your vision] on paper": "Thriving on Order," *Inc.,* December, 1989, p. 47.

Page 91 "I will build a car": Robert Lacey, *Ford: The Men and the Machine* (New York, NY: Ballantine Books, 1986), p. 93.

Page 92 "Hitler knows that he will have to break us": William Manchester, *The Last Lion, Alone* (Boston, MA, Little, Brown, and Company, 1988) p. 686.

Page 94 "People don't call themselves visionaries": V. Woodruff, "Giving the Globe a Nudge: Ted Turner," *Vis a Vis,* August, 1988, p. 58.

Chapter 3: Strategy

Page 95 "Strategy is easy": A. Rock, "Strategy vs. Tactics From a Venture Capitalist," *Harvard Business Review,* November-December, 1987, p. 63.

Page 100 The tank: William Manchester, *The Last Lion: Visions of Glory* (New York, NY: Dell Publishing, 1983), pp. 510–512.

Page 101 Stages of industry evolution: Michael Porter, *Competitive Strategy* (New York, NY: The Free Press, 1980), pp. 158–162.

Page 105 David Birch: D Birch, "Trading Places," *Inc.,*April, 1988, p. 42.

Page 106 "His all pervading hope": Winston S. Churchill, *The Gathering Storm* (Boston, MA: Houghton Mifflin Company, 1948), p. 222.

Page 106–107 Statistical Department: Churchill, *The Gathering Storm,* p. 468.

Page 107 "Sharp, scratchy, harsh, almost unpleasant individuals": T. Watson, "The Greatest Capitalist in History," *Fortune,* August 31, 1987, p. 24.

Page 111 "Don't grow too fast": Interview on HP-TV video, viewed by the authors.

Page 113 Osborne: K. Baron, "Spectacular Failures," *Peninsula,* July 1989, p. 40.

Page 115 Examples of rapid growth leading to arrogance: Baron, "Spectacular Failures," pp. 40–50.

Page 116 University National Bank Case Example: "Small Business: Second Thoughts on Growth," *Inc.,*March 1991, pp. 60–66, and K. Moriarty, "University National Bank and Trust Company," *Stanford Business School* Case S-SB-125.

Page 117 "If you're diversified": Larry Ansin, talk given at Stanford Business School, October, 1990.

Page 121 Cargill: M. Berss, "End of an Era," *Forbes,* April 29, 1991, p. 41.

Page 122–123 Tensor: T. Gearreald, "Tensor Corporation," *Harvard Business School Case* #9-370-041.

Page 123 "It's a good thing we're not a publicly owned company": J. Pereira, "L .L. Bean Scales Back Expansion Goals To Ensure Pride in Its Service Is Valid," *Wall Street Journal,* July 31, 1989.

Page 134 Porter's caveats: Porter, *Competitive Strategy,* pp. 158–162.

Chapter 4: Innovation

Page 135 "... all progress depends": Jorgen Palshoj, "Design Management at Bang and Olufsen," in *Design Management,* ed. Mark Oakley (Oxford, England: Basil Blackwood, 1990), p. 42.

Page 138 "This 'telephone'": M. Miller, "Sometimes the Biggest Mistake is Saying No to a Future Success," *Wall Street Journal,* December 15, 1986, p. 30.

Page 138 "The concept is interesting and well formed": P. Ranganath Nayak and John M. Ketteringham, *Breakthroughs!* (New York, NY: Rawson Associates, 1986) p. 318.

Page 138 "We don't tell you how to coach": Nayak and Ketteringham, *Break-throughs!,* p. 238.

Page 138 "So we went to Atari and said": Steve Jobs, talk given at Stanford Business School, May, 1980.

Page 138 "You should franchise them": Vance H. Trimble, *Sam Walton* (New York, NY, Dutton, a division of Penguin Books, 1990) p. 99.

Page 138 "We don't like their sound": M. Miller, "Sometimes the Biggest Mistake is Saying No to a Future Success," *Wall Street Journal,* December 15, 1986, p. 30.

Page 138 National Cash Register: Daniel J. Boorstin, *The Americans: The Democratic Experience* (New York, NY: Vintage Books, 1974), p. 201-202.

Page 138 "What's all this computer nonsense": Nayak and Ketteringham, *Break-throughs!,* p. 158.

Page 139 Drill for Oil: Boorstin, *The Americans: The Democratic Experience,* p. 46.

Page 139 "The airplane is useless.": Basil H. Liddell Hart, *The Real War* (Newport Beach, CA: Books on Tape, Inc.,1989), cassette 3, side 1.

Page 139 "The television will never achieve popularity": William Manchester, *The Glory and the Dream,* (New York, NY, Bantam Books, 1990) p. 240.

Page 139 Ideas behind the MacIntosh: T. Simmers, "The Big Bang," *Peninsula,* July, 1988, pp. 46–53.

Page 139 McDonald's: Ray Kroc, *Grinding it Out: The Making of McDonald's* (New York, NY: Berkley Publishing Corporation, 1977), pp. 5–13.

Page 139 Personal Publisher: S. Bandura, "T/Maker: The Personal Publisher Decision," *Stanford Business School Case* #S-SB-111.

Page 139 Tylenol: Lawrence G. Foster, *A Company that Cares: One Hundred Year Illustrated History of Johnson & Johnson* (New Brunswick, NJ: Johnson & Johnson Company, 1986), p. 123.

Page 139 Oxydol and Lava Soap: Schisgall, *Eyes on Tomorrow: The Evolution of Procter & Gamble* (Chicago, IL: J.G. Ferguson Publishing Company, 1981), p. 112.

Page 139 WETODRY: Minnesota, Mining, and Manufacturing Company, *Our Story So Far: Notes from the first 75 Years of 3M Company* (St. Paul, MN: Minnesota, Mining, and Manufacturing Company, 1977), pp. 64–65.

Page 140 Xerox: Chester Carlson: "Sometimes the Biggest Mistake is Saying No to a Future Success," *Wall Street Journal*, December 15, 1986, p. 30.

Page 141 Stew Leonard's: Ron Zemke and Dick Schaaf, *The Service Edge: 101 Companies that Profit from Customer Care* (Markham, Ontario: Penguin Books, 1989), pp 317–321.

Page 142 Wal-Mart LCT: Zemke and Schaaf, *The Service Edge,* p. 362.

Page 142 L. L. Bean: "L. L. Bean, Inc.," *Harvard Business School Case* #9-366-013.

Page 144 Fax machine: P. Drucker, "Marketing 101 for a Fast-Changing Decade," *Wall Street Journal*, November 20, 1990.

Page 144 3M Post-It™: Nayak and Ketteringham, *Breakthroughs!*, pp. 50–74.

Page 144 Federal Express: Nayak and Ketteringham, *Break- throughs!*, p. 318.

Page 144 Debbie Fields: Debbie Fields, *One Smart Cookie*, (New York, NY, Simon And Schuster, 1987) pp 56–58.

Page 144 David Sarnoff: Boorstin, *The Americans: The Democratic Experience*, p. 154.

Page 145 Windham Hill: Michael Ray and Rochelle Myers, *Creativity in Business* (New York, NY, Doubleday, 1986) p. 128.

Page 145 Microwave oven: Nayak and Ketteringham, *Break-throughs!*, p. 195.

Page 145: Sony: Akio Morita, *Made in Japan* (New York, NY: E.P. Dutton, 1986), p. 79.

Page 145–146 "Consumers, when confronted with something new": Jean-Pierre Vitrac, "Prospective Design," in *Design Management*, ed. Mark Oakley (Oxford, England: Basil Blackwood, 1990), p. 305.

Page 146 "Certainly the search": Nayak and Ketteringham, Break-throughs!, pp. 17–18.

Page 148 Personal Publisher: S. Bandura, "T/Maker: The Personal Publisher Decision," *Stanford Business School Case* #S-SB-111.

Page 148 "Like most great ideas": Steve Jobs, talk given at Stanford Business School, May, 1980.

Page 149 Band-aids™: Foster, *A Company that Cares*, p. 82.

Page 149 "In my age group": Nayak and Ketteringham, *Break-throughs!*, p. 119.

Page 150 L. L. Bean: J. Skow, "Using the Old Bean," *Sports Illustrated*, December 2, 1985.

Page 151 Baby Powder: Foster, *A Company that Cares,* p. 32.

Page 151 Ballard Medical Company: T. Richman, "Seducing the Customer: Dale Ballard's Perfect Selling Machine," *Inc.,* April, 1988, pp. 95–104.

Page 152 "Of course, this is a somewhat unscientific": Paulo Viti and Pier Paride Vidari, "Design Management at Olivetti," in *Design Management,* ed. Mark Oakley (Oxford, England: Basil Blackwood, 1990), p. 305.

Page 152 "What's important is experimentation": Vinod Khosla, talk given at Stanford Business School, October, 1988.

Page 153 Edison: J. Collins, "The Bright Side of Every Failure," *San Jose Mercury News,* March 29, 1987, P. PC 1.

Page 153 "Gordon the Guided Missile": John Cleese, speech given December 9, 1987. The speech is reproduced by Video Arts of Northbrook, Illinois.

Page 154 "The key to the Post-it™": Nayak and Ketteringham, *Break-throughs!,* p. 57.

Page 154 "It [the popcorn]": Nayak and Ketteringham, *Break-throughs!,* p. 185.

Page 155 "I see Jennifer, Bill, and me": B. Maxwell, "Powerfood's First Year," *Powerbar News,* December, 1987, pp. 1–4.

Page 156 Novellus: V. Rice, "A Model Company," *San Jose Mercury News,* February 21, 1991, p. B1.

Page 157 Ford Model B: Robert Lacey, *FORD: The Men and the Machine* (New York, NY: Ballantine Books, 1989), p. 82.

Page 157 Motorola product failures: Harry Mark Petrakis, *The Founder's Touch: the Life of Paul Galvin of Motorola* (New York, NY, McGraw-Hill Book Company, 1965) pp. 102, 129, 167, 180.

Page 161 "People are allowed to be persistent": R. Burgelman, "Intraorganizational Ecology of Strategy-making and Organizational Adaptation: Theory and Field Research,"

Stanford Graduate School of Business Research Paper #1122, p. 24.

Page 161 Intel's internal venture program: Burgelman, "Intraorganizational Ecology," p. 17.

Page 165 "You have to balance the 'flakes'": Vinod Khosla, talk given at Stanford Business School, October, 1988.

Page 165 "If you want the best things to happen in corporate life,": G. Melloan, "Herman Miller's Secrets of Corporate Creativity," *Wall Street Journal*, May 3, 1988, p. 31.

Page 167 Benjamin Franklin: Daniel J. Boorstin, *The Americans: The Colonial Experience)* New York, NY: Vintage Books, 1958), pp. 251–259.

Page 167 "Conventional wisdom": Debi Coleman, interview with authors, August, 1991.

Page 169 Boston Celtics: Interview on CBS Sports during the championship series, May, 1988.

Page 170 "...they did the work": John Tracy Kidder, *The Soul of a New Machine* (Boston, MA: Little, Brown and Company, 1981), pp. 272–274.

Page 171 Herman Miller: Melloan, "Herman Miller's Secrets."

Page 171 Merck: From a talk given by Merck CEO Roy Vagelos at Stanford Business School, February 15, 1990.

Page 171 Rosenberg and Birdzell: Nathan Rosenberg and L. E. Birdzell, Jr., *How the West Grew Rich* (New York, NY: Basic Books, *Inc.,* 1986).

Page 172 "You have to find a new structure for U.S. industry": "The Thinking Man's CEO," *Inc.,* November, 1988, pp. 29–42.

Page 172 "If you are going to have literally hundreds": Paul Cook, talk given at Stanford Business School, April 17, 1981.

Page 177 Herman Miller: Melloan, "Herman Miller's Secrets."

Page 178 "You win one game": Kidder, *The Soul of a New Machine*, p. 228.

Page 179 Ben and Jerry's: Paul Hawken, *Growing a Business* (New York, NY: Firside, 1988), p. 149.

Page 179–180 Federal Express: Zemke and Schaaf, *The Service Edge*, p. 479.

Page 180 William McKnight: Mildred Houghton Comfort, *William McKnight: Industrialist* (Minneapolis, MN: T.S. Denison & Company, *Inc.,*1962), pp. 132, 139, 191.

Page 182 "Regis McKenna: Ray and Myers, *Creativity in Business*, p. 91.

Page 183–184 Paul Galvin: Petrakis, *The Founder's Touch*, p. 209.

Page 184 Herman Miller: Melloan, "Herman Miller's Secrets."

Page 184 Claude Rosenberg: Talk given at Stanford Business School, November 8, 1984.

Page 185 Ted Nierenburg: Talk given at Stanford Business School, December 5, 1984.

Chapter 5: Tactical Excellence

Page 187 "God is in the details": "Thoughts on the Business of Life," *Forbes*, August 19, 1991, p. 152.

Page 188 Hemingway: Theodore A. Rees Cheney, *Getting the Words Right* (Cincinnati, OH: Writer's Digest Books, 1983), p. introduction 3.

Page 188 *Inc.*, CEO survey: J. Case, "The Origins of Entrepreneurship," *Inc.,*June, 1989, p. 62.

Page 189 Compaq, Apple, and IBM profits per employee: Compaq, Apple, and IBM 1990 annual reports.

Page 189 "The key ingredient turned out to be": Vance H. Trimble, *Sam Walton* (New York, NY, Dutton, a division of Penguin Books, 1990) pp. 120–122.

Page 191 "The bulk of the causes": W. Edwards Deming, *Out of the Crisis* (Cambridge, MA: Massachusetts Institute of Technology, Center for Advanced Engineering Study,

1986). This quote is repeated by Deming over and over in his seminars, and is repeated in various forms throughout his book. To gain a complete understanding of this quote, we highly recommend reading Deming's *Out of the Crisis.*

Page 192 Richard Barber: R. Barber, "How L. L. Bean Restored My Soles—And Warmed my Soul," *Wall Street Journal,* December 18, 1990, p. A12.

Page 194 Airplane parts manufacturer: Peter F. Drucker, *Concept of the Corporation* (New York, NY: The John Day Company, 1972), pp. 157–158.

Page 195 Federal Express: P. Ranganath Nayak and John M. Ketteringham, *Break-throughs!* (New York, NY: Rawson Associates, 1986) pp. 314–322.

Page 196 Deming Prize: Mary Walton, *The Deming Management Method* (New York, NY: Perigee Books, 1986), pp. 3–21.

Page 198 Stew Leonard's: Ron Zemke and Dick Schaaf, *The Service Edge: 101 Companies that Profit from Customer Care* (Markham, Ontario: Penguin Books, 1989), pp 317–321.

Page 198 Marriott: Zemke and Schaaf, *The Service Edge,* pp. 117–120.

Page 200 Whole Foods: B. Posner, "The Best Little Handbook in Texas," *Inc.,* February, 1989, pp. 84–87.

Page 201 Jim Miller: Zemke and Schaaf, *The Service Edge,* pp. 516–519.

Page 202 Parisan: Zemke and Schaaf, *The Service Edge,* pp. 356–359.

Page 202 Dominos: Zemke and Schaaf, *The Service Edge,* pp. 301–304.

Page 203 Stew Leonard's: Zemke and Schaaf, *The Service Edge,* pp. 317–321.

Page 203 Home Depot: C. Hawkins, "Will Home Depot be 'The Wal-Mart' of the '90s'?," *Business Week,* March 19, 1990, p. 124.

Page 206 Herzberg study: F. Herzberg, "One more time: How do you motivate employees?," *Harvard Business Review,* September-October 1987, pp. 109–120.

Page 206 L. L. Bean: Zemke and Schaaf, *The Service Edge,* pp. 378–381.

Page 207 Marriott: Zemke and Schaaf, *The Service Edge,* pp. 117–120.

Page 207 Deluxe: Zemke and Schaaf, *The Service Edge,* pp. 446–449.

Page 207 Bob Evans: Zemke and Schaaf, *The Service Edge,* pp. 293–296.

Page 208 Shewhart Cycle: Deming, *Out of the Crisis,* p. 88.

Page 210 Federal Express: Zemke and Schaaf, *The Service Edge,* p. 479.

Page 212 "I don't see how we can get": J. Skow, "Using the Old Bean," *Sports Illustrated,* December 2, 1985.

Page 217 Watson of IBM: T. Watson, "The Greatest Capitalist in History," *Fortune,* August 31, 1987, p. 24.

Page 218 Studies on worker motivation: D. Yankelovich and J. Immerwahr, "Putting the Work Ethic to Work," *Social Science and Modern Society,* Volume 21, No. 2, January-February, 1984, pp. 58–76.

Page 219 Federal Express: P. Ranganath Nayak and John M. Ketteringham, *Break-throughs!* (New York, NY: Rawson Associates, 1986) pp. 314–322.

INDEX